1995

W9-ANH-139

THE AMERICAN PARTY SYSTEM
AND THE AMERICAN PEOPLE

PRENTICE-HALL FOUNDATIONS OF MODERN POLITICAL SCIENCE SERIES

Robert A. Dahl, Editor

THE AGE OF IDEOLOGY-POLITICAL THOUGHT, 1750 TO THE PRESENT, Second Edition
by Isaac Kramnick and Frederick M. Watkins

THE AMERICAN PARTY SYSTEM AND THE AMERICAN PEOPLE, Third Edition
by Fred. I. Greenstein and Frank B. Feigert

THE ANALYSIS OF INTERNATIONAL RELATIONS, Second Edition
by Karl W. Deutsch

CONGRESS AND THE PRESIDENCY, Third Edition
by Nelson W. Polsby

DATA ANALYSIS FOR POLITICS AND POLICY
by Edward R. Tufte

MODERN POLITICAL ANALYSIS, Fourth Edition
by Robert A. Dahl

MODERN POLITICAL ECONOMY
by Norman Frohlich and Joe A. Oppenheimer

THE POLICY-MAKING PROCESS, Second Edition
by Charles E. Lindblom

PUBLIC ADMINISTRATION
by James W. Fesler

third edition _____

THE AMERICAN PARTY SYSTEM AND THE _____ AMERICAN PEOPLE

FRED I. GREENSTEIN
Princeton University

FRANK B. FEIGERT
North Texas State University

Prentice-Hall Inc., Englewood Cliffs, New Jersey 07632

Library of Congress Cataloging in Publication Data

Greenstein, Fred I.
   The American party system and the American people.

   Bibliography: p.
   Includes index.
   1. Political parties--United States. 2. United
States--Politics and government--1945-
   I. Feigert, Frank B. II. Title.
JK2265.G75 1985   324.973   84-22864
ISBN 0-13-028473-4

Editorial/production supervision
and interior design: **Marjorie Borden**
Manufacturing buyer: **Barbara Kelly Kittle**

PRENTICE-HALL FOUNDATIONS OF MODERN POLITICAL SCIENCE SERIES

Robert A. Dahl, Editor

Printed in the United States of America

10 9 8 7 6 5 4 3 2 1

ISBN 0-13-028473-4 01

Prentice-Hall International, Inc., *London*
Prentice-Hall of Australia Pty. Limited, *Sydney*
Editora Prentice-Hall do Brasil, Ltda., *Rio de Janeiro*
Prentice-Hall Canada Inc., *Toronto*
Prentice-Hall of India Private Limited, *New Delhi*
Prentice-Hall of Japan, Inc., *Tokyo*
Prentice-Hall of Southeast Asia Pte. Ltd., *Singapore*
Whitehall Books Limited, *Wellington, New Zealand*

CONTENTS

PREFACE

PREFACE TO THE THIRD EDITION

This is a thorough revision of the widely read 1970 and 1963 editions. When Fred Greenstein and Stan Wakefield asked me to undertake this revision—too many years ago—I was both delighted and discomfited: delighted because I was happy to be associated with this work, and discomfited because of the inevitable necessity of tampering with Fred's fine prose. I have tried to do the latter as little as possible, keeping the original flavor of the book as well as its intellectual framework.

The book has been expanded to include the substantive changes that have taken place, as well as to reflect current scholarship. In this revision I have rejected the "party-is-dead" approach as a trendy artifact of some weak research and, perhaps, some wishful thinking. On the other hand, it is vital to note the many significant changes in the party system and the ways we reflect that in our behavior as citizens.

Much is owed to many people in the preparation of any book, whether initially or in revision. The greatest debt, of course, I owe to Fred Greenstein for his patience, good humor, and willingness to allow me to expand on his analysis. Stan Wakefield of Prentice-Hall initiated this collaboration, and he knew when to prod and when to be understanding. Marjorie Borden did a superb job as our production editor, even to the extent of taking dictated art changes over the phone. And, it might be added that all three managed to deal with my illegible handwriting—no mean feat at all. Additional help was provided by—and thanks go to—Bob Brookshire, David McClure, and David Molta. Finally, this book would not have been possible without the data provided by the Center for Political Studies, University of Michigan, which bears no responsibility for the use made herein.

Frank B. Feigert

PREFACE TO THE SECOND EDITION

Two points were made in the Preface to the first (1963) edition of this work—one of them about the converging bodies of empirical literature on the American party system on which I was drawing, and the second about the intrinsic limitations of the general task I had set for myself: that of evaluating the party system. On each of these points my original assertions can be reiterated with elaboration and qualification. In addition, a third set of prefatory remarks now needs to be added, taking note of historical events and change since the first edition, for no one could write about American party politics in 1969 in precisely the fashion that it was possible to write in 1963. But first the two points of "old business."

(1) The times were propitious, I argued in the first edition, "to write on party politics and electoral behavior in the United States."

> Empirical political research blossomed in the post-World War II years. The "empiricist" or "behaviorist" entered the scholarly scene, accompanied by much intradisciplinary polemic about the mertis of "scientific" study of politics. Fortunately, there was more than polemic; fresh research began to accumulate, theorizing about politics became increasingly more sophisticated and there was increasing effort to confront theories with data which might test their validity. This book draws extensively on findings which were reported in the past decade. In the recent past, research on electoral psychology has begun to connect meaningfully with our understanding of various political institutions. New and theoretically productive investigations of local, state, and federal party politics have been reported. It has become possible to begin integrating what scholars have found at various levels of government and to relate these observations with findings from the voting studies.

The resulting accrual of new insight into the parties made it possible, I pointed out, to see relationships and connections that had not hitherto been widely discussed: for example, the parallels noted in Chapters 3 and 5 of both editions between the findings of electoral behavior research and the findings of research on politics in nonpartisan jurisdictions and in primary elections, especially those in one-party states. Since 1963 the expansion of empirical research has been so substantial that on some issues where one speculative essay with selective and illustrative data existed then, as many as a dozen specialized research reports are available now. This almost geometric increase in research evidence has occurred with respect to almost all of the topics dealt with in this work. Paradoxically, where the most research has been done, the greatest clarity has not necessarily emerged. Thus in the fifth chapter of this edition, after noting a large number of recent studies of the politics of nonpartisanship and several studies of the relationship between the party competitiveness of a political jurisdiction and the kinds of policies it produces, I conclude that the verdict on these matters is still unsettled (see pp. 66–70 and pp. 76–77).

Why should greater knowledge seem to produce greater confusion? The answer is that different studies use somewhat different procedures and assumptions; furthermore, the various bodies of data employed are not invariably comparable. For the moment, therefore, the state of understanding of some aspects of the party system is rather like that of the elephant which the several blind men were attempting to describe. Nevertheless, it is a mistake to think either that the understanding of elephants would be better if the blind men simply sat in their armchairs, spinning out a priori pronouncements about pachydermal characteristics, or that the confusion will be permanent. Indeed, in some other empirical areas (compare the discussion of voter psychology in the two editions of this work, for example) the research evidence now fits together in a remarkably coherent and illuminating manner.

(2) On the second matter, that of attempting to evaluate the party system, I introduced the following caveat in the Preface to the first edition:

> In order to give unity to the discussion (and at the risk of oversimplification), I have introduced three criteria for assessing the functions served by the American party system for the American people. The parties are examined in terms of their contribution to democracy, stability, and "effective policy-making." It should be evident to the reader that the criteria have been used impressionistically—to suggest rather than to demonstrate. If we were even to begin to explore the conceptual and methodological problems involved in using such criteria satisfactorily, a quite different and far more technical book would emerge. Yet hopefully the three loosely explicated criteria will help to provide students with some over-all framework for organizing their thinking about the uses of political parties.

The caveat still stands, though the evaluative aspect of this book has undergone a degree of change. Conceptual advances and increasing expectations for conceptual rigor have marked the years between the editions. Consequently, while I still eschew the program of conceptual clarification and indicator construction that would be involved in using such criteria definitely, I have rewritten and expanded upon (if briefly) the exposition of the criteria and their implications. I also have attempted to specify which of my judgments and conclusions are essentially empirical—and can be straightforwardly derived from the available evidence—and which of them cannot even in principle be so derived without introducing value premises of the sort that are intrinsically controversial in that what one individual finds congenial another may not. Finally, I have simply changed or elaborated on some of my own value-premise-based judgments about the party system. Here I was bound to be influenced by the shape of partisan and other politics in the United States since 1963.

(3) In 1964 the Republican party nominated precisely the kind of candidate who, according to the thesis argued in the first edition, the GOP "should" not nominate—on pain of suffering a major defeat. Since the 1964 Republican candidate was overwhelmingly defeated, this aspect of the argument of the first edition was strengthened rather than refuted by the passage of events. But not all of the developments of the 1960s are so easily absorbed without altering the various lines of interpretation and judgment in the previous edition. At one point or another it has been necessary to discuss or allude to: the substantial challenge to the two major parties in 1968 by the third party led by former Alabama Governor George C. Wallace; the contention and violence in the streets in connection with the 1968 Democratic Convention; the decision of President Johnson not to seek re-election; urban violence; the assassination of a president, a senator, and a world-famour leader of American blacks; the rise of issue-oriented, ideological activists in both parties; and the increased politicization of at least a segment of the nation's youth.

Some of these widely proclaimed developments and events point to what appear to be enduring changes. Other may be ephemeral. (One hopes so in the case of assassinations!) In all, while I take account of the rise of various kinds of "new politics," my assumption is that announcements of the demise of the "old politics" of bargaining and compromise are as premature as were the famously inaccurate early reports of Mark Twain's death.

Among the many people who helped me on the two editions, I would like particularly to mention Charles R. Adrian, James D. Barber, Richard W. Boyd, Robert A. Dahl, Charles Gilbert, John Grumm, Anthony King, Duane Lockard, Roger Masters, William K. Muir, Jr., James Murphy, Russell Murphy, Thomas O'Neill, James Payne, Nelson Polsby, Richard Scammon, Allan Sindler, Donald Stokes, and Clement Vose.

Fred I. Greenstein, 1970

chapter 1

_____ INTRODUCTION

We shall be concerned, in this book, with American political parties and the American people. What does the party system do for Americans? What functions does it serve? Have political parties contributed usefully to life in the United States, or is it possible that their activities have justified George Washington's warning that "the effects of the spirit of party" would be "baneful"?

Several generations ago there would have been little hesitation on the part of most solid, thoughtful citizens in accepting Washington's assessment. A great deal of the legislation and reform activity during the first two decades of the twentieth century explicitly sought to weaken or destroy political parties. If this could be done, it was thought, the avenues of communication between people and their government would be freed from the interference of self-serving party politicians. On the other hand, serious thinkers about American politics have usually maintained that parties perform certain necessary functions, and have dedicated considerable scholarly effort to the study of these functions. However, since the 1960s, parties again began to fall into disregard with the general public, as well as with journalists and scholars. Reform efforts, from groups thoroughly committed to parties, have also had the effect of weakening the parties even further. A notable example of this is the attempt to reform campaign finance, which has had the unintended effect of weakening the formal party organization.

The widespread suspicion of politics and politicians that is elicited by

1

every public opinion poll dealing with the topic suggests that a great many contemporary Americans agree with turn-of-the-century reformers. That is, they believe the parties have *not* made useful contributions—that they have actually had negative effects on the country. In contrast, the bulk of students of politics and political leaders recognize the need for parties in the operation of modern political systems. Many of them, however, are not pleased about how the party system now works. Thus, for example, in recent years we have seen some prominent Republicans advocating very much the same kind of reforms in national convention delegate selection as have been put in place since 1980 by the Democrats.

If we were to attempt to catalogue all the functions, both positive and negative, that political parties may perform for a nation and its various subgroups, the cataloguing alone would exceed the length of this book.[1] Therefore we must sharpen our inquiry. We shall concentrate on aspects of American party politics that help us to answer three very broad but vital questions which can be asked about any political institution:

1. Does the institution—in this case the American political party system—contribute to the degree to which the political system is *democratic?*
2. Does the institution foster, or does it hamper, the *stability* of the political system?
3. How, if at all, does the institution effect the *adequacy of governmental policy-making?*

For our purposes a political system can be considered democratic if citizens have a relatively high degree of control of the actions of their leaders—relative, that is, to the degree of control that citizens of other political systems have of *their* leaders. In no national political system do citizens influence even a simple majority of their leaders' actions. Nevertheless there are very great differences between systems like Canada, the Netherlands, and the United States, in which public efforts to influence political leaders are expected, accepted, and often successful, and systems like South Africa or China, in which open opposition to the government in power is not countenanced.

The criteria of stability and effectiveness of policy-making are more elusive than the criterion of democracy. "Stability" is a term sometimes used simply to refer to the persistence, with only gradual, evolutionary change, of some political pattern: in this sense a coup-ridden nation which regularly employed assassination as a means of replacing leaders could be described as "stable" if the system maintained a "steady-state" over the years. But "stability" commonly also has the further connotation of *nonviolent* political pattern-maintenance. For present purposes we can think of a political system as stable to the degree that it performs its tasks without violence and without abrupt, disruptive, and arbitrary changes in governmental policy, governmental staffing, and (perhaps most important) in the very ground-rules by which government and politics proceed.

"Adequacy of policy-making" has an even greater number of connotations than stability. "Adequacy" can, for example, refer to the swiftness with which decisions are made, the internal consistency of government policies, their consistency over periods of time, the likelihood that policies will accomplish their stated purposes, or the frequency with which policies that cope with the challenges of the present and the future actually get made. Furthermore, analyses of adequacy will reach different conclusions depending on the analyst's own values about which policy outcomes are adequate. "Adequacy" provides a handy initial basis for pointing to a cluster of more specific criteria about how the policy-making process of a political system performs, but we frequently shall find it necessary to qualify the term in order to make explicit the sense in which it is being used.[2]

With the three obviously very broad questions of how the party system contributes or fails to contribute to democracy, stability, and effectivensss of policy-making in mind, it will be possible to carry out a selective examination of the role of parties in four arenas of American politics. First, after briefly analyzing the citizen base of the American political system (Chapter 2), we shall consider (Chapter 3) the role of parties in the electorate—their impact on public opinion and voting. Here our concern is mainly, though not exclusively, with citizen control of leaders. Then we shall go on to analyze organized party politics, beginning with the activities of parties at the local level (Chapter 4). Our principal concern will be with the implications for political stability of a fascinating, if fading, species: the old-time urban machine. But we shall also look at some modern variants of the machine: reform party organizations and nonpartisan politics. Then our focus will shift to the remarkably diverse kinds of state party systems in the United States (Chapter 5). Here we return to the question of popular control, although policy-making also is a concern. The examination of local and state party activities provides a foundation for moving on to consider the national parties (Chapter 6), especially their connection with policy-making. Following this we briefly reconsider (Chapter 7) the three key questions raised above.

Before we proceed, two warnings are in order. The first bears on our consideration of how the parties contribute or fail to contribute to democracy and stability. It cannot be argued that by themselves the parties cause either phenomenon. Social scientists are increasingly convinced that there are fundamental non-political prerequisites of stable democracy. Stable democracies tend to have, for example, relatively advanced economies and literate populations. They also tend to have certain non-institutional political prerequisites such as well-developed traditions among the politically active acknowledging the legitimacy of opposition to incumbent governmental leaders. It is exceedingly unlikely that the introduction of new political institutions (say the constitution and party system of the United States or Great Britain) would transform a nation without such preconditions—for example, Bangladesh—into a stable democracy. But neither does this mean that a nation's political institutions are unimportant. Social factors and political traditions operate through institutions. Nations and other political units which are quite similar socially and in their general traditions sometimes differ in political organization, and, as we shall see, these differences can have significant consequences.[3]

A second warning. The raw materials for a definitive appraisal of American parties are not fully developed. Like jazz and like the writings of Poe, Melville, and Faulkner, American parties were granted serious attention by domestic scholars only after they were "discovered" by foreigners. An Englishman, James Bryce, writing in the late nineteenth century, was responsible for the first extended discussion of American parties which was not a mere partisan broadside or campaign history.[4] Within a few years after Bryce's initial effort, publications about American parties began to proliferate. Today they make a mountainous pile. Nevertheless, a good bit of the research over the years has been unsystematic and anecdotal. Too often studies have been insufficiently comparable with one another to produce reliable, cumulative understanding of the parties. Moreover, much of the writing on the American parties has consisted of broadly cast, rather repetitive debates about the overall merit of the party system—often by disputants who, since they disagreed on their criteria for appraisal, engaged in little more than a ritual ballet.

These difficulties have increasingly been remedied. It has become more common for students of parties to try to isolate important empirical questions which must be answered in order to assess the party system, to state these questions carefully in the form of hypotheses, and to attempt to test the hypotheses rigorously. There also is a greater tendency for the work of one scholar to be built on that of his predecessors. Nevertheless, there are sizable gaps in our knowledge about political parties. A great deal of what we think we know is based on shaky evidence and is subject to complex qualifications. Therefore, what follows should be read in a scientific spirit, with the awareness that knowledge is provisional, that the verities of the past often have proved to be errors, and that many present verities will encounter the same fate. This should not be a source of discouragement, since advances in understanding are possible only if we make our beliefs explicit and test them against reality.

NOTES

[1]For general remarks on the different notions implicit in discussions of the "functions" of political parties see Howard A. Scarrow, "The Function of Political Parties: A Critique of the Literature and the Approach," Journal of Politics, 29 (November 1967), 770-90. See also

Frank J. Sorauf, "Political Parties and Political Analysis," in William Nisbet Chambers and Walter Dean Burnham, (eds), *The American Party Systems: Stages of Political Development,* 2nd ed. (New York: Oxford University Press, 1975).

²Contemporary political scientists have devoted more effort to studying how policies are made than to evaluating policy-making procedures or to examining the policies themselves. Although there have been recent efforts to direct scholarly efforts into policy analysis, there are still no agreed-upon standards for evaluating policy. To attempt to develop them here would leave little space for examining the party system. On the analysis of policy see the essays in Austin Ranney, ed., *Political Science and Public Policy* (Chicago: Markham, 1968) and Charles E. Lindblom, *The Policy-Making Process* (Englewood Cliffs, N.J.: Prentice-Hall, 1968).

³For representative selections from the growing literature on the prerequisites of stable democracy, see Seymour M. Lipset, *Political Man* (Garden City, N.Y.: Doubleday, 1960), Chaps. 2 and 3; Dean E. Neubauer, "Some Conditions of Democracy," *American Political Science Review,* 61 (December 1967), 1002-1009; Robert A. Dahl, *Modern Political Analysis,* (2nd ed.; Englewood Cliffs, N.J.: Prentice-Hall, 1970), Chap. 6.

⁴James Bryce, *The American Commonwealth* (London: Macmillan, 1888), 2 vols.

chapter 2 _____

THE CITIZEN BASE
OF THE AMERICAN
_____ POLITICAL SYSTEM

Often study of government and politics focuses on institutions and processes, ignoring the role of the public. In examining the nature and extent
of democracy in the United States, for example, we may ask ourselves if the
judicial branch is becoming too strong, or if there is an adequate way to
balance the powers of the executive and legislative branches. Often we also
focus on particular events and personalities. Why is unemployment up?
What can be done about the latest oil spill? Is the president fulfilling the
campaign promises?

Important as these kinds of questions are, we must also understand
the role of citizens in our system, or in any other system for that matter. It
is inadequate to concentrate exclusively on the readily visible parts of the
body politic—public officials, party leaders, interest groups, and other
widely publicized participants. At least since the time of Plato, the more
searching political theorists have acknowledged the necessity of also understanding the base on which the leaders rest—the citizenry whose countless
acts of acquiescence, indifference, and defiance empower or weaken
leaders.

Because of their belief in the importance of the citizen base of political
systems, Plato and Aristotle would not have been surprised at the failure of
democracy to take root in many of the former colonial nations that have
entered the world community in recent decades. Noting the high illiteracy
rates of these countries, their overpopulation, and the bare subsistence lev-

els at which their citizens exist, they would surely have argued that in these nations the raw material is not present for anything but an autocratic—or anarchic—mode of politics.

What of our own system? Are we a democracy simply because we tell ourselves that we are? Does the United States meet the requirements for a democracy? By formal institutional criteria it would seem that we do. The Constitution provides that no one branch of government can exercise excessive power, to the exclusion of the others, or of the citizenry. A great many offices (some 800,000) are elective, at the federal, state, county, and local levels.

Simply showing that citizens have opportunities to participate and that the branches of government are limited does not show that we have an effective democracy. There are many requirements in the nature of the citizenry that a democratic system must meet. Most political analysts would include the following among them:

(1) Active citizen participation in the game of democratic politics. More than lip service is necessary in a democracy. A passive commitment to the democratic process is not sufficient. Rather, citizens must be willing to attempt to control their leaders through some form of participation. Minimally, this is usually regarded as the act of voting. This may be supplemented through a wide variety of other forms of participation. Moreover, the act of participation, no matter what form, must meet standards of rationality. One such standard is that citizens be guided by information about government and its leadership. Along with this, citizens must have at their disposal criteria for evaluating leadership performance.

(2) Citizens' feelings of efficacy in the democratic process. It is not sufficient for citizens to feel a commitment to an abstract notion such as "democracy," or to participate in the process. In order to ensure that both continue, it is essential that citizens feel that their participation is worthwhile, that it results in some outcome that might not otherwise occur. Whether they indeed have an impact on the process, they must feel that they do, or that they can if the present leadership is not performing up to expectations. There is an intimate relationship between this criterion and the other two. If citizens feel that their participation is worthless, their commitment may drop, along with their participation. Of course, some will participate more out of habit than anything else. Nonetheless, citizens are unlikely to continue participation in a process, or feel much commitment to the rules governing it, if they feel that they have little or any influence in it.

So much for the abstract criteria for an effective democracy. To what extent do Americans meet these requirements? The thesis of this and the following chapter is that, as a whole, the American people meet these requirements quite imperfectly. This may be jarring to some, but, as the data will show, our civics lessons have been learned imperfectly. Nevertheless, for various reasons, especially because of the existence of institutions which tie the public and politicians together, we have a political system that most of us would consider both democratic and stable.

With the development of modern public-opinion polling techniques, it is possible to make rather precise statements about the citizen base of our political system. These must be taken for what they are—statements at any one given time, or at several points in time. An often fatal flaw in the use of such data is the assumption that citizen attitudes are frozen in time. Thus, sometimes politicans, ahead in the surveys, become complacent, only to find, too late, that they have been defeated. Citizen attitudes can be highly volatile and unstable.

By examining responses to poll questions over time, it is possible to detect trends in attitudes. It is with such trends that we are concerned in the present chapter and the following one.

Before we proceed further, however, we must deal with the nature of the data which provide the basis for our assessments. For the uninitiated, there may be a tendency either to accept polling results as unquestionable or view them as representing some arcane "science." For others, just the opposite holds true; they refuse to believe that opinions can ever be accurately gathered, measured, and analyzed. The truth lies in between, especially when the operations are done by the better academic and commerical survey organizations and are intelligently interpreted. By various sampling procedures, it is possible for interviewers to ask representative cross-sections of the population questions about their political activities, opinions, and information. If the sampling procedures are properly followed, the findings are almost always quite close to what would have been established if the entire population had been interviewed.[1] And if the questions are worked skillfully, they provide genuine insight into public opinion, information, and participation.

In this chapter we present a series of "photographs," frames of moving picture taken over time, to show the extent to which the public meets our criteria for democratic citizenship—participation and efficacy. In Chapter 3 we analyze the question of participation further by looking at the active and inactive electorate, and go, as it were, to view the motion picture, examining the dynamics of opinion formation and electoral choice.

HOW COMPETENT IS THE AMERICAN CITIZENRY AT THE GAME OF POLITICS?

For a country that prides itself on having the oldest written and still operative constitution, there are certain problems in considering ourselves a democracy. These center around the level and types of participation in which we engage, our information level, and the holding of general political opinions.

Level of Political Participation

We can turn first to the minimal act in a democracy, voting in national elections. One indication of the degree to which Americans are politically active is available without turning to public-opinion surveys: the number of voters who actually vote can be compared with the potential electorate (the voting-age population). Such a comparison confirms that numerous (and, in recent years, an increasing percentage of) American fail to perform the rather undemanding act of voting.

In the eight presidential elections between 1952 and 1980, roughly four out of ten adults were non-voters. Since 1960, there has been an almost steady decline, to the point where almost half of the adults are non-voters. In the congressional elections for those years, elections which lack the stimulus of a nationally-fought and publicized contest, the turnout was lower by about 4%, and also showed a distinct decline. When we examine the off-year congressional elections, the results are even more depressing. In this time period, roughly six out of ten adults did not vote for members of Congress. Indeed, in 1978, little more than a third of the potential electorate voted.

Several reasons can be offered for these trends—the absence of real contests in some instances, the absence of any opposition in certain congressional races, and so forth.

Whatever the reasons, it is obvious that there is nothing approaching a desirable minimum level of voting in the United States. We should add this point here: When reasons for non-voting are brought up, there is an invariable mention of political cynicism, a point with which we deal further later in this chapter, when we examine the second criterion—efficacy—for popular democracy. And, when cynicism is mentioned, it is by now a cliché to mention Watergate and the subsequent resignation in disgrace of a president. A quick glance at Figure 2-1 should make it clear that the overall decline in the level of voting preceded Watergate. The Watergate burglary took place in June 1972, but presidential involvement in the cover-up was not clear until after there was a 5 percent drop-off in 1972 from the previous presidential election.

Of course, it is possible that turnout statistics underestimate citizen political activity. It occasionally has been argued that there are many Americans who are deeply interested in politics but who fail to vote simply because of the similarity of the two major parties and their candidates. This is the "Tweedledee and Tweedledum" argument, drawn from the empty-headed identical twins in Lewis Carroll's *Alice in Wonderland*. There are some survey data to support this point, inasmuch as 37 percent of Americans recently reported that they saw little difference between the two par-

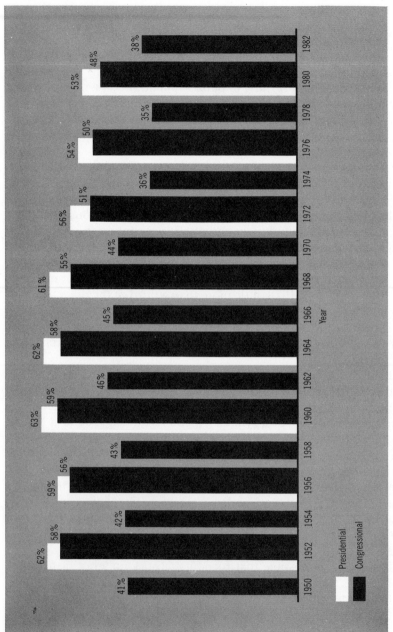

Source: *Statistical Abstract of the United States,* 1979 and 1984.

FIGURE 2-1 Participation in Recent Presidential and Congressional Elections

ties.[2] However, this is somewhat questionable, since 31 percent in a 1980 Gallup Poll answered that they would support a new party of the middle, between the polarized Democratic and Republican parties.[3] Hence for these people we have "Tweedledee, Tweedledum" and a third variant— "Tweedlemiddle." And they are not objecting to a lack of difference between parties, but rather seeking even less difference than now exists.

There are many reasons for non-voting. Some citizens are kept home on election day because of illness or bad weather, are unable to fulfill state residency requirements, or are prevented by other mechanical impediments from voting.[4] Therefore, a more detailed characterization of public political participation would be useful.

In addition to voting, we must consider various other modes of political participation and involvement. These range widely and include newsgathering, campaign activity, cooperating with others in an interest group, and making contact with public officials.[5] Table 2-1, which summarizes responses to questions regarding individuals' political activity during the eight presidential compaigns from 1952 through 1980, makes it clear that if turnout statistics are at all misleading it is because they *over*estimate public political involvement. While a majority of voters surveyed reported that they had gone to the polls in the current year's presidential election,[6] half admit that they have missed a presidential vote at one time or another. And while anywhere from 62 to 80 percent report having read something about the present campaign in the newspapers, less than half report following it assiduously or being "very much interested" in it. Moving on to somewhat more demanding citizen endeavors, we find that a third or fewer Americans practice the indoor sport of attempting to persuade some fellow citizen how to vote; less than a fifth wear a button or sport bumper stickers; a tenth claim to have made a financial contribution or attended a meeting; and a twentieth or fewer work for the parties or candidates, belong to political clubs or organizations, or attend more than a single meeting. As far as registering a political opinion via some means other than the ballot box, approximately a quarter have ever written a public official, and a mere 3–8 percent have ever sought expression through the letters-to-the-editor columns.

Of special interest here is the fact that these findings have remained virtually constant over almost three decades. In this time, television has grown into a medium which can bring campaigns into most households. Further, this has also been a time when major changes have taken place in extending and securing the franchise. As a result of sweeping legislation in the mid-1960s, large numbers of minority group-members were able to vote for the first time. The Twenty-sixth Amendment also allowed eighteen-year-olds to vote, starting with the 1972 presidential election. Yet, despite such changes in the potential electorate, the activity level has remained low.

TABLE 2-1   Proportion of Adult Americans Engaging in Varying Kinds of Political Activities

	1952	1956	1960	1964	1968	1972	1976	1980
Voting								
Reports having voted in current year's presidential election[a]	73%	73%	74%	78%	76%	73%	72%	62%
Registered to vote (those who are certain they are)	NA[b]	75	78	82	83	79	77	72
Reports having voted in all elections for president since old enough to vote	43	42	46	50	53	49	44	43
News attention								
Read something in the newspaper about year's presidential campaign	79	69	80	79	75	73	73	62
Read regularly (1952: "quite a lot") about the campaign	39	NA	43	40	36	43	34	22
Very much interested in campaign	37	30	38	38	39	32	37	29
Campaign activity								
Talked with someone and tried to persuade him or her how to vote	27	28	33	31	33	32	37	29
Wore a campaign button or put sticker on car	NA	16	21	16	15	14	8	6
Contributed funds to a candidate or party	4	10	12	11	9	10	9	9
Worked for one of the parties or candidates	3	3	6	5	6	5	4	3
Belongs to political club or organization	2	3	3	4	3	NA	NA	3
Attended a political meeting, rally, or dinner during campaign	7	10	8	9	9	9	6	7
Attended two or more meetings, etc.	NA	NA	3	4	NA	NA	NA	NA
Political communication								
Has written a public official, expressing an opinion	NA	NA	NA	17	20	27	28	NA
Has written a letter to the editor, expressing a political opinion	NA	NA	NA	3	2	7	8	NA

[a]Note that for each of the presidential elections about 10 percent more of the survey respondents report having voted than the aggregate election-date statistic in Figure 2-1 shows. The aggregate statistic is computed with total vote as the numerator and the voting-age population as the denominator. A number of categories of voting-age individuals are underrepresented or left out in public-opinion polls, and these are groups that tend not to vote (for example, the institutionalized and non-citizens). Furthermore, some small percentage of the non-voting population bends the truth when answering survey interviewers and claims to have voted. See Aage R. Clausen, "Reponse Validity: Vote Report," *Public Opinion Quarterly*, 32 (Winter 1968-69), 588-606; Michael W. Traugott and John P. Katosh, "Response Validity in Surveys of Voting Behavior," *Public Opinion Quarterly*, 43 (Fall, 1979), 359-377.
[b]Not asked.

Source: Regular election-year polls of the Survey Research Center, Center for Political Studies, University of Michigan. These and other findings are summarized in John P. Robinson et al., *Measures of Political Attitudes* (Ann Arbor, Mich.: Survey Research Center, 1968), pp. 591-625.

Level of Political Information

It is obviously impossible for every citizen to be his or her own well-qualified political expert—a walking guide to the political system. Even by very generous standards, however, the American public is remarkably ill-informed about the structure and progress of our government. This is the case despite a constantly increasing level of education and great public access to the mass media. (At minimum level, most American homes have a television set and a radio; many also subscribe to one or more newspapers and magazines.)

What has been the combined impact of these two forces—education and the media—on our level of information? While not testing this question directly, the data in Table 2-2 provide very little to reassure those who would place their faith in an increasingly informed electorate. The table reports responses to two questions concerning the partisan composition of the House of Representatives. While a majority could supply the correct answer (except after the 1980 election), a substantial percentage of people were unable to do so. On the second question, which calls for ability to report on recent election results, the failure of citizens to monitor public affairs through the media is especially evident, since elections are widely publicized and surveying occurred very soon after the elections.[7]

We know that much crucial factual information about the basic structure of the political system is not widely shared. Polls have shown that somewhat more than half of the population does not know the number (not to speak of the names) of the senators sent by their state to Washington. Slightly less than half know the length of the terms of senators and representatives—a piece of information of no small consequence if one conceives of the voter as responsible for rewarding and punishing elected officials at the polls.

It is conceivable, of course, that knowledge of the structure of government is a mere "civics book matter," and is not vital to effective citizenship. Let us, therefore, look at one further aspect of public political

TABLE 2-2 Basic Information-Holding by the American Public

	1960	1964	1968	1972	1976	1980
"Which party had the most members in the House of Representatives *before* the elections?"						
Correct answer (Democrats)	64%	64%	70%	63%	61%	71%
Incorrect, don't know, unable to answer	36	36	30	37	39	29
Totals	100%	100%	100%	100%	100%	100%
"Which party had the most members in the House of Representatives *after* the elections?"						
Correct answer (Democrats)	55%	79%	49%	56%	58%	15%
Incorrect, don't know, unable to answer	45	21	51	44	42	85
Totals	100%	100%	100%	100%	100%	100%

Source: Center for Political Studies, University of Michigan.

information—awareness of the names and duties of the nation's leaders. It would be difficult to maintain that citizens can control their leaders without knowing who these individuals are. In fact, however, the occasional systematic efforts to assess public awareness of leaders have consistently shown that very large numbers of Americans are unaware of very large numbers of their leaders.

Table 2-3 reports the results of a survey taken in early spring 1980, regarding public knowledge of various political leaders and "media stars." Leading all personalities and well ahead of those in public affairs was Mary Tyler Moore. Indeed, the three most widely known figures were television personalities. About a third of those interviewed were able to correctly identify our Secretary of State—less than half of those who recognized Don Rather. Another Cabinet officer was recognized by only 13 percent and the president of the AFL-CIO was recognized by one in twenty respondents.

Focusing more closely on the citizen's own representative in Congress, Table 2-4 shows that only about two out of every five Americans can name their representatives, and less than one out of five know of any congressional votes or actions for the district. Moreover, as in other studies, there was evidence of the absence of information about the rudimentary fact of the length of the congressional term, with only slightly less than a third able to tell when their representative would next come up for re-election.

It is possible, of course, that we have overstated the case. In Table 2-2 (also see Table 2-4), we show a degree of ignorance about such aspects of the House of Representatives as which party is in control and the name of one's own representative. There is, to be sure, a contradictory point of view, arguing that, if voters are given the name of the incumbent, they are

TABLE 2-3 Proportion of Americans Able to Correctly Identify Various Political and Non-Political Figures

FIGURE TO BE IDENTIFIED	PERCENTAGE CORRECT
Mary Tyler Moore	93
Phil Donahue	83
Dan Rather	69
Eric Heiden, Olympic speed-skating star	59
Jane Byrne, Mayor of Chicago	39
Kurt Waldheim, U.N. Secretary-General	39
Frank Borman, former astronaut	38
Ron Guidry, pitcher for New York Yankees	36
Cyrus Vance, Secretary of State	34
Lee Iacocca, Chairman of Chrysler Corporation	31
Patricia Harris, Secretary of Housing and Urban Development	13
Lane Kirkland, President of AFL-CIO	5

Source: Roper Poll, 3/29/80–4/5/80. We are indebted to Everett Carll Ladd and Marilyn Potter of the Roper Center, University of Connecticut, for these data.

TABLE 2-4   Proportion of Americans Knowing Their Congressional Representative and Various Things about Him or Her

	PERCENTAGE CORRECT
1. Do you happen to know the name of the present Representative in Congress from your district?	43
2. Do you happen to know when he or she comes up for election next?	30
3. Do you know how he or she voted on any major bill this year?	19
4. Has he or she done anything for the district that you definitely know about?	14

Source: 1965 AIPO survey, reported in November 1965 *Gallup Opinion Index.*

able to recognize that name. Thus, when they walk into the polling place and are faced with a ballot they are not acting in total ignorance.[8] But this is a far cry from informed political participation!

The Holding of Political Opinions

Are many citizens ill-informed about the actions of government and the issues with which it deals? Or is the unhappy picture we have drawn about citizen knowledge of their government mistaken? It could easily be argued, for instance, that "textbook" information about who controls Congress or the names of representatives is not as relevant to citizens as are the issues facing government. In short, the presence of public current issues may be more important than answers to a "civics quiz."[9]

One problem lies in disagreement over how to best interpret surveys. For instance, a major source of the thesis that American voters are uninformed is work done in the 1950s and 1960s.[10] This work has come under serious question, and one well-received study suggests that, although the findings may have been valid for that time, new data and interpretations show that American voters are remarkably more sophisticated than they had earlier been.[11] Yet, this finding has since been challenged by others who find that the new interpretations may be based on faulty research procedures.[12] Thus, when scholars themselves are at odds over the answers to certain questions, it is impossible to paint an entirely valid picture of the American voter.

Nevertheless some findings are clear. One is that Americans rarely express a "no opinion" on an issue, when a survey question is posed to them which gives them a choice of responses. Indeed, rarely does this answer exceed 15 percent. But many of those who express "opinions" do so on the basis of almost no prior thought, and some on total unfamiliarity with the issue at hand.[13]

This becomes especially evident in responses to open-ended questions in which the respondent is asked to come up with his or her own wording in formulating an answer. Under these circumstances, the proportion of people expressing an opinion plummets. Take, for instance, the data in Table 2-5. Over the years, just before the elections, pollsters have asked citizens if there is anything about each candidate that they like or dislike. As can be seen, the percentage who confess they have no opinion is consistently high, ranging from 27 to 63 percent. And, we have not even attempted to undertake an analysis of just what opinions are offered. They range from rather specific responses about policies or ideology to such extremely vague responses as "I just like him." In short, even when we include virtually all open-ended responses no matter how vague, we still see that a substantial proportion of the American public cannot express themselves as to why they prefer or reject a given candidate in any election year.

Lest our photograph of the state of public opinion become a caricature, we should add that the public is not totally devoid of opinions. At least a few members of the electorate are close observers of and commentators on public affairs. For many other voters the fine points of governmental policy are not clear, but the general outlines of what the individual prefers are: "I don't know much about government, but I know that I like." Thus, since its inception, nation-wide polling has regularly shown that certain kinds of public attitudes are firmly established and consistently held. These, in general, are attitudes which bear on broad values, on overall policy directions. It was totally evident, for example, from the polls conducted during the several years before the United States entered World War II that the sympathies of most Americans were with the Allied, not the Axis, cause. After Pearl Harbor, devotion to winning the war was intense and widespread.[14] In subsequent years there has been consistent further documentation of broad consistencies in public assessments of many domestic and international issues.

TABLE 2-5   "No Opinions" on Presidential Candidates

YEAR	FOR DEMOCRATIC CANDIDATE	AGAINST DEMOCRATIC CANDIDATE	FOR REPUBLICAN CANDIDATE	AGAINST REPUBLICAN CANDIDATE
1952	50%*	63%	35%	54%
1956	55	51	25	55
1960	42	48	39	61
1964	27	56	61	29
1968	50	39	46	45
1972	60	31	33	53
1976	39	43	42	45
1980	46	34	51	39

*Percentages represent the proportion of all surveyed who either stated that they had "no opinion" in favor of or against that candidate or, if they had an opinion, could not offer it.

Source: Center for Political Studies, University of Michigan.

The effects of question wording on responses *might* account for some of the findings we have shown. For instance, compare responses to questions asked in the aftermath of the Three-Mile-Island accident in 1979, when there was public concern about the safety of nuclear power, and about possible government controls. As we can see in Table 2-6, wording can lead to quite different responses and interpretations. The first wording seems to reveal 64 percent concern about the safety of nuclear plants; the second a mere 30 percent concern. This does not mean, of course, that public attitudes are simply a shapeless mush. In both cases reservations were expressed regarding the safety of nuclear power. The inconsistency in assessments surely was affected by the range of options offered.

DO AMERICAN CITIZENS FEEL THAT THEY ARE EFFECTIVE AT THE GAME OF POLITICS?

Thus far we have found that Americans do not fulfill our first requirement for a democracy. They do not participate at a very high level. They claim to hold and express opinions, but do not necessarily base them on much information or show a capacity to articulate them. What of our other criterion? Do they feel that their participation is meaningful? Do they feel they have an effect upon what the government does?

We can approach these questions several ways, but each points to the same conclusion. Americans do not have strong feelings of political efficacy. In fact, there has been a marked decline in such feelings over the past three decades. Consider the standard set of questions which has been used to measure sense of political efficacy since 1952. The results of these sur-

TABLE 2-6 How Question Wording Affects Public's Response to a Question: Views of Two Comparable Samples About Nuclear Power

QUESTION	RESPONSES	
"There are differences in opinion about how safe atomic energy plants are. Some people say they are completely safe, while others say they present dangers and hazards. How do you feel—that it would be safe to have an atomic energy plant someplace near here or that it would present dangers?"	Safe	28%
	Would present dangers	64
	Dont't know	8
		100%
"All in all, from what you have heard or read, how safe are nuclear power plants that produce electric power—safe, somewhat safe, or not so safe?"	Very safe	21%
	Somewhat safe	46
	Not so safe	30
	Not sure	3
		100%

Sources: The first question was asked by the Roper Poll, 9/27/80–1/4/80; the second was asked by the poll conducted by ABC News/Lou Harris Associates, 4/4/79–4/9/79. We are indebted to Everett Carll Ladd, Jr., and Marilyn Potter of the Roper Center, University of Connecticut, for these data.

veys, shown in Figure 2-2, suggest that Americans do not especially feel that their votes are worthwhile, or that they can otherwise affect government and the officials they elect. The figure further shows the long-term trend in the decline in sense of political efficacy. This is especially strong in terms of belief that ability to affect government is worthwhile and doubt whether public officials care what the average citizen feels about issues.

There are other indications that American people have gradually come to feel less effective about their participation in politics. Many studies have shown, for instance, that there has been a greater tendency to be distrustful of the government, and to express cynicism about it and its officials.[15] It should also be pointed out, however, that wide-eyed naiveté regarding the political process can also have its costs. If the citizens of this or any other country blindly trusted the elected leadership to do what is "right," then public opinion would be unlikely to be a check on government

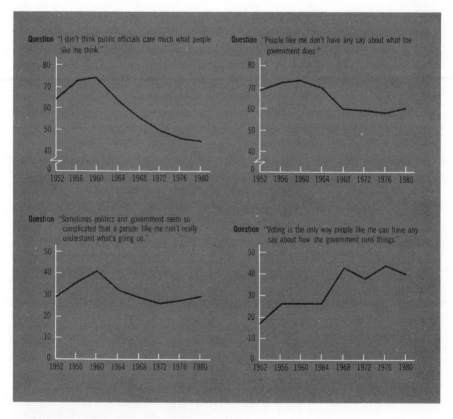

Source: Center for Political Studies, University of Michigan.

FIGURE 2-2 Percent Agreeing with Statement

at all. A healthy public skepticism of government, its leaders, and the effectiveness of its policies can contribute to ensuring that the political leadership is at least periodically responsive to the general public. So, as discouraging as the decline in feelings of efficacy seems, there may be a brighter side.

IS DEMOCRACY IN PERIL?

Our photograph of the American electorate provides the unhappy image of a citizenry ill-equipped to control its leaders effectively and undevoted to fundamental democratic principles. Nevertheless, the reader is correct if he or she suspects that these findings tell only part of the story.

The survey findings reported in this chapter are, after all, curiously discontinuous with the common-sense impression that the United States is a nation ranking high in democracy and stability. Election of public officials up to and including the president has continued uninterrupted from the early days of the republic. Many of the choices made by the electorate have—by anyone's standards—been meaningful. Who, for example, would argue that governmental policy would have been the same if Bryan had defeated McKinley in 1896, or if Hoover had defeated Roosevelt in 1932, or if Carter had won in 1980? In 1968 the unpopularity of an administration policy in the realm of greatest presidential autonomy—foreign affairs and military policy—contributed to President Johnson's decision not to run for re-election and to a variety of changes in military strategies in Vietnam (decisions to stop bombing the north, to join in negotiations with North Vietnam, etc.). And, especially important, after each presidential election (with the exception of that of 1860) the defeated parties have readily acceded to the decision of the voters. Even in 1968, when the recurrent strand of violence in American society stood in especially clear relief, there was no sign whatsoever that American political leaders had come to consider violence an acceptable means of managing political change. And, although minor party dissidents cannot be said to have been completely free from harassment in the United States, the American Independent Party of former Alabama Governor George Wallace was able to find a place on the ballot in every state in 1968 as was John Anderson in 1980. In general, restraints on free expression do not remotely approximate those in the many nations that bar electoral competition and enforce a single political orthodoxy.

A good bit of the disparity between the impression gained by examining the attitudes and information of a cross-section of the electorate and our overall common-sense impression of American politics disappears when we go on (as we do in the following chapter) to analyze the members of the political community in terms, not of a static snapshot, but rather with a view to characterizing the dynamics of electoral behavior, the division of political labor within the electorate, and the basic division of labor between citizens and their political leaders. The findings reported here should not be forgotten, however. They afford us a notion, which will be reinforced in Chapters 4 and 5, of what politics may be like when a crude, direct-democracy approach to the problems of government is adopted, an approach which conceives of politics in terms of the simple transformation of public attitudes into public policy. Fortunately, there are "devices"—among them political parties—which intervene between "raw" citizen opinion and the actions of governmental leaders. These make public control of leaders more complex—but also more workable—than the direct-democracy model would seem to suggest.

NOTES

[1]On sampling and public opinion research, the classic work is Mildred Parten, *Surverys, Polls, and Samples* (New York: Harper, 1950). See also Frederick F. Stephan and Philip J. McCarthy, *Sampling Opinions* (New York: Wiley, 1958); Earl R. Babbie, *Survey Research Methods* (Belmont, Cal.: Wadsworth, 1973); Charles H. Backstrom and Gerald D. Hursh-Cësar, *Survey Research* (2d ed.; New York; Wiley, 1981).

[2]Source: Center for Political Studies. Also see Sidney Verba and Norman H. Nie, *Participation in America: Political Democracy and Social Equality* (New York: Harper and Row, 1972), especially Chs. 6 and 8. A useful summary of the literature on this point can be found in Lester Milbrath and M. L. Goel, *Political Participation* (2d ed.; Chicago: Rand McNally, 1977).

[3]*Gallup Opinion Index,* 177 (April/May 1980), 64–65.

[4]One study, undertaken and reported before the passage of the Twenty-sixth Amendment, is of more widespread interest than its title might suggest. Philip E. Converse and Richard Niemi, "Non-Voting Among Young Adults in the United States," in William J. Crotty, Donald M. Freeman, and Douglas S. Gatlin, eds., *Political Parties and Political Behavior* (2d ed.; Boston: Allyn & Bacon, 1971), pp. 443–466.

[5]See Verba and Nie, *op. cit.,* especially Chs. 3 and 4

[6]But see the note to Table 2-1 for an explanation of why the polls show a higher percentage of turnout for any particular election than the election results would seem to indicate.

[7]Comparison to other nations is not especially comforting, either. A five-nation study more than twenty years ago showed that roughly one-third of our population (as compared to 27 percent in Great Britain, 24 percent in Germany, 55 percent in Mexico, and 60 percent in Italy) could not name more than one Cabinet position. Another third (as compared to 34 percent in Great Britain, 40 percent in Germany, 21 percent in Mexico, and 23 percent in Italy) could name five of the positions, or about half of those which then existed.

[8]Thomas E. Mann, *Unsafe At Any Margin* (Washington: American Enterprise Institute, 1978), especially Chp. 3.

[9]Benjamin I. Page, *Choices and Echoes in Presidential Elections: Rational Man and Electoral Democracy* (Chicago: University of Chicago Press, 1978), p. 32.

[10]Angus Campbell, Philip E. Converse, Warren E. Miller, and Donald E. Stokes, *The American Voter* (New York: Wiley, 1960); Philip E. Converse, "The Nature of Belief in Mass Publics," in *Ideology and Discontent*, David Apter, ed., (New York: Free Press, 1964), pp. 206–261.

[11]John C. Pierce and Douglas D. Rose, "Nonattitudes and American Public Opinion," *American Political Science Review*, 68 (June 1974), 626–649; Norman H. Nie, Sidney Verba, and John R. Petrocik, *The Changing American Voter* (Cambridge, Mass.: Harvard University Press, 1976).

[12]George F. Bishop *et al.*, "The Changing Structure of Mass Belief Systems: Fact or Artifact?" *Journal of Politics*, 40 (August 1978), 781–87; Ronald B. Rapoport, "What They Don't Know Can Hurt You," *American Journal of Political Science*, 23 (November 1979), 805–815; George F. Balch, "Statistical Manipulation in the Study of Issue Consistency: The Gamma Coefficient, " *Political Behavior*, 1 (1979), 217–41. A useful bibliography on some of the points raised by those who question the findings in *The Changing American Voter* may be found by consulting George F. Bishop, "Experiments in Filtering Political Opinions," *Political Behavior*, 2 (1980), 339–69.

[13]Herbert Hyman and Paul Sheatsley, "The Current Status of American Public Opinion," *National Council for the Social Studies Yearbook*, 21 (1950). Reprinted in Daniel Katz, et al., eds., *Public Opinion and Propaganda* (New York: Dryden, 1954), reference on p. 37. The "don't know" response can be significantly affected by the presence or absence of a "filter question," as well as by the question wording itself. On this point, see George F. Bishop, "Experiments in Filtering Political Opinions."

[14]Jerome Bruner, *Mandate from the People* (New York: Duell, Sloan, 1944).

[15]See, for example, Arthur H. Miller, "Political Issues and Trust in Government: 1964 - 1970," *American Political Science Review*, 68 (September 1974), 951–72; also, in the same issue, Jack Citrin, "Comment: The Political Relevance of Trust in Government," 973–88, and Arthur H. Miller, "Rejoinder to 'Comment' by Jack Citrin: Political Discontent or Ritualism?", 989–1001.

chapter 3 _____

CITIZEN POLITICS:
The Behavior
_____ of the Electorate

Although polls and election statistics reveal that many Americans do not vote, some engage in doorbell ringing and other more demanding kinds of participation. Still others are far more politically active and potent than virtually anyone caught up in the broad net of the usual public-opinion survey. These are the thousands of individuals in actual leadership positions—for example, elected and appointed officials at various levels of government, directors of interest groups and other associations, key figures in the communications industry, directors of some of the great tax-free foundations, academic policy advisors who move in and out of government, and elder statesmen such as former presidents.

It follows from such uneven distribution of activity that the views of some citizens have more political impact that the views of others. We therefore cannot be content simply with studying the behavior of the undifferentiated general public in our assessment of the citizen base of the political system. We must go on, as we do in the present chapter, to consider the behavior of the effective public. After our analysis of the composition of groups in the electorate and their relative effectiveness, we shall examine the dynamics of electoral choice.

GROUPS IN THE ELECTORATE AND THEIR BEHAVIOR

Who Participates in Politics?

One way to answer the question is to define the non-participant. Over several decades, certain characteristics have been evident. The typical stay-at-home is more likely to be low in occupational skills and education level. Figure 3-1 identifies the politically active members of the electorate and showing variation in voting levels. The range of participation from group to group is striking. Taking extreme cases, in 1980 almost nine out of ten of the citizens in professional and managerial occupations interviewed by the University of Michigan Survey Research Center reported that they had voted; only six out of ten skilled, semi-skilled, and unskilled workers reported having exercised the franchise.[1]

FIGURE 3-1   Electoral Turnout of Key American Categoric Groups: 1980 Presidential Election

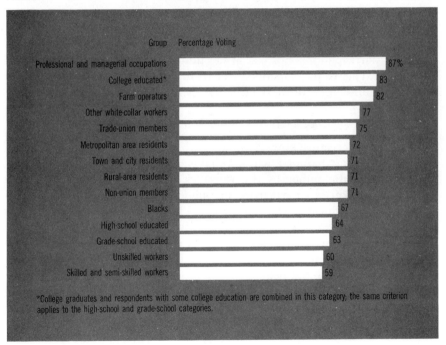

*College graduates and respondents with some college education are combined in this category; the same criterion applies to the high-school and grade-school categories.

Source: National survey conducted by the Center for Political Studies, University of Michigan. A very extensive breakdown of group differences in voting turnout is provided in U.S. Bureau of the Census, *Current Population Reports, Special Studies, Series P-23, No. 102*, "Nonvoting Americans," (Washington: Government Printing Office, April, 1980). The present findings are taken from the less detailed CPS findings in order to parallel those reported in Table 3-2 on the party support of these groups. On why poll findings indicate higher turnout than do aggregate election statistics, see the note to Table 2-1.

Of course, it is immediately evident that these "groups" are not discrete entities. Voters are not necessarily *either* college-educated *or* professionals. There is an overlap in population categories. For instance, very young voters—the lowest turnout category in many surveys—include the well-educated and also young people with only grade-school training. There is greater turnout for college educated youths than for those who have received less schooling.

The relationship between political participation and various indices of social standing or social advantage has been consistently found over the years.[2] What about the decline in participation? There is no conclusive explanation, but one study of the long-term decline in voter turnout in presidential elections from 1960 to 1980, concluded that the combined effect of two changing attitudes accounted for roughly two-thirds of the decline. These attitudes were party identification and feelings of governmental responsiveness. Fewer voters had loyalties to parties and fewer felt that government is essentially responsive.

As might be expected, there are differences between groups in terms of participation other than voting. One study focused on individuals who actively practiced their citizenship through consistent attention to public affairs and participation—not just at election time. It found that the more attentive and active participants differ from the general public in the same ways that non-voters differ from voters.[3]

What Are the Characteristics of the Active Participants?

A happier picture emerges of the citizen base of the political system than was seen in Chapter 2 when we take account of group activity levels and then rate the public by the yardstick of political competence. The groups most likely to participate in politics tend also to be the better-educated and politically better-informed. Thus, in Table 3-1, which shows how the findings reported in Table 2-2 differ by education levels, for the 1980 elections, we see that college-educated people are much more likely to know which party controlled the House of Representatives before and after the election than are the people who have only a grade-school education. This is not to say that the college-educated are models of civic virtue (almost eight out of ten were unable to say who controlled the House after the election—despite heavy media discussion on election night and thereafter of the nature of split control, with President-elect Reagan facing a Democratic House), or that all of the low-education citizens are uninformed. Furthermore, it obviously does not follow that because an individual knows such facts he or she can wisely comprehend the events that follow, leading up to his or her next election choices. But it is the case that the tendency to vote and the tendency to know something about the subject matter of

TABLE 3-1 Information-Holding and Education, 1980

	EDUCATION		
	(0-8 Years)	(9-12 Years)	(More Than 12)
"Which party had the most members in the House of Representatives *before* the election?"			
Correct answer (Democrats)	50%	66%	85%
Incorrect, don't know, unable to answer	50	34	15
Totals	100%	100%	100%
"Which party had the most members in the House of Representatives *after* the elections?"			
Correct answer (Democrats)	10%	10%	23%
Incorrect, don't know, unable to answer	90	90	77
Totals	100%	100%	100%

Source: Center for Political Studies, University of Michigan.

voting go together, and that such information cannot always be dismissed as "trivia."[4]

Thus one of the attributes of the "general public" which was revealed in Chapter 2—low political participation—seems to be neutralized when we shift our perspective and examine the "differentiated public." We might add, too, that feelings of political efficacy have commonly been found to increase with educational level. Because the active citizens tend to be those who feel most effective politically, as well as those who are most committed to democratic ground-rules, there emerges a public which exceeds the general public in their effect on public law-makers. As we indicated in Chapter 2, there is some question as to whether participation increases feelings of political efficacy, or whether those who are most efficacious in the first place are more likely to participate.

Regardless of such questions, it should be clear that this differentiated public under-represents the nation's poorer and less well-educated citizens. In this respect, we depart from any ideal one may hold of a democracy in which all citizens are of equal influence. Second, even the more highly active, democratically oriented, and relatively well-informed segments of the "differentiated public"—for example the college graduates in the surveys we have considered—fall considerably short of some idealized "perfect" citizenship. For instance, although Table 3-1 shows that college-educated people are generally more aware of Congress and their representative, it does not show that only one out of four had written their representative in the past twelve months. This brings us to another, quite different sort of control relationship between citizens and their leaders.

Who Supports Which Party in the United States?

One of the most persistent stereotypes we hold in politics is the image we have of ourselves in terms of party support. Reduced to its essentials, the stereotype holds that Republicans are better-educated (with the implication of being "smarter"), of higher income, hold higher status jobs, and are more likely to live in the suburbs. Democrats not only represent the other side of this coin, but are more likely to be Catholics, Jews, blacks, and perhaps a trifle shabby to boot! An oddity of this picture is that Independents—those who support neither party with any regularity—are idealized in the folklore of American politics for their sagacity. And, in terms of education, income, and so on, the popular image of Independents closely parallels that of Republicans.

One trouble with stereotypes is that they may hold just enough water to be accepted uncritically. In this case, they have been fostered somewhat by the national parties themselves. Democrats commonly speak of themselves as being the "party of the little person," seemingly representing the average person against the rapacity of large corporations. Republicans, on the other hand, portray themselves as being in favor of sound fiscal practices, such as those used in business. The distorted images the two parties project of each other certainly do not help, either. Democrats are portrayed as profligate spenders who are not above getting the country into war in order to improve economic conditions. Republicans must bear the burden of being accused of fostering depressions, unemployment, and general economic bad times. The images which voters hold of parties may become even more mixed as a result of developments in the late 1970s and the 1980 election. President Carter, for instance, adopted what many thought was the Republican banner of fiscal conservativism, even though his budget was consistently unbalanced. And, Reagan campaigned with the avowed intention of reducing unemployment, an old Democratic theme. In this sense, some of those who profess to see little or no differences between the parties may be more informed than we might otherwise have thought.

When we consider the electorate in terms of its group makeup, we find that there is indeed some justification for one set of stereotypes—that of the broad groupings that "normally" vote for one party or the other. In doing so we must make allowances for the peculiarities of each campaign and the candidates for president who head their respective tickets. Each of the major parties has tended to have a somewhat different clientele of supporters among the groups in society. When we look at group party-support patterns, it becomes clear that in spite of the paucity of political information and carefully considered opinions in the population, the citizen's vote *does* seem to relate his needs and interests to the actions of officials in a rational way.

For instance, it has long been assumed by many observers that congressional candidates were the primary beneficiaries of party-line voting. That is, while some voters may hop about on the ballot, voting for a Democrat here and a Republican there, there might be some consistency in the vote, based on party identification, starting with members of Congress and going further down the ballot. Further, this was often assumed to be the case, *necessarily,* since so many voters did not know the name of their representative, or at least so it seemed. Yet, some recent research has shown that there is a tendency for voters to "choose the preferred candidate in congressional elections instead of automatically voting their party or bowing to the incumbent . . . "[5] The basis of this preference can be any of several factors, ranging from group identifications to personal knowledge of the candidates to issue appeals made, and so forth. These factors are not necessarily unrelated, by any means. Indeed, there is probably, in many voters' minds, a link between their own group identifications and party identification, but it is apparently not one which is unquestionable. In 1980, for instance, the Reagan-Bush ticket for the Republicans made a major effort to direct its campaign to blacks, a constituency which had largely been ignored in the past. To prove this point, we might examine Table 3-2, which shows the dominant voter support patterns over several elections involving incumbent presidents.

These elections provide considerable variation, such as margin of victory and the circumstances of the elections. The 1948 election, for instance, was a very close "upset" in which in incumbent President Harry S. Truman defeated New York Governor Thomas E. Dewey; the 1956 election provided incumbent Republican Dwight D. Eisenhower a substantial majority; in 1964, Democratic President Lyndon B. Johnson defeated his Republican adversary Barry Goldwater in a record landslide; incumbent Republican Richard M. Nixon won in 1972 with yet another record vote over his Democratic challenger, George McGovern; the 1980 election saw incumbent Democratic President Jimmy Carter lose to Republican Ronald Reagan, affected by the independent candidacy of former Republican Representative John Anderson.

What is remarkable about the social background data we see in Table 3-2 is the general consistency of group support for one or the other major party. For an indication of the Republican core vote, for instance, note the groups that gave a plurality of their support to the GOP not only in its winning year of 1956, but also in its losing year of 1948.[6] *Every* population group gave more support to the Democrats than to the Republicans in the Democratic avalanche of 1964, but even in that year the Republican core groups held more solidly for that party than did the rest of the population. These categories of consistent Republican voting are the professional and

TABLE 3-2   The Voting of Major American Social Groups: Survey Research Center Findings in the 1948, 1956, 1964, 1972, and 1980 Elections

GROUP CHARACTERISTIC[a]	VOTE REPUBLICAN					VOTE DEMOCRATIC				
	1948	1956	1964	1972	1980	1948	1956	1964	1972	1980
Education										
Grade School	16%	35%	14%	33%	20%	35%	24%	54%	22%	36%
High School	29	41	22	44	33	34	34	54	62	27
College	54	62	40	53	45	17	28	48	31	26
Occupation of family head										
Professional and managerial	58	57	35	55	39	14	27	50	26	28
Other white-collar	38	48	30	46	39	38	30	54	27	27
Skilled and semi-skilled	15	39	16	43	29	52	32	57	23	29
Unskilled	12	24	11	26	32	33	29	56	29	22
Farm operators	13	40	29	62	52	25	34	52	17	6
Trade union affiliation of family head										
Member	13	36	12	44	29	55	39	68	31	38
Non-member	32	46	28	46	38	26	25	47	23	25
Type of community										
Metropolitan areas	32	43	17	43	24	46	35	63	31	40
Towns and cities	30	46	28	49	41	28	25	50	21	22
Rural areas	12	38	42	45	40	25	29	52	20	24
Religion										
Protestant	28	44	29	46	38	25	25	47	21	29
Catholic	25	43	18	45	35	49	36	66	30	30
Race										
White	29	46	28	49	41	33	29	51	21	24
Black	10	12	0	8	1	18	23	64	54	61

managerial occupations, the college-educated, and the residents of those areas that are so often thought to be the quintessence of Republicanism, America's towns and smaller cities. Also "carried" by the Republicans in both their winning year and the year when they were defeated by only a small margin are a pair of population groupings that are too large and amorphous to be treated as clienteles to which parties can appeal directly—Protestants and non-union members.

When we follow these results into the 1972 and 1980 elections, both won by Republicans in a time when the parties were often said to be undergoing significant change, what do we find? Republicans made substantial gains among those of lower education and across all occupational categories, especially those considered to be less skilled. Reflecting this somewhat is the increased Republican vote among union members.

TABLE 3-2 (Continued)

GROUP CHARACTERISTIC[a]	VOTE OTHER					NOT VOTING				
	1948	1956	1964	1972	1980	1948	1956	1964	1972	1980
Education										
Grade School	4%	1%	0%	3%	1%	45%	40%	32%	42%	43%
High School	4	1	—[b]	4	5	33	26	24	30	35
College	8	—	—	3	12	21	10	12	13	18
Occupation of family head										
Professional and managerial	3	1	0	3	8	25	15	15	17	24
Other white-collar	5	1	0	3	9	19	21	16	24	25
Skilled and semi-skilled	4	1	—	3	5	29	28	27	31	38
Unskilled	5	—	0	4	2	50	47	33	41	44
Farm operators	4	—	—	5	12	58	26	19	17	24
Trade union affiliation of family head										
Member	5	2	0	5	5	27	23	20	21	28
Non-member	4	1	0	3	8	38	28	25	28	30
Type of community										
Metropolitan areas	5	1	0	2	8	17	21	20	10	28
Towns and cities	5	1	—	4	7	37	28	22	26	30
Rural areas	4	1	—	4	6	59	32	25	32	30
Religion										
Protestant	5	1	—	3	5	42	30	24	30	28
Catholic	5	1	0	4	7	21	20	16	21	29
Race										
White	4	1	—	3	8	34	28	21	26	28
Black	8	1	0	2	1	64	64	36	36	34

[a]Cell entries represent percent of that group voting Republican, Democratic, other, and not voting, that year.
[b]Less than 0.5 percent.
Source: Center for Political Studies, University of Michigan.

On the Democratic side we find three groups consistently providing a plurity of support for that party, even in the face of Eisenhower's 1956 triumph—unskilled workers, blacks, and union members. Clearly, legislation designed to combat the consequences of urban decay and slums is more likely to seem urgent to members of the Democratic core groups (especially the first two of them) than to those from the Republican-leaning strata of the population. Further evidence of this traditional Democratic coalition—which formed during the years of Franklin D. Roosevelt's New Deal—can be found by noting the additional groups picked up by the Democrats in 1948 and carried with special one-sidedness in 1964—Catholics (in many cases representatives of the ethnic groups which emigrated from Europe between the middle of the nineteenth century and World War I), residents of metropolitan areas, and the grade-school and high-school educated.

However, as implied by our mention of Republican gains in certain population groupings, there was also a noticeable loss for the Democrats in the 1972 and 1980 elections, among what are normally considered their core voting groups—the relatively less educated and less skilled, and union members. Nonetheless, Democrats still have a major "hold" on these groups, and have shown some off-setting gains among others. Before we jump to conclusions about how the nature of support for the two parties has changed, we should remember that our data show the elections at eight-year intervals. Hence, we do not show the victories for Eisenhower (1952), Kennedy (1960), Nixon (1968), or Carter (1976). A closer look might suggest that the changes in social class support for the candidates of the two major parties might be more apparent than real, a product of candidate images rather than genuine shifts in party support.

Many Americans object to group analyses of political behavior—especially if they touch on social class. And, members of one or another grouping do not necessarily wish to have themselves taken for granted as "belonging" to one or the other party. But, group voting patterns have a long history in the United States. References to them can be found as far back as colonial times; in fact, the competition of social groups during the period of the Articles of Confederation was an important consideration in the minds of the Founding Fathers when the Constitution was framed.[7] Analysis of group voting is one of the standard tools of the working politician. As might be suspected from the discussion in the preceding chapter, one of the most difficult tasks faced by an elected official is somehow to reach down to the grassroots and gain insight into his or her actual or potential sources of support. To do this effectively, it is necessary to find some means of categorizing the electorate, of pinpointing groups which may be responsive—or antagonistic—to different appeals. By necessity, therefore, working politicians become students of the sociology of the electorate. (As we have mentioned and shall discuss again shortly, the politician's use of shorthand procedures for classifying and analyzing the public is paralleled by the voter's similar use of a number of elementary "simplifying" devices which make possible the act of political choice.)

Table 3-2, although it indicates the group bases of each party, also suggests that the popular objection to class interpretations of American politics has some merit. Neither party has exclusive "control" of any of the population groups. Each party is sufficiently heterogeneous to receive some support from all groups. And, from election to election, the winning party is capable of advancing—and retreating—within the groups which ordinarily provide the other party's core supporters. Reading almost any line of Table 3-2, for instance, shows a certain ebb and flow of support for each major party. An analysis of the 1980 elections along these lines is suggestive of the extent to which the party coalitions have stayed alove.

> The basic structure of party coalitions is intact: the Democrats still attract a disproportionate share of . . . their traditional groups, and the Republicans do the same. . . . There has, however, been a weakening of the partisan loyalties of the union families, the non-Protestants, and the Southerners. The traditional coalition of the Democratic Party is now so watered down that the Democrats are in trouble, despite their continuing lead in party identification.[8]

There is a single important exception in Table 3-2 to the rule that no party monopolizes *all* of any group, applying to only one of the three elections there summarized. In 1964, the Survey Research Center interviewers did not encounter a single black Goldwater supporter. This is not to say that in the general population there were absolutely no black voters for the Republican (although a few black precincts did in fact go 100 percent for Johnson); it simply indicates that black voters were overwhelmingly pro-Democratic in that year.

The circumstances of the one-sided black vote for Johnson in 1964 are instructive. Johnson had just actively presided over the passage of a major civil rights bill. Goldwater's vote against that bill had been widely publicized. In 1968 the Republican candidate also did very poorly among blacks; the Survey Research Center found only 3 percent black support for Nixon. One of Mr. Nixon's first political "signals" after assuming the Presidency (on the occasion of a ceremonial visit to the Washington ghetto) was to let it be known that he hoped to establish his, and his party's, stock among blacks. While it is easy to exaggerate the degree to which political leaders are moved by electoral calculations, it is worth noting that President Nixon's margin of victory had been so close that even a tiny splinter of the black vote was not to be scorned. Furthermore, the advantages of bidding for further support in this population group—strategically placed as it is in populous, closely competitive states—were obvious. As can be seen, however, Nixon's 1972 support among blacks was not especially high.[9]

However, this is not to say that black voters are wholly wed to the Democrats. In 1969, Mayor John Lindsay of New York City, a Republican who had been defeated in his own party's primary election, ran on the ticket of a New York third party (the Liberal Party). He was re-elected with overwhelming support from black areas of the city. Lindsay ran against Democratic and Republican candidates who emphasized the kinds of "law and order" issues that came in the late 1960s to be seen by many voters as a surrogate for direct expression of racial antagonisms. The variability of voting among blacks, a group low in the resources that normally make for effective political participation, provides a striking illustration of how group voting can serve to express citizens' needs and desires.[10] This was probably never so clearly demonstrated at a national level as by Reverend Jesse Jackson's campaign for the Democratic party's presidential nomination in 1984. His candidacy served to register several million blacks and other minorities who had previously stayed outside normal electoral politics.

Let us attempt to state the implications of voter sociology for democratic politics in a reasonably general fashion: *Under conditions of reasonably close balance between the parties, politicians who want to gain office have a substantial incentive to adopt what might be described as a "flexibly responsive" stance to the principal groups in the electorate.* They need to be sufficiently responsive to the central groups in their own clientele to hold the support of these groups and encourage them to turn out at the polls. At the same time, they have reason to be sufficiently flexible to win at least some votes from members of groups that supply the core constituents of the other party. Conditions of close party balance do not in fact obtain everywhere in the United States, as we shall see in Chapter 5. But in some political jurisdictions there *is* close party competition; in many others the minority party at least poses an occasional threat; and in the nation's most important jurisdiction, the presidential electoral arena, the party balance is sufficiently close to produce occasional outcomes like President Nixon's 1968 popular vote plurality of 0.68 of 1 percent.

Such evenness of electoral balance encourages more than simple response to group demands; it encourages entrepreneurial efforts by politicians to anticipate (and shape) group desires even before they are fully crystallized. In such enterprising efforts by politicians to establish links with the diverse groups of the electorate we find a partial explanation of the seeming contradiction noted at the end of the previous chapter: the American electorate appears to exercise considerable (though scarcely perfect) control over the political actions of its leaders—even though most members of the electorate appear to be strikingly low in political activity and attentiveness.

THE DYNAMICS OF ELECTORAL CHOICE

The study of group voting takes us only part of the way to an understanding of electoral behavior. For a more thorough knowledge of voters we must move to a level of analysis closer to the actual processes of choice— from voter sociology to voter psychology. What are voters' motivations? What criteria guide their electoral choices?

The *New Yorker* cartoonist George Price once memorably portrayed the decision-making of a totally criteria-less voter. Price sketched a voting booth, the curtains drawn. Spinning in the air over the booth was a flipped coin. From our examination of the electorate en masse in Chapter 2, we might expect that for many citizens the act of voting is precisely as arbitrary as it was for Price's coin-flipping voter. But this clearly is not the case. If all voters were random in their choices none of the groups shown in Table 3-2 would vary far from a 50-50 split.

A Classification of Elections

One way to approach the subject of voter choices is to examine what has happened in an historical context. That is, we can look at presidential elections, see what preceded and what followed them, and then come to some understanding of what may have been the dominant orientations of voters in each of those elections.

There are several ways of doing this. One is the use of a three-election typology.[11] The first type of election in this scheme is the so-called *maintaining election*. In this type, the dominant party majority in the electorate remains the majority, and literally maintains its control by voting for the party which is already in power in government. One problem with this scheme is immediately apparent. At what office level shall we make our distinctions? For instance, if we look at Table 3-3, we see that the dominant election type has been maintaining, at least for presidential elections. Were we to examine a lower-level office, that of U.S. Representative or Senator, we could come to the conclusion that maintaining elections are virtually the only kind we have, since the Democrats controlled both the House and the Senate for all but four years, 1933-1981! Hence, we might simply come to believe that party identification has such an overwhelming impact on the electorate and therefore on the ways in which ballots are cast that change is virtually impossible.

Yet, as we saw in Table 3-2, there is something of a shifting basis of support for our two major parties, even though there is an apparent "core" for each. Hence, voters are not necessarily attached so firmly to a single party that they vote simply on the basis of party identification. Nor, for that matter, should we assume that maintaining elections reflect this for all voters. Instead, voters can consider other matters besides party identification when they cast their votes, and many do. When most voters temporarily shift their allegiances and vote for a candidate of the apparent minority party, we refer to a *deviating election*. It is a deviation in large part because a subsequent election shows that the prevailing party majority is still there. Take the 1952 and 1956 presidential contests, for example. After twenty years of Democratic control of the White House, Eisenhower was able to capture the presidency in two successive elections. However, we classify these two as "deviating" because, in part, the following elections (Kennedy in 1960; Johnson in 1964) restored the Democrats to control. Further, at the next lower office levels, the Democrats were able to maintain their control of the House and Senate, with the single exception of the 1952 elec-

TABLE 3-3   Types of Elections in the United States

MAINTAINING	DEVIATING	REALIGNING
	Dominant Voter Orientation:	
Party	Candidate	Issue
1864		1860
1868		
1872		
1976		
1880		
	1884	
1888		
	1892	
		1896
1900		
1904		
1908		
	1912	
	1916	
1920		
1924		
1928		
		1932
1936		
1940		
1944		
1948		
	1952	
	1956	
1960		
1964		
	1968	
	1972	
1976		
	1980? or	1980?

tions. In sum, it would appear that candidate orientation (the perceptions of candidates held by the voters), at least at the the presidential level, was the dominant factor in Eisenhower's victories. The same might be said for the 1968 and 1972 elections in which Nixon defeated Democrats Humphrey and McGovern, but could not lead his fellow Republicans to control of either house of Congress. Assuming that this typology of elections is valid, then it would appear that deviating elections, often based on candidate orientation, are the second most common type, but trail maintaining (party identification-based) elections by a significant margin.

We might add, parenthetically, that history is an obvious test of how to classify any single election. Hence, to some observers the 1968 election initially appeared to be of our third variety, a *realigning election*, in which a new majority is created and fundamental party allegiances shift in a rather significant manner. Such elections are typically based on a major issue or set of issues, so major that it might appear to be traumatic to some. In 1968 we appeared to have such a set of issues, centering around such questions as our participation in the Vietnam War and what has been called the "Social Issue."[12] The latter was a cluster of issues involving race, social order, minority rights, and the role of government. Yet the Democrats in 1968 and through 1974 continued to control the Congress, and the Republicans were unable to establish a new majority. Hence we can call the 1976 Carter election "maintaining," rather than deviating from a new Republican majority in the electorate.

How shall we describe the 1980 presidential election? *Some* signs of a realignment were present, but were they sufficient to make the Republicans a new majority on a more or less permanent basis? Accompanying such a shift should also be a significant change in what voters expect from government. In short, there should be a newly dominant public philosophy which would guide and shape the nature of the issues to be considered, and how government would approach those issues. A dominant issue in the 1980 election was the economy, with a peculiar but now-familiar combination of recession and inflation. Also at question was a set of issues involving America's role in world affairs. Iran had held more than 50 Americans hostage for over a year at the time of the election. America was unable to stop armed Soviet expansion into Afghanistan. There was considerable negative candidate orientation against President Carter. And, aside from this, a serious independent candidacy by John Anderson threatened both major parties. Was this a realignment, or the beginnings of one? Given the ways in which Congress reacted to President Reagan's program in his first two years, it *might* appear that a new public philosophy had emerged. On the other hand, it could also be that Congress was reacting both to the President's personal appeals to them, and to the *appearance* of a new public philosophy. At this writing it is too early to tell, especially since Congress was split in party control. However, it is clear that some voters are drifting in their party allegiances, with a potential for instability in party-developed public policy.

This possibility is quite important to the failure of our party system, so let us examine it in more depth. A realigning election, in one case, created a whole new majority party out of what had previously been a minority: In 1860, the Republican party, then only six years old, won the presidency in a four-way race, and established itself as the majority party for many years to come. Slavery and states' rights were the traumatic issues of 1860. The 1896 election, which we have termed realigning, kept the Republican majority but also reshaped it, giving it an urban base where before it had been more of a rural party. The primary issues of that time were "free coinage of silver" and the personality of the Democratic candidate, William Jennings Bryan. The 1928-1936 period may be thought of as a "realigning electoral era." Certainly, the Republicans captured the presidency in 1928, but they did so at the cost of their recently won urban constituency, which essentially moved back to the Democrats. This was brought on, in part, by the candidacy of the Democratic standard-bearer, Governor Alfred E. Smith of New York. Smith's Catholicism was a highly emotional and significant issue. By 1932, holding onto their newly regained urban base, the Democrats under Franklin Delano Roosevelt were able to capture both the presidency and Congress as the nation was undergoing its most significant economic depression. By 1936, Roosevelt had created a new majority which essentially followed his New Deal public philosophy of governmental activism. This New Deal coalition of liberals, labor, minorities, and the South served as the backbone of the Democratic party for many years, as we saw in Table 3-2, but was badly shaken by the Nixon victories in 1968 and 1972, and Reagan's 1980 election as well. The essential point is that not only were the Democrats dominant in the 1932-1980 era, giving up Congress for only four years, but their liberal policies set the agenda for that time as well. Even though the nation elected Republicans Eisenhower and Nixon in this period, the governing philosophy of the country remained essentially unaltered.

A Second Look

It is generally not difficult to accept the three-fold typology of elections we have discussed here. But it is also possible to make too much of it. For instance, even though party identification may be the dominant force in maintaining elections, it is not the only one. Some voters may be guided in their choices by party identification, but rarely to the exclusion of the factors of candidate qualities and issues. It is probably safe to say that in such elections most voters find ways unconsciously to bring their perceptions of the candidates and issues into harmony with their underlying party identification.

In the same vein, while some voters may be persuaded by a candidate's appearance or general image, to the exclusion of other considerations, this does not necessarily mean that party identification is ignored, or that candidate evaluations cannot be made on the basis of issues. Indeed, one of the major ways in which candidates are evaluated is on their positions regarding certain issues, such as foreign or economic policy. Another way is for voters to conclude that Candidate X would be better or worse for certain groups, such as farmers, consumers, labor, small business, and the like.[13]

It is also entirely likely that the scheme we have presented here places far too much stress on maintaining elections as being essentially reflective of party identification. For instance, one could argue that, starting at least as early as the 1936 election, most people have been voting, at least at the presidential level, on the basis of candidate orientation. Candidates have always had their strong as well as weak points, and voters have been able to react to these. The second election of Franklin Delano Roosevelt may be safely said to have been a watershed in electronic campaigning. From the distant viewpoint of the several decades which have since elapsed, it is easy to forget the role played by radio in the days before television. Yet Roosevelt was one of the best candidates any media consultant could want. From his inaugural address in 1933, when he told the nation that "the only thing we have to fear is fear itself," he made masterful use of the radio, reaching more Americans than had any office-holder before him. His "fireside chats" as President, during the worst days of the Depression, kept him in the public eye, as did his leadership during World War II. In those years, the Democratic party he led secured a strong grip on the Congress and on many lower offices as well. Did Roosevelt profit from the Democratic majority? Or was that majority created by him, and did his party profit by his leadership?

Similar questions can be asked about the succeeding maintaining elections. In 1948, while his opponent Thomas Dewey slowed his campaigning in the last several weeks, President Truman took his "whistlestop" campaign train to the people, monopolizing headlines. The "give 'em hell, Harry" theme which developed was an advertising executive's dream, in the way it communicated an image of a feisty common man taking on his opponents. Did Truman win because of party identification? Or, again, did he bring a majority into Congress and other offices as well?

The 1960 and 1976 elections could be defined as "reinstating elections," a term coined to describe the return to power of a previous majority, presumably followed by at least one maintaining election.[14] Certainly, the 1960 election bears all of the hallmarks of this, when, after eight years under Republican President Eisenhower, John F. Kennedy narrowly won election. Yet, there may be a clue here, for Kennedy did not do so well with the public as did his party in Congress. Both positive and negative candidate orientations may have been at work. On one hand, Kennedy's Catholicism was a major issue for many voters. On the other, the "Great Debates" of 1960 seemingly cost his opponent, Vice President Nixon, an edge in the polls which was never regained. It might seem that, in 1960, Kennedy was helped by the party identification of the majority Democrats. Or, could we conceivably turn this analysis around and conclude that party identification was barely sufficient to overcome the electoral handicap of his religion!

Was 1976 a "maintaining" or "reinstating" election? At first glance it might seem that Carter, who won office over incumbent Republican President Ford, may have profited from his party identification. However, it should also be remembered that that election took place in a very specific and unusual context. Little more than two years earlier, Ford had assumed office after the first resignation of a U.S. president. Shortly thereafter, Ford gave ex-President Nixon an unconditional pardon. In 1976, for both contenders, candidate orientation may have been operative. In Ford's case, there was a record to defend, including his pardon of Nixon. Carter had a minimal record of public service, but stressed the stylistic theme of "trust."

In 1964, President Johnson may also have been the beneficiary of candidate orientation. Running against "Mr. Conservative," Barry Goldwater, Johnson had in a year's incumbency built a record as one who knew how to make things work in Washington, thereby impressing the more liberal wing of his party. For others, notably in the South, LBJ's stance in favor of civil rights legislation suggested that he was no longer one to be trusted. Indeed, Goldwater carried only six states, his native Arizona and five others in the Deep South.[15] It would seem that not only Johnson's generally positive image, but a strongly negative orientation toward Goldwater, may have been the deciding factor in that campaign.[16]

What we have described to this point are the three major criteria by which voters make their choices. These three are *issue orientation, candidate orientation,* and *party identification.* Let us briefly examine them in greater detail, to come to an appreciation of the dynamics of the voting decision.

Orientations Toward Issues and Electoral Choice

Highly issue-oriented voters gather information and weigh the policy alternatives posed in a campaign. Their choices are based on their agreement or disagreement with the candidate's expressed views on the crucial problems of the day. These citizens doubtless best fit the standard civics-book conception of how voters *should* make their choices. By and large, they will be *"ideologues."* That is, they will have a reasonably self-conscious and overarching view of the good life, usually expressed in the form of a liberal or conservative philosophy.

Ideology provides a remarkably keen tool for assessing new political issues as they arise—liberal or conservative ideologues will quite readily be able to decide where they stand on policies as diverse as parity price supports, offshore oil reserves, free trade—and possibily even free love. Their need to be consistent will lead them to abandon a traditional party or a once-supported candidate if either should stray from the path of purity. But voting research suggests that ideologues are quite rare in the United States. Even people who simply *tend* to view the political world in liberal or conservative terms probably make up little more than a tenth of the electorate.

One could expect that issue-oriented voters would be more informed on political matters, and this is normally the case. Whether such information-holding is at all objective is another story entirely. It is rather difficult to conceive of a person possessed of some ideological leaning happily accepting information which disagrees with his or her philosophical framework. Among social psychologists, this is called "selective perception."[17] Put in a more homely phraseology, people may see what they want to see, and hear what they want to hear. However—and the point must be emphasized—this is not limited to those who are primarily issue-oriented in their voting preferences.

The extent to which voters are indeed issue-oriented has been a subject of much debate among political scientists. One study suggested that "ideologues and near-ideologues" comprised about 15 percent of the voting population, at least for the 1950s era.[18] Another study, focusing on the 1960s and the early 1970s concluded that, although this low figure might have been the case earlier (and the point was not readily conceded), this was not the case for later elections. In three successive presidential elections, 1964–1972, those who made ideological and near-ideological evaluations of candidates comprised at least 30 percent of voters, falling in 1976 to 23 percent.[19] Is this really the case, or has this interpretation relied, as alleged by others, on conceptual and methodological flaws?[20]

While we cannot resolve this question, we can state with some certainty that issue orientation of a less thorough-going sort is sufficiently widespread to affect election outcomes significantly. In 1980, for example, incumbent President Carter was faced with the burden of defending his administration's record on the issues of inflation, unemployment, and foreign policy. Surveys clearly indicated that voters were aware of these problems, at least in a general sense, as well as of Carter's personal performance. We cannot say with any certainty at this time whether the dominant motivation was issue orientation or candidate orientation. The 1980 picture is even further muddied by the fact that Democrats held on to their majority in the House, while losing the Senate and the presidency.

Findings of this sort serve to indicate that issue orientation does have an impact on voting, even when an election is apparently not of the realigning variety. But, at the same time such findings underscore the imperfect nature of that impact: of the voters who were drawn to the kind of views President Carter had been expressing on inflation, for instance, about 40 percent voted for Reagan. Conversely, Carter received the support of 35 percent of those who held views on this issue similar to those of Reagan.

Orientations Toward Candidates and Electoral Choice

Few readers will be surprised to learn that the personal attractiveness (or unattractiveness) of a candidate may have a considerable effect on the behavior of voters—an effect which is independent of the policies espoused by the candidate. In recent decades the personal appeals of Presidents

Roosevelt and Eisenhower were especially potent. The Eisenhower attraction has been carefully studied, both through examination of the many "trial-heat" presidential surveys conducted before Eisenhower stated a party affiliation or even avowed an interest in running for office, and by analysis of voter response during the two Eisenhower campaigns. "Liking Ike" seems to have resulted, to a remarkable degree, from perception of the General's personal attributes. The appeal of these qualities was especially great in a number of the population categories (e.g., high-school graduates) which ordinarily give strong support to the Democrats.[21]

In the Survey Research Center election studies, candidate orientation has been studied by tabulating the frequency of positive and negative references to the candidates in response to the questions "Is there anything about X that would make you want to vote *for* him?" and "Is there anything about X that would make you want to vote *against* him?" The consistent finding has been that the higher a voter "scores" a candidate in answering these questions, the more likely a voter is to cast his or her ballot for that candidate.

There are problems with such assessments, however. They may tend to ignore the total number of persons who never respond for or against either major party candidate, or else they focus on candidate attributes which may have little or nothing to do with how well (or poorly) each candidate may perform if elected. On this latter point, for instance, an early study showed that, between 1952 and 1956, after four years of Eisenhower's presidency,

> references to his skills as leader and administrator were fewer in 1956 than before. It was the response to personal qualities—to his sincerity, his integrity and sense of duty, his virtue as a family man, his religious devotion, and his sheer likeableness—that rose substantially in the second campaign. These frequencies leave the strong impression that in 1956 *Eisenhower was honored not so much for his performance as President as for the quality of his person.*[22]

TABLE 3-4   The Absence of Performance-Related Candidate Evaluations*

CANDIDATE'S PARTY	1952	1956	1960	1964	1968	1972	1976
Democratic candidate							
Positive = 0	81.0%	85.7%	77.1%	76.3%	82.3%	92.6%	84.0%
Negative = 0	95.7	91.6	91.4	88.0	87.0	75.2	72.0
Republican candidate							
Positive = 0	74.9	69.4	83.6	88.2	83.4	86.5	76.8
Negative = 0	91.9	78.5	92.2	85.7	85.9	90.6	88.0
N =	1614	1762	1954	1571	1557	1119	2870

*Cell entries represent the percentage of the voting-age population who had no evaluations of each candidate as regards potential job-performance as president.

Source: Frank B. Feigert and David L. McClure, "Candidate Evaluation: Limits to Rationality" (paper presented at the annual meeting of the Southwestern Political Science Association, Dallas, 1981).

TABLE 3-5   Favorable and Unfavorable Attitudes Towards the Candidates, 1952 - 1972

YEAR	PERCENTAGE FAVORABLE AND UNFAVORABLE TOWARDS EACH CANDIDATE					
	Democrat Positive	0	Negative	Republican Positive	0	Negative
1952	24.8	69.1	6.0	30.3	61.0	8.7
1956	21.1	66.4	12.5	38.6	41.8	19.6
1960	32.1	53.5	14.4	36.2	55.7	8.1
1964	37.6	47.6	14.7	15.0	61.7	23.3
1968	22.1	55.2	22.7	19.6	60.1	20.3
1972	6.7	63.4	29.9	18.0	69.3	12.6

Source: Compiled from David G. Lawrence, "Candidate Orientation, Vote Choice, & the Quality of the American Electorate," *Polity*, 11 (Winter 1978), 236. The "0" category represents voting-age respondents "with either no overall evaluation favoring either candidate or identical and offsetting evaluations of both." Ibid., 235.

In a similar vein, one analysis tried to make the point that candidates are assessed on the basis of their ability to perform the job of President. What was ignored, however, was the startling proportion of people who were either indifferent or had "identical and offsetting evaluations of both. [candidates]."[23] In Table 3-5, for instance, we see that the proportion of such respondents is roughly four to seven out of ten. On the basis of these data, it is concluded that "candidate orientation can provide a second route to rational voting, and it is a route often taken where it exists."[24]

The key phrase here is "where it exists." One can look at the same data we have shown in Table 3-5 and still have questions as to what proportion of the voting-age population has candidate evaluations at all. In another study, examining candidate orientations during the elections of 1952-1976, it was found that roughly seven to nine out of every ten respondents interviewed had no performance-related evaluation at all, positive or negative, for either the Democratic or the Republican presidential candidate. Further, those without *any* evaluations, whether of a general or a specific nature, comprised a significant proportion of those actually voting.[25]

The conclusions are disquieting at best. It is part of our political mythology that Americans generally "vote for the man." Evidently, this notion is in need of a good bit of qualification. If electoral choices were made simply on the basis of candidate's personal characteristics, the voting of various groups would probably exhibit very little continuity from one election to the next—as manifested, for example, by the patterns of election returns from high- and low-income precincts, or from urban and rural sections of a state. But actually the continuities are impressive, except (to anticipate our discussion in Chapter 5) when political parties are not a part of the electoral process. In 1896, for instance, the Democratic party virtually repudiated the conservative policies of its President, Grover Cleveland, and nominated William Jennings Bryan, a man who represented almost the antithesis of Cleveland. Nevertheless, a large proportion of Bryan's support came from precisely the same Democratic areas which had backed Cleveland four years earlier.[26] Evidently, virtually any candidate named by the Democrats would have been supported by these areas.

But, personal characteristics are not always unrelated to potential performance. Integrity, for instance, was a candidate characteristic stressed in 1960 by the Democrats, who pinned the label of "Tricky Dick" on Vice-President Nixon. Again, in 1968, the integrity question cast a small shadow on Nixon's campaign for the presidency. How many voters considered themselves "right" when Nixon became the first president to resign from the White House, the object of accusations that he had participated in obstructing justice by covering up the involvement of White House employees in the Watergate break-in two years earlier? And, one could argue that Carter's 1976 campaign, waged in large part on the style issue of trust, was not only necessary for his election, but also for the restoration of some faith in our government.

Identifications with Parties and Electoral Choice

Clearly, some voters base their choice on relatively short-run factors tied in to a specific election campaign. These are the voters who are guided mainly by issues and candidacies. While there are some issues which are relatively enduring, there are also any number which crop up in the last several weeks after the conventions. For that matter, not until the nominees have been selected and the formal campaign is underway is it at all clear which issues are to be emphasized by the candidates, and in what ways. Yet, a remarkable proportion of voters regularly report that they made up their minds *before* the presidential nominating conventions, and many additional voters decide immediately after the conventions—that is, before the campaigns "officially" begin.[27]

On what basis are such election decisions made? For many citizens a vote is a standing decision to support a particular political party. Party identification—the third criterion for electoral choice—has usually been by far the strongest of the lot, although there is now some debate as to whether it remains a strong influence.[28] If we were to learn where a voter stood on just one of the three criteria—issues, candidates, and party—knowledge of the last would enable us to make the most accurate prediction of his or her vote. In any election some party identifiers, especially those whose loyalties are not strong, will vote for the opposing party, normally on the basis of issue or candidate preferences. But it is considerably more likely that a voter's choice on election day will be inconsistent with either of these preferences than it is that party defection will take place.[29]

The term "party identification" refers to what might appear to be one of the simpler and more fragile of political phenomena—namely, the individual's subjective attachment to the Republicans or Democrats (or, in the case of an infinitesimal proportion of the electorate, to some other political party). This psychological orientation, which in fact proves to be durable and most influential, is measured in the University of Michigan voting studies simply by asking: "Generally speaking, do you usually consider yourself as a Republican, a Democrat, an Independent, or what?"[30] The possession of a party identification should not be confused with a generalized belief that parties are a "good thing." While most Americans claim to prefer the present party system to various possible alternatives, by and large Americans do not think of the parties as performing the various positive functions many political scientists attribute to them.[31] There are many factors that might seem to discourage party identification in the United States in addition to the widespread negative attitudes toward partisanship and partisan conflict: for example, the American parties do not have formal membership procedures, and, as we have seen, many Americans are not deeply interested in politics. Nevertheless, *about three out of every five American adults identify with one or the other major political party.*

In the United States an individual's identification is usually an evolutionary outcome of the largely inadvertent and unintended political learning that is absorbed from family, peer group, neighborhood, schools, and mass media, remarkably early in childhood. By the age of ten (fifth grade), more than one-half of all American children consider themselves little Republicans or Democrats, whereas at this age the capacities for abstraction that are necessary for issue orientation are largely unformed, and orientations toward candidates and political leaders in general are immature in the sense that children tend to be idealistically uncritical of those individuals in public life of whom they are aware.[32] Children do not invariably acquire the party preference held by their parents: a major national survey of high-school seniors and their parents reveals much more inter-generational political difference than would be suspected from the widespread reports by adults that they identify with the same party their parents supported. Nevertheless, among parents who are party identifiers there is better than a fifty-fifty chance that the child will hold the same party identification by age seventeen, at which time the incidence of party identification has typically been about 10 percent lower than it is in the adult population. Of those children who do not share their parents' party loyalty, the greatest number have not formed party identifications. The relatively few children who actually "oppose" their parents in partisanship tend to balance each other out (4 percent of the adolescent population appear to be Republican defectors from Democratic parents and 4 percent to be Democrats from Republican backgrounds): by and large these are not principled departures or the consequences of adolescent rebellion, but rather the result of drift and what the report on this inquiry calls "lack of cuegiving and object saliency on the part of parents.[33]

Changes of party identification during adult life are rare; the few voters who change appear largely to be less-involved supporters of the parties; shifts out of and into each party evidently are of about the same magnitude, since the aggregate distribution of party identifications in the electorate as a whole is amazingly constant, setting the terms of partisan conflict for entire epochs. The present distribution appears to have formed in the early 1930s, when, under the stress of unemployment rates of as high as 25 percent, the electorate shifted from a plurality of Republican identifiers to a Democratic plurality.[34] The precise contemporary pattern of party identification can be seen in Table 3-6 which summarizes statistics from fifteen national samplings conducted at two year intervals, beginning with the Survey Research Center's first attempt to measure party identification. During that time some two-thirds to three-quarters of the population was willing to express a party preference. Some slippage has occurred in recent years. This may be the beginning of a slow drift in the direction of the oft-proclaimed increasing "independence" of the electorate, especially because, at least until 1980, the slippage had been consistently toward independence (29 percent - 1968; 34 percent - 1972; 37 percent - 1976; 33 percent - 1980). What is remarkable, however, is the relatively tenacious hold by the Democrats, who have rather consistently maintained a 3 to 2 advantage. This, it should be noted, has held even in the face of Republican presidential victories in 1952, 1956, 1968, 1972, and 1980, including congressional victories in 1952 (both Houses) and 1980 (Senate only).

Do these relatively recent changes in party identification mean that a massive change is underway? Some scholars have been predicting a major change in our party system, to be indicated at least in part by the weakening of traditional party loyalties. There is some evidence that this is now underway. However, the very slowness of the changes in party identification suggest either that the electorate is slow to give up its traditional partisan attachments, and/or that something else is happening. That "something else" is a fairly simple phenomenon—the entrance of new voters into the system, as well as the passing on of older voters.

These new voters basically formed their partisan identities at an early age. For the young child, party identification is so barren of supporting information that he or she may be able to say "I am a Republican" or "I am a Democrat" without even knowing the party of the incumbent president. One study found that it was not until seventh grade that even a few children differentiate between the parties in terms of their policy positions.[35] As they approach and reach adulthood, few manage to stay in this state of blissful ignorance. But, there seems to be a natural tendency to develop images of the parties which are consistent with their previous identifications.

Party identifications seem to have an impact on voting because they are, as it were, first on the scene.

Even among adults party identifications are temporally prior to issue

TABLE 3-6 Party Identification, 1952 - 1980

	1952	1954	1956	1958	1960	1962	1964	1966	1968	1970	1972	1974	1976	1978	1980
Strong Republican	13%	13%	15%	13%	14%	11%	11%	10%	9%	9%	10%	8%	9%	8%	10%
Weak Republican	14	14	14	16	13	16	13	15	14	15	13	14	14	12	14
Independent	22	22	24	19	23	23	23	28	30	31	34	36	37	39	35
Weak Democrat	25	25	23	24	25	25	25	27	25	24	26	21	25	24	23
Strong Democrat	22	22	21	23	21	21	26	18	20	20	15	18	15	15	16
Apolitical*	4	4	3	5	4	4	2	2	2	1	2	3	1	3	2

*Individuals are classified as "apolitical" if they do not claim either party identification or independent status, or if they answered "don't know" when asked for their party identification by an interviewer.

Source: Center for Political Studies, University of Michigan.

and candidate orientations in that as new issues and candidates arise over the years they are perceived and judged by voters who already are possessed of party identifications. Thus party becomes not only a criterion for voting, but also a criterion for shaping the other criteria. Voters may describe their election choices in terms of their views of the issues and candidates and in doing so they may accurately portray their impressions of what has motivated them; they are likely to fail to appreciate what often lies *behind* their issue and candidate preferences—party identifications and the group experiences which foster and reinforce partisanship.

THE POLITICAL SIGNIFICANCE OF PARTY IDENTIFICATIONS

Just as voting on the basis of issue orientation seems to many Americans to be closest to the ideal of citizen participation, so party voting seems to be further from that ideal. To many observers, party is a blind criterion for political choice—one which leads merely to "brand label" voting. Yet, if there is truth to the following observation of James Bryce, the pervasive influence of party on voting may not be unfortunate in terms of maintaining democracy and promoting political stability:

> To the great mass of mankind in all places public questions come in the third or fourth rank among the interests of life, and obtain less than a third or fourth of the leisure available for thinking. It is therefore rather sentiment than thought that the mass can contribute, a sentiment grounded on a few broad considerations and simple trains of reasoning; and the soundness and elevation of their sentiment will have more to do with their taking their stand on the side of justice, honour, and peace, than any reasoning they can apply to the sifting of the multifarious facts thrown before them, and to the drawing of the legitimate inferences therefrom.[36]

Bryce's observation is to a considerable degree true—public evaluations of government and politics do tend to be confined to "broad considerations" and "simple trains of reasoning." That one of the most important of these considerations has been party is probably of great consequence for both the political system and the voter.

For those voters who still rely principally on party identification in making their choices, party labels simplify their tasks to a remarkable degree. They enable the voters to respond to the infinitely complex events of the contemporary political world in terms of a few simple criteria. Without such criteria, detailed research on the issues of the day would be necessary to make any sort of meaningful electoral choice. Perhaps even more important than the usefulness of party labels as devices to simplify issue questions is their usefulness for sorting out candidates and public officials. Given the vast complexity of American government, with its divisions between executive and legislature and between the federal, state, and local levels, there is immense value to an instrument which enables the voter, in one burst of exertion, to evaluate all the public officials he must select. Without party labels choice becomes almost impossible, especially at the state and local levels, where dozens of public officials—down to the tax collector and the county sheriff—may be on the ballot.

Although party labels, and voting on the basis of party identifications, are great political simplifiers, they are not complete blinders. Where powerful issues and striking candidates have not emerged to become the focus of public attention, most of the electorate votes on a party basis. Under such circumstances, elections will be decided by the underlying distribution of party identifications in the population. By taking account of the 3-to-2 Democratic plurality among part identifiers—but also of the lower turnout rate of Democrats (due to the lower educational and occupational levels of their core supporters)—it has been estimated that there is a "natural" Democratic majority of about 53 percent in any election which involves a ratification of party preferences.[37]

The vote distribution in a low-intensity party-voting election— Carter's 1976 close victory over Ford—is reconstructed in Figure 3-2, which shows the independent vote, the proportion of the population that identifies strongly and weakly with each of the main parties, and indicates the turnout levels and the party division in each of these five categories. As can be seen, each party held onto virtually identical proportions of its strong identifiers; there were similar defection rates among weak identifiers (but compare these to the 1980 data below) and the independents were fairly closely divided in favor of President Ford. Republican turnout was higher in both categories than was that for the Democrats, but not enough to make up for the fact that 40 percent of the electorate consisted of Democratic identifiers and only 27 percent of Republican identifiers. The low-intensity 1976 election provides a rather good model of voting in congressional elections, since the elections for Congress rarely raise burning issues or attract great attention (in fact most people know little about Congress, as we saw in Table 2-2. It is not surprising that there was a Democratic majority in all but two of the two-year congressional terms between 1932 and 1980. Republican candidates, Eisenhower in 1956 and Nixon in 1968 and 1972 were elected without carrying Congress for their parties; this has never been the fate of a Democrat in the modern era.

Party identifications clearly do not dominate voting to the exclusion of other factors. Given party identification, the "normal" expectation in presidential elections would be about 53 percent Democratic. Yet, there has been some considerable fluctuation around this, ranging from a low of

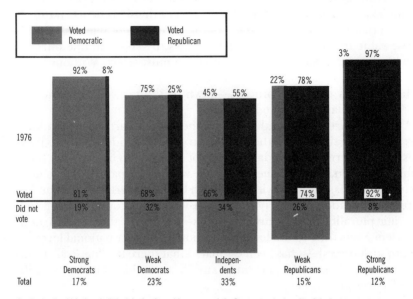

An election in which there is little defection from either party and the Democrats win, in spite of the lower turnout of their identifiers; Carter's victory in 1976.

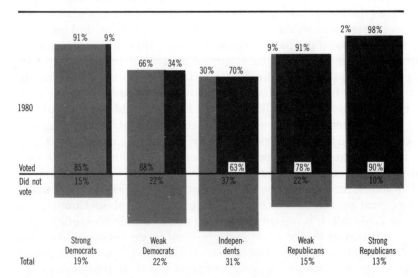

An election in which the minority (Republican) party wins by holding its identifiers and winning the votes of many independents and majority party identifiers; the Reagan victory of 1980.

Source: Center for Political Studies, University of Michigan.

FIGURE 3-2 The Ingredients of Election Outcomes: (1) the proportion of identifiers with each party; (2) party defection rates; (3) the independent vote; (4) differential turnout.

about 40 percent (McGovern, 1972; Carter, 1980) to a high of about 60 percent (Johnson, 1964). For the Republicans to wrest victory from the Democrats in this era of apparent Democratic dominance in the electorate, they must turn out to vote in higher proportions, and a great many Democrats must defect. The lower half of Figure 3-2 shows this, for 1980. As we see, reflecting the information from Table 3-6, the Republicans were still very much in the minority. Only in and following the very rare realigning election is there much shift in the distribution of party identification. Neverthelesss, Reagan's popularity, coupled with an absence of any intense support for Carter and the Democrats' unpopular record led to virtually perfect party support among Republicans, strong support from Independents, and very substantial Democratic defections, especially among weak identifiers.[38]

Thus, although the dead weight of voters' "standing decisions" has a major effect on election outcomes, the nation's electoral decision is also dependent on the voters' evaluations of current issues and candidates. Furthermore, the various elements in the equation of voting behavior—party identification, differential group turnout, response to current issues and candidates—are such as to make any single national election a matter of considerable uncertainty. This prevents the politicians from becoming complacent and stimulates the more politically interested and active members of the electorate to pay attention to the spectacle and drama of the campaign.

Although the outcomes of national elections are ordinarily in doubt, a result of the prevalence and stability of party identifications and of the link between party identifications and group voting differences is that many aspects of politics become predictable. In the present era, Democrats—or at least northern Democrats—can be relatively sure that their core support will come from citizens in the lower educational and blue-collar occupational levels. Republicans can generally be confident of their business, professional, college-educated, and small-town stalwarts.

Politicians in both parties are led to advance policies consistent with group interests by the need to maintain the backing of their core groups. This contributes to differentiation in the policies supported by leaders of both parties. At the same time, since each of the parties also needs—and seeks—support from the more or less uncommitted groups (such as white-collar workers and farmers) *and* from groups in the other party's coalition, party differences are not likely to be so sharp that changes in party control of government lead to radical reversals of governmental policy. The cross-cutting nature of party appeals also tends to keep political cleavage from reaching the point at which some elements of the public or leadership consider revolutions and coups preferable to elections because they do not care to risk the possibility that intolerable policies will be put into effect by their opponents.

NOTES

[1]Scholars have long debated just how much each factor in these clusters of interrelated attributes contributes to turnout. For instance, would the citizen of "high" education but "low" occupational status be more likely to vote than the citizen with the opposite characteristics? An exceptionally refined study along these lines, which makes a powerful case for the primary impact of education, is Raymond E. Wolfinger and Steven J. Rosenstone, *Who Votes?* (New Haven, Conn.: Yale University Press, 1980). It should be noted that one of the principal determinants of low voting turnout in the United States has been the exceptionally demanding—by the standards of other countries—requirements for voter registration. For very convincing documentation see Stanley Kelley, Jr., Richard E. Ayres, and William G. Bowen, "Registration and Voting: Putting First Things First," *American Political Science Review*, 61 (June 1967), 359–79. On why poll findings tend to exaggerate the actual turnout, see the note to Table 2-1.

[2]William S. Maddox, "The Changing American Nonvoter, 1952-1978," paper prepared for the annual meeting of the Southern Political Science Association, Galtinburg, Tenn., 1979. See also Howard L. Reiter, "Why is Turnout Down?" *Public Opinion Quarterly*, 43 (Fall 1979), 297–311, and several articles in the special issue of *American Politics Quarterly*, 9 (April 1981).

[3]James N. Rosenau, *Citizenship Between Elections* (New York: Free Press, 1974), Ch. 7. These findings are generally consistent with most research on political participation. For a useful bibliographical review, see Lester W. Milbrath and M. L. Goel, *Political Participation* (2d ed.; Chicago: Rand McNally, 1977), especially Ch. 4. Also Paul R. Abramson and John H. Aldrich, "The Decline of Electoral Participation in America," *American Political Science Review*, 76 (September 1982), 502–21.

[4]On "civic virtue" and education, see the excellent discussion and illustrations provided in Wolfinger and Rosenstone, *op. cit.*, pp. 17–20.

[5]Thomas E. Mann, *Unsafe At Any Margin* (Washington: American Enterprise Institute, 1978), p. 103.

[6]A more detailed analysis would, of course, also deal with the overlap between categoric groups referred to earlier in this chapter—by determining, for example, whether college graduates at the lower occupational levels were as Republican in their voting as college graduates at the higher occupational levels. For an especially sophisticated analysis taking account of these factors, see Angus Campbell, et al., *The American Voter* (New York: Wiley, 1960), pp. 295--332.

[7]The following episode from the period of the Articles of Confederation provides as good an example as any that politics based at least in part on social-class cleavages is not without precedent in America. The 1787 Massachusetts gubernatorial election, which followed Shays' Rebellion, has been described by historians as a struggle between a candidate representing the poor debtor classes, John Hancock, and a candidate of the state's more prosperous citizens, Governor James Bowdoin. (Bowdoin had ordered the suppression of the insurrection of the state's western farmers.)

Shortly after his defeat, Bowdoin's supporters reported the following breakdown of the vote in Boston:

	Bowdoin	Hancock
Physicians	19	2
Clergymen	2	0
Lawyers	17	3
Independent gentlemen	50	0
Merchants and traders	295	21
Printers	8	4
Tradesmen	328	279
Laborers, servants, etc.	5	466
	724	775

Not to be outdone, Hancock's forces reported their own analysis:

	Bowdoin	Hancock
Usurers	28	0
Speculators in public securities	576	0
Stockholders and bank directors	81	0
Persons under British influence	17	0
Merchants, tradesmen, and other "worthy" citizens	21	448
Friends of the Revolution	0	327
Wizards	1	0
	724	775

(*Massachusetts Centinel,* April 4 and 7, 1787, reprinted in Peter H. Odegard and E. Allen Helms, *American Politics* [New York: Harper, 1957], pp. 24, 25.)

[8]Robert Axelrod, "Communication," *American Political Science Review,* 76 (June 1982), 396. See also Everett Carll Ladd, Jr., *Where Have All the Voters Gone?* (2d ed.; New York: Norton 1982) Chap. 2.

[9]It is instructive to note here that black leaders also became aware, about this time, of the favorable implications for minorities of the essentially anti-democratic device of the Electoral College. Research has shown that abolishing the Electoral College would disadvantage blacks who are concentrated in urban and populous areas, depriving them of their important "swing" or deciding vote for their states in close presidential elections. Judith Best, *The Case Against Direct Election of the President* (Ithaca, N.Y.: Cornell University Press, 1975), especially Ch. 4. See also Senate Judiciary Committee, *Direct Popular Election of the President* (Washington: Government Printing Office, 1975).

[10]For an essay arguing that voting studies, in general, tend to underestimate voter's rationality, see V. O. Key, Jr., *The Responsible Electorate* (Cambridge, Mass.: Harvard University Press, 1966). Also see the comments on Key's thesis, as well as the more general findings referred to in the text above, in the SRC report on the 1968 election: Philip E. Converse, et al., "Continuity and Change in American Politics: Parties and Issues in the 1968 Election," *American Political Science Review,* 63 (December 1969), 1083–1105. An important milestone in this "revisionist" approach to voter rationality is Norman H. Nie, Sidney Verba, and John R. Petrocik, *The Changing American Voter* (enlarged ed.; Cambridge, Mass.: Harvard University Press. 1979).

[11]V. O. Key, Jr., "A Theory of Critical Elections," *Journal of Politics,* 17 (February 1955), 3–18, and "Secular Realignment and the Party System," *Journal of Politics* 21 (May 1959), 198–210.

[12]Richard Scammon and Ben Watenberg, *The Real Majority* (New York: Coward, Mc Cann, 1970).

[13]Campbell, et al., pp. 234–40.

[14]See Campbell, et al., *Elections and the Political Order* (New York: Wiley, 1966), p. 94.

[15]See Bernard Cosman, *Five States for Goldwater* (University: University of Alabama Press, 1966).

[16]Warren E. Miller, Arthur H. Miller, and Edward J. Schneider, *American National Election Studies Sourcebook, 1952-1978* (Cambridge, Mass.: Harvard University Press, 1980), Tables 2.46 and 2.50.

[17]Bernard Berelson and Gary Steiner, *Human Behavior* (New York: Harcourt, Brace and World, 1964), pp. 100–21.

[18]Campbell, et al., *The American Voter,* pp. 227–34.

[19]Nie, Verba, and Petrocik, p. 367.

[20]See Chap. 2, note 12 (p. 20).

[21]Herbert Hyman and Paul Sheatsley, "The Political Appeal of President Eisenhower," *Public Opinion Quarterly,* 17 (Winter 1953-54), 443–60.

[22]Campbell, et al., *The American Voter,* p. 56. Emphasis added.

[23]David G. Lawrence, "Candidate Orientation, Vote Choice, and the Quality of the American Electorate," *Polity,* 11 (Winter 1978), 235.

[24]*Ibid.,* 246.

[25]Frank B. Feigert and David L. McClure, "Candidate Evaluation: Limits to Rationality," paper presented at the Annual Meeting of the Southwestern Political Science Association, Dallas, 1981.

[26]Lee Benson, "Research Problems in American Historiography," in Mirra Komarovsky (ed.), *Common Frontiers of the Social Sciences* (Glencoe, Ill.: Free Press, 1957), pp. 162–163.

[27]Roughly one-third, on average, decide before the conventions and another third, more or less, immediately after. See Miller, Miller and Schneider, *op. cit.,* Table 6.56.

[28]See note 10.

[29]Angus Campbell and Donald E. Stokes, "Partisan Attitudes and the Presidential Vote," in Eugene Burdick and Arthur J. Brodbeck, eds., *American Voting Behavior* (Glencoe, Ill.: The Free Press, 1959), pp. 356–57.

[30]Following this the voter is asked if he or she considers himself or herself either a strong Democrat or strong Republican. If the initial answer from the respondent indicates that he or she is an Independent, the respondent is then asked whether he or she "leans" toward one of the political parties.

[31]The only systematic study in this area is Jack Dennis, "Support of the Party System by the Mass Public," *American Political Science Review,* 60 (September 1966), 600–615. The Dennis study is of a sample of Wisconsin citizens, and that state (because of its historical connections with Progressivism) may be somewhat more anti-party then the rest of the nation. Among Dennis' findings are that 54 percent of Wisconsinites believe that "the parties do more to confuse the issues than to provide a clear choice on them," whereas only 20 percent reject that assertion; 53 percent agree with the statement "Our system of government would work a lot more efficiently if we could get rid of conflicts between parties altogether," and only 34 percent disagree; 82 percent choose voting for "the man regardless of his party label"; and so forth. That the Wisconsin findings are not wholly untypical of the rest of the nation is indicated by a 1968 Gallup national survey which obtained virtually the identical distribution of attitudes on "voting for the man rather than his party." The national findings did, however, indicate that anti-partisanship does not extend itself to positive preferences for some other kind of party system: 67 percent of the national population was "generally satisfied with the choice of parties we have now" and only 27 percent favored a new party; and the 27 percent was of such diverse backgrounds that it could not have readily been aggregated into a single third party. *Gallup Opinion Index,* October 1968.

[32]Robert D. Hess and Judith V. Torney, *The Development of Political Attitudes in Children* (Chicago: Aldine, 1967), especially pp. 9 and 90. Fred I. Greenstein, *Children and Politics* (New Haven, Conn.: Yale University Press, 1965), Ch. 4.

[33]That is, the parties are not important to the parents and therefore the children are not exposed to enough partisan communication to learn what the parents' preferences are. M. Kent Jennings and Richard G. Niemi, "The Transmission of Political Values from Parent to Child," *American Political Science Review,* 62 (March 1968), 169–84.

[34]As shown in Table 3-3, the last previous realignments seemed to have occurred in 1896, when declining Republican plurality was substantially altered and strengthened, and just after the Civil War, when the nation polarized into a Republican-dominated North and a Democratic South. See the citations in note 10; Campbell, et al., *Elections and the Political Order,* chap. 4; and Walter Dean Burnham, *Critical Elections and the Mainsprings of American Politics* (*New York: Norton, 1970*).

[35]*Greenstein, op. cit.,* p. 68.

[36]James Bryce, *The American Commonwealth* (3d ed.; New York: Macmillan, 1904), vol. 2, pp. 250–51.

[37]Philip E. Converse, et al., "Stability and Change in 1960: A Reinstating Election,"

American Political Science Review, 55 (June 1961), 269–80; Philip E. Converse, "The Concept of a Normal Vote," in Campbell, et al., *Elections and the Political Order,* pp. 9–39.

[38]On the other hand, when the Republicans in 1964 nominated a candidate who was unable to hold many of the identifiers of his own party and who had virtually no appeal among the Democratic core groups, the Democrats won by a record majority. The implications of this aspect of electoral behavior for national party politics are considered in Chapter 6. On the 1964 election see Philip Converse et al., "Electoral Myth and Reality: The 1964 Election," *American Political Science Review,* 59 (June 1965), 321–36.

chapter 4 _____

LOCAL POLITICS:
Old-Time Machines and
_____ Modern Variants

So far our protagonist—the party system—has entered this account in only a shadowy way. We have seen the parties as objects of voter identification— that is, as psychological reference groups in the decision as to whether or not to vote, and then perhaps how to vote. For voters, parties are relatively long-term factors to be weighed against the short-term forces of candidacies and changing issues.

We have not as yet considered another aspect of parties, their activities as *organized* groups, although we have referred briefly to the response of party politicians to voters. It is appropriate to begin examining party organization at the grassroots level, for observers are uniformly agreed that the farther one moves from local politics in the United States, the more difficult it is to find evidence of organized party activity. When a local political party is capable of organizing to constantly "deliver" the vote, it is often pictured as a "machine." This evokes images of urban "bosses" who control a great many resources, public as well as party in nature. However, it might be wise if we were to first look at the nature of machines before we simply assign them to an urban dustheap, a relic of things past.

THE NATURE OF MACHINES

In any setting, when a political party organization can develop a long-range basis of voter support, the opportunity develops for a political party machine. The very word "machine" implies something that is both efficient and unstoppable, responsive to the wishes of the person who pushes the buttons.

However, it is not sufficient simply to have an assured base of voter support. Areas of traditional Democratic or Republican dominance can exist for reasons other than organizational presence and activity. Indeed, if the electorate in a particular area is overwhelmingly one-party, there may be little incentive for a machine to develop, since election is assured simply by winning the party's nomination. Instead, there are several characteristics of a community and its party system which can lead to the development of a machine as well as its maintenance.

Scarce Resources

Political scientists are fond of describing the political system as that which is responsible for the allocation of scarce resources,[1] whether these be monetary resources or jobs, status, power, and the like. However, political parties have acted for the system in distributing such resources, long before the formal system itself got involved in such questions. For instance, this country once existed without any formal system of social welfare. The poor remained poor, and were likely to go unemployed and hungry. When party organizations found that they could mobilize jobs (governmental, or in private industry from "grateful" constituents who appreciated the government services the party could provide) in exchange for votes, the incentive to organize was obvious. Given a steady base of votes, the party could expect to win elections often enough to "provide for their own" by controlling the ways in which government spent money and allocated its resources.

Hierarchical Organization

As we shall see, American parties are rarely tightly organized and controlled, at least at the state and national levels. Such organization is possible, however, and has been found more often at the local level, at least in the past. It should be added here that this has not been the case in all counties and cities, by any means, and there is a very real question as to how many urban machines exist at this time.

The "machine" is pictured as conforming to the hierarchical pattern found, for example, in corporations or military units. At the top of the organization there is a single chief, or at any rate a unified board of directors. The various local levels are staffed by subordinates who carry out instructions from above and exercise the degree of discretion expected for their level. To the degree that they conform to this pattern, party machines have had a command structure similar to many European parties and to some American third parties, such as the Socialists and Prohibitionists.

How does such a machine operate at the local level? One of the first prerequisites is the presence of a single figure, sometimes known as "the boss." The late Mayor Richard Daley of Chicago, for instance, was often known as "Boss Daley," if not always in the local newspapers.[2] The leader or "boss" consolidated power in his hands. Included in this was control over the party's nominations, certainly one of the scarcer resources available. In order to win approval for one's candidacy, a record of service to the party and the leader was essential. Depending on the locale and the personality of the leader, pledges of financial support for the party may have been required as well. In New York City, for instance, the "going price" for a nomination to various judicial positions once included a pledge equal to a year's salary for the position.[3]

Personal style of the bosses varied greatly. Some were widely known for their corruption, for taking large sums of money from those who would gain favors from either the party or the city government itself. The awarding of contracts, for instance, could usually be discretionary, and not always to the lowest bidder. Thus, it would be fairly easy for a corrupt party boss to pass the word to his followers that the X Corporation, even if it submitted the lowest bid for building a city hospital, could not conceivably do a good job, but that the Y Corporation could, and the contract would be awarded accordingly.

Other bosses may not have been corrupted by money, but may have simply built up the resources of the party and managed to control them personally. For instance, despite numerous allegations that he was financially corrupt and could be "bought," Mayor Daley apparently never committed the financial abuses of power so common among some other city bosses, notably Boss Pendergast of Kansas City, Mo., who was sent to prison for income-tax evasions.[4] It may be, instead, that Daley is the archetype of those who are corruptible not in the sense of financial but personal power.

In order to command the resources of partronage, nominations, and control over local government activities, the boss or leader has typically had control over a number of individuals with very specific tasks, but all of whom are characterized by a high degree of personal loyalty to the leader. Their loyalty, in turn, is rewarded by such things as nondemanding but financially worthwhile city or county jobs. Each of these "lieutenants" (note the military terminology so often used in these descriptions) also has a cadre of individuals who report to him and are both held accountable and rewarded.

An example of this might be in the conduct of a voter registration drive. The boss can establish a quota for new voter registrations and tell each of his lieutenants (or ward captains, in some cases) how many new registrants each must produce by the close of registration. The lieutenants can then set a quota for each precinct leader, who may very well have block leaders with their own quotas to meet by established deadlines. At designated times, the individuals actually engaged in registering the voters report to the precinct leaders, these to the ward captains, and these to the boss, who can adjust quotas, reward those doing a good job, or threaten to punish those who are not meeting their quotas. Since punishment could lead to a loss of one's livelihood, efforts to meet the quota will be redoubled if necessary, and excuses are not accepted.

Control of Patronage

We have mentioned that one of the necessities of a "machine" type of party organization is the control of scarce resources. This control typically belongs to the "boss" or leader. One of the most effective resources, when carefully managed, is that of patronage, or the granting of jobs based on party allegiance. While many governmental jobs are covered by civil service or merit systems, there are many that are not. Loyal service to the party, especially at the local level, can result in the faithful getting jobs, and it is assumed that everything will be done by these people to hold onto their positions as well as to advance in rank and salary.

We should make it clear that this material incentive, getting a job, is not the only one available to the party organization. If this were the case, then there would be little to attract workers to the party in this day and age, since the merit system is widespread. We return to this point later in this chapter. However, *where* such rewards are possible and *when* they are managed effectively, the party can profit in terms of votes as well as financially. The late Mayor Daley of Chicago, for instance, reportedly controlled some 35,000 city jobs and another 10,000 in private industry "grateful" to him for the services and protection he provided. Conventional wisdom has generally suggested that each patronage job is worth some three to seven votes at the polls. Thus, even before any actual organizational work for the election, there was a base of 135,000 to 315,000 votes for the Daley machine in Chicago. Further, when his fellow Democrats controlled Cook county and the Illinois governor's mansion as well, there was an even greater potential for controlling the election, through strictly legal means.

In order to keep their jobs, patronage workers are usually expected to contribute to the party. This may take the form of registering voters, getting out the vote on election day, and the like. Another form of contribution may be financial, including direct payment to the party as well as buying (and selling) tickets for party fund-raisers, such as cocktail parties, picnics, and testimonial dinners. Given a sufficiently broad base of patronage workers, the party organization can often expect to do quite well, maintaining offices with paid professional staff (another form of patronage) and being amply prepared for the expenses of conducting campaigns.

At this writing the future of patronage is somewhat clouded. The general increase in merit systems and several court decisions have raised serious problems for those party organizations which have been based on the "glue" of patronage. In two decisions, the Supreme Court has held that dismissing employees for belonging to the "wrong" party—that is, the one which lost the last election—violates freedom of association and belief. If former patronage positions cannot be vacated, if the old rule that "to the victor belong the spoils" is set aside, then the party organization is deprived of a significant resource. Further, the hiring of employees for political reasons can be seen as an example of discrimination against those who do not belong to the party controlling the government.[6]

The local party machine is said to be a declining, if not dead, phenomenon. There is considerable evidence that urban machines are declining, but completely reliable assertions on this cannot be made because knowledge of the distribution of types of local party organization is imperfect. Note also that we have qualified our statement for urban parties only, since we know all too little about the ways in which rural party organizations operate. Indeed, one could argue that the possibilities of machine politics are even greater in rural areas, away from the scrutiny of major competing media, and where his ability to deal directly with local politics can make the boss very much a fixture.

A close study of that darkest of dark areas in American government, county government, might well demonstrate that patronage in the traditional sense is alive and well. Most political practitioners in the South, and indeed in all those areas identified by Daniel Elazar as having a "traditional" political culture,[7] are aware of the great political strength of local sheriffs. The reason for this strength is simple—the sheriff has a paid staff of political operatives (deputies) at his disposal. It is not much of an exaggeration to note that the duties of a deputy sheriff are often (a) to re-elect the sheriff and (b) to enforce the law, in that order. Because of the nature of these machines, a sheriff's support is considered very valuable by other politicians running for election. This transferable power of a sheriff can be contrasted with that of another extremely powerful county office, that of county tax assessor. This, like the office of sheriff, is often held for life or, if not for "good" then for just "not obnoxious" behavior. The power of the assessor, however, lies in the authority to adjust property assessments and therefore taxes, not in the existence of a political machine. (You support or oppose a candidate for assessor at your financial peril.) Candidates for governor do not actively vie for the assessor's support as they do for that of the sheriff and his deputies.

Much of the anecdotal and analytical literature on patronage and machine politics focuses on the urban experience. Much of American political folklore, however, centers on rural leaders. It is, moreover, at the local level that the anomalies of American politics are most striking. Examination of these anomalies has a way of illustrating the rich and varied nature of American politics. To cite but one example let us look briefly at St. Landry's Parish (county), Louisiana, in the early 1960s. It is an article of faith among political analysts that black voter registration was at its lowest during this period in the rural South. How, then, does one explain rural St. Landry Parish with some 10,000 registered black voters in the pre-Voting Rights Act era of the '60s? The answer lies in the struggles over the sheriff's office. The incumbent "Cat" Doucet was not the choice of the "respectable" elements of the parish. Unlettered (he once predicted he would win in a "landscape") and colorful, he was a strong supporter of Huey Long and his political heirs and followers. To remain in office, Doucet had to expand the electorate. Increasing black voting strength was his solution. Having expanded the vote it was also necessary to control it. With all balloting done on lever voting machines, this was not as easy as it once had been. Consequently, the rumored methods ranged from the straightforward, paying opponents not to vote, to the ingenious—handing out left shoes to 100 heads of families in a given precinct. If he got over 100 votes in that precinct, everyone got a right shoe; under 100 votes and nobody got a right shoe! Given the poverty of that part of the rural South, shoes were always needed. And, given the extended family structure of south Louisiana, feet could be found to fit any size shoe. Doucet always got well over his minimum vote.[8]

There is no census of local parties, urban or rural, covering either the present time of the ostensible heyday of bosses and machines, and there is reason to believe that the standard accounts exaggerate the ubiquity of organized urban parties in the past[9] and may have underestimated their contemporary prevalence.[10] In the 1950s an effective old-style Democratic organization was put together in the once Republican-dominated city of Philadelphia. Recent changes in the social composition of many big cities—as the more prosperous citizens move to the suburbs and leave the central cities to the socially disadvantaged (low-income groups and, increasingly, black and Hispanics)—also raise the possibility that a resurgence of old-style party organization could be in the offing. This, of course, assumes the presence of the factors which we have been discussing—control of scarce resources, including patronage, and the presence of a "boss" who can control an hierarchical organization. Countering this possibility, among other things, is the increased use of individualistic campaigning, ignoring the formal party organization at all levels.

At the state level, the major parties rarely approximate the machine model. As we shall see in Chapter 5, state political parties usually are alliances of autonomous and sometimes feuding factions. At the national level our parties are notoriously unhierarchical, lacking discipline, unity of control, and the ability to manage resources such as patronage. The one attribute of our national parties that has most impressed observers, in fact, is their disorganization. Hence, any pretense at organization in the classic sense, as it relates to our parties, can be found only at the local level, and then in many cases in retrospect.

Whatever the future may hold for urban machines, their past is of great interest to anyone who cares to reflect on the functions served by American parties. Therefore, we shall look at the remarkable rise of this pattern of organization in the nineteenth century, at the factors which maintained it, and at the forces that have tended in recent years to sap machine strength. Then, after briefly considering some present-day manifestations of organized local politics and two contemporary variants on the city machine, we can make some assessment of old-style party organizations.

WHY URBAN MACHINES DEVELOPED

By the mid-nineteenth century, tightly disciplined party organizations, staffed by professional and semiprofessional politicians, their activities extending into every corner of the community, began to be evident in many American cities. Through their monopoly of control over nominations for public office, these organizations and their "bosses" (the men in effective control of the parties, whether or not they actually held party office) became for all practical purposes the city governments, just as in contemporary Great Britain the majority party leader is the effective national leader even though the monarch is nominally sovereign. Organized local politics became as much a part of the unique political formation which developed west of the Atlantic as did disorganized national politics.

Urban party organizations were not unknown in America even in colonial times. Few writers on American parties have been able to resist reproducing John Adams' diary entry for February 1763, describing the activities of the Boston Caucus Club:

> This day learned that the Caucus club meets at certain times in the garret of Tom Dawes, the Adjutant of the Boston regiment. He has a large house, and he has a movable partition in his garret which he takes down, and the whole club meets in one room. There they smoke tobacco til you cannot see from one end of the garret to the other. There they drink flip, I suppose, and they choose a moderator who puts questions to the vote regularly.

A central concern of the Caucus club was the choice of nominees for public office. In Tom Dawes' garret, Adams reports, " . . . selectmen, assessors, collectors, fire-wards, and representatives, are regularly chosen before they are chosen in the town."[11]

The urban bosses and their organizations probably could not have arisen if certain board preconditions had not existed in American society and culture. These include the tradition of freewheeling individualism and pragmatic opportunism that developed in a prosperous, sprawling new society unrestrained by feudalism, aristocracy, monarchy, an established church, and other traditional authorities. This is the state of affairs which has been commented on by countless observers, even before de Tocqueville, and which has been used to explain such disparate phenomena as the failure of socialism to take hold in the United States, the recurrence of popularly based assaults on civil liberties, and even the peculiarly corrosive form which was taken by American slavery.[12]

It also is possible to identify five more direct determinants of the form that urban party organization took in the nineteenth century, three of them consequences of the Industrial Revolution and two of them results of political institutions and traditions which preceded industrialization.

Meteoric urban growth. Cities grew with dizzying speed as the nation's economic base shifted from agriculture to industry. In 1850, on the eve of industrialization, only one American city exceeded 250,000 in population. A mere 3½ million Americans lived in what the Bureau of the Census described as "urban territory"—cities and towns of over 2,500 population—in contrast to 20 million rural residents. By 1890 eleven cities had more than 250,000 residents and three had more than a million. Urban population had increased sixfold, while rural population had only doubled.

When great masses of people are uprooted from their small face-to-face communities and thrust into metropolises, they find that the basic requirements of existence change profoundly. All kinds of public services which formerly were unnecessary become essential for survival. Highly developed transportation arrangements must be set up to insure a constant supply of food and other resources. Within the city there is a need for streets, street-lighting, bridges, and mass transportation systems. Backyard outhouses and compost heaps are no longer satisfactory sanitary arrangements; sewers must be installed and garbage hauled. With the breakdown of old neighborhood relationships, control of delinquency cannot be based on informal social pressure aided by a town constable; a sizable police force (and prison system) must be organized. The need for these and many other services, such as fire-fighting, building inspection, and hospitals, places overwhelming demands on government.

Disorganized governmental structures. Nineteenth-century city governments were not geared to meet the challenges of urban growth. City governmental structures had been inherited from the day when every citizen knew his neighbor and the tasks of public officials were minimal. Following Jacksonian traditions, most of the major municipal officials—mayors, council members, tax collectors, city clerks—were individually elected, sometimes annually. As each was responsible only to the voters who had supported him, there was little incentive for one official to cooperate with another. The power to undertake positive governmental activity was restrained by countless checks and balances, with authority divided among the numerous officials, the often large and unwieldy city councils, and a plethora of boards and commissions. Unless some informal means of bringing about cooperation among public officials could be found, governmental stalemate—rather than coordinated attacks on the problems of urban growth—was bound to result.

Needs of dependent populations.   It is difficult for us today to appreciate the precarious, unsettled conditions of life that existed for the great bulk of ninteenth-century city-dwellers. The rural-born American migrant to the city found the transition to an impersonal brick and concrete jungle exceedingly difficult. For immigrants from abroad—forced as they were to adopt a new culture and (except for the Irish and English) learn a new language—the difficulty was compounded. From the Civil War to World War I, when legislation restricting immigration was passed, the United States somehow managed to incorporate more than 25 million immigrants, most of whom settled in the cities.

The assimilation of this horde of newcomers was unplanned. Governmental facilities to ease the dislocations they had to undergo were largely nonexistent; private facilities were inadequate. To make matters even more difficult for the immigrant, doctrines of rugged individualism and Social Darwinism made a virtue of struggling in the face of such inadequacies. A contemporary account of working conditions in the New York garment industry in the 1890s gives the reader some feeling for the immigrants' early encounters with their new homeland:

> In the . . . "sweat shops" unhealthy and unclean conditions are almost universal, and those of filth and contagion common. The employes are in the main foreign-born and newly arrived. The proportion of female labor is large, and child labor is largely used. Wages are from a fourth to a third less than in the larger shops. As to hours, there is no limit except the endurance of the employes, the work being paid for by the "task," and the task so adjusted as to drive from the shop any employe who, whenever he is given a bench, will not work to the limit of physical endurance, the hours of labor being rarely less than twelve, generally thirteen or fourteen, frequently from fifteen to eighteen hours in the twenty-four.
> The lot, however, of these "sweat-shop" workers is luxury compared to that of those engaged in tenement home work. The homeworker is generally a foreigner just arrived, and frequently a woman whose husband is dead, sick, or worthless, and whose children keep her at home. Of these tenement homeworkers there are more women than men, and children are as numerous as both. The work is carried on in the one, two, or three rooms occupied by the family, with its subtenants or boarders. No pretence is made of separating shop work from household affairs. The hours observed are those which endurance alone limits. Children are worked to death beside their parents. Contagious diseases are especially prevalent among these people; but even death disturbs from their occupation only the one or two necessary to dispose of the body.[13]

Needs of business. The needs of the lower strata of the city were for rudimentary requirements of survival and—often equally important—for some measure of personal recognition in an alien environment. Businesses, large and small, legal and illegal, also had needs. Streets had to be maintained in the vicinity of the plant. Permission to build and expand had to be obtained. Freedom from overly vigorous enforcement of ordinances affecting plant safety, working conditions, and disposal of industrial waste might be desired. For some businesses the prime need was to operate without governmental interference. For others, such as contractors, utilities producers, and transit corporations, the need was to do business with the government itself; that is, to engage in the profitable pursuit of ministering to the process of urban growth.

Unrestricted suffrage. Finally, because even the lowliest of citizens was, or could become, a voter, a class of politicians developed building upon the conditions referred to above. One important party service to new immigrants was initiation into citizenship. As raw and unvarnished as machine procedures were, it is difficult to conceive of another institution which could have so effectively greeted such a vast host of bewildered individuals, conferring on them an invaluable commodity—the vote. City machines sometimes literally herded disembarked immigrants into naturalization and voter-registration ceremonies. Yet as corrupt as these activities of urban politicians were, they had the immediate effect of reducing the hopelessness of the immigrant's condition.

HOW THE CITY MACHINES OPERATED

These five factors—the qualitative changes in the requirements of caring for populations once they became densely concentrated; the fragmentation of urban government; the grinding poverty and loneliness of urban life; the presence of businesses in need of governmental favor; and the existence of the right to vote and of competing groups of politicians seeking voter support—furnished the raw materials with which the classical city political machines operated.

The party organizations served as brokers, responding to the conditions of urban life and—for a broker's commission—meeting at least some of the needs of various groups of citizens. A key determinant of organization effectiveness was the capacity of partisanship to unite what law and tradition had separated. By confining nominations for public office to party politicians—each of them beholden to the organization, rather than to a private constituency—parties were able to pull all the diverse threads of urban government into a reasonably unified command structure. City governments, once unified, could decide on and carry out policies designed to meet the problems of urban growth and, at the same time, confer benefits on business groups, both those who wanted to deal with government and those who wanted freedom from public harassment.

Underlying the parties' ability to do all this was the assiduousness with which they met the needs of the large mass of urban citizenry. The votes of these citizens—the prime source of machine strength—were won through a 24-hours-a-day, 365-days-a-year social-service operation. The newly naturalized citizens had no conception of the value of their votes; but politicians did, and therefore were disposed to do whatever seemed necessary to court favor. Jobs, welfare activities, and symbolic recognition were of particular importance.

Employment.   The immigrant (and for that matter the native-born city-dweller) was aware of the importance of getting and holding a job, often desperately so. Few people had the savings to weather more than brief periods of unemployment. There were no effective governmental programs, such as unemployment insurance, to deal with these contingencies. Thus the parties could offer a service that would be immediately appreciated. Countless municipal jobs were available to be filled by the loyal party voter and worker—jobs in the police, fire, and sanitation departments; jobs maintaining and cleaning city buildings; and, especially important, not only public jobs but also private jobs in the many businesses and industries which were in some way indebted to the machine.

Patronage is the classical lubricant of party machinery. Even the promise of a few jobs, as newspaperman Frank Kent has shown, could be sufficient to enable a precinct organization to achieve its basic goal: filling the party column on the ballot with organization nominees. A precinct, Kent noted, was likely to contain about 600 voters.[14] Discounting independents and the other party's registrants, only about 250 of the voters were eligible to participate in primaries; and of these, only about 125 could be expected actually to vote. Therefore, about 65 sure votes would insure control of the nominations by the party in the precinct.

Where were these 65 votes to come from? To begin with, the precinct captain himself (usually a minor city employee) could be counted on to swing both his own vote and that of four other family members, Kent explained. By judicious award of election-day patronage (paid poll-watching jobs, rental of the polling place) to citizens with similar influence over their kinfolk, his safe-vote total could be increased to 35.

> He is still shy about thirty votes, enough to make him sure in the primaries. But he has not yet counted the office holders. There are in every precinct some of these, and they mostly hold their jobs because of the recommendation of the precinct executive [captain]. There are street cleaners or lamp lighters whom he has put to work through the ward executive who has the pull at the City Hall. There are members of the Police Department or firemen

whom he helped put on the force. Or there may be aspirants for jobs of one sort or another who cannot get them without the precinct executive's backing.

There are very few precincts anywhere in which there are not at least ten persons living who are under party organization obligations of one sort or another for the offices they hold. In many precincts there are a good many more. But take seven as the average, and if each one of the seven is worth his five family votes—and it is extremely rare that he is not—then the precinct executive has got his total of sixty-five votes and a little more.[15]

Welfare activities. Party organizations were not merely employment agencies. A broadly conceived notion of the welfare state and its functions, financed by the proceeds of machine services to business, was reflected in the daily practices of effective organization politics. Tammany Hall sachem George Washington Plunkitt, turn-of-the-century philosopher-king of old-style urban politics, explained:

What holds your grip on your district is to go right among the poor families and help them in the different ways they need help. I've got a regular system for this. If there's a fire in Ninth, Tenth, or Eleventh Avenue, for example, any hour of the day or night, I'm usually there with some of my election district captains as soon as the fire engines. If a family is burned out I don't ask whether they are Republicans or Democrats, and I don't refer them to the Charity Organization Society, which would investigate their case in a month or two and decide they were worthy of help about the time they are dead from starvation. I just get quarters for them, buy clothes for them if their clothes were burned up, and fix them up til they get things runnin' again. It's philanthropy, but it's politics, too—mighty good politics. Who can tell how many votes one of these fires bring me? The poor are the most grateful people in the world, and, let me tell you, they have more friends in their neighborhoods than the rich have in theirs.[16]

A family at the bottom of the urban heap often needed more than financial help. It often needed a friend in court, an intermediary between the impersonal governmental authority and a youngster accused of some minor delinquency or a family breadwinner who had just been informed that his pushcart license could not be renewed. Note a few of the entries in Riordon's account of a day in the strenuous life of Plunkitt:

2 A.M.: Aroused from sleep by the ringing of his door bell; went to the door and found a bartender, who asked him to go to the police station and bail out a saloon-keeper who had been arrested for violating the excise law. Furnished bail and returned to bed at three o'clock.

8:30 A.M.: Went to the police court to look after his constituents. Found six "drunks." Secured the discharge for four by a timely word with the judge, and paid the fines of two.

9 A.M.: Appeared in the Municipal District Court. Directed one of his district captains to act as counsel for a widow against whom dispossess proceedings had been instituted and obtained an extension of time. Paid the rent of a poor family about to be dispossessed and gave them a dollar for food.

11 A.M.: At home again. Found four men waiting for him. One had been discharged by the Metropolitan Railway Company for neglect of duty, and wanted the district leader to fix things. Another wanted a job on the road. The third sought a place on the Subway and the fourth, a plumber, was looking for work with the Consolidated Gas Company. The district leader spent nearly three hours fixing things for the four men, and succeeded in each case.[17]

Recognition.   The most compelling needs of the nineteenth-century urbanite were protection and the elementary requirements of physical survival, but few people are content to remain for long at so low a level of aspiration. City organizations were well geared to meet needs for more than bread alone.

One of the first reactions of new arrivals thrust into a strange nation is to acquire a sense of ethnic awareness. In the old country there often was no more need for the Czech, Italian, or Pole to be aware of his nationality than there is for the proverbial fish to realize his watery surroundings. If a European peasant had loyalties beyond the immediate family, they were likely to be to a village, or perhaps a province. In the New World, however, one's nationality stood out as a unique attribute, and often as a symbol of underprivileged status. Furthermore, in the United States there was freedom to express group aspirations. Immigration, therefore, stimulated a paradoxical sense of Old World identity, which, for many groups, had never existed in the Old World.[18]

The upper-crust urban reformers who in the mid-nineteenth century began to band together to resist machine corruption were oblivious to immigrant desires for recognition and skeptical concerning the contribution of the immigrants to American life. These early reformers were typically prosperous local citizens whose objection was more to the abuses of the machines than to the depressed social conditions that made machines possible. Solid middle-class descendants of early settlers, these reformers typically excluded the Irish, Jews, blacks, and other recent immigrants from southern and eastern Europe. Machine politicians, on the other hand, were not standoffish. The Chicago arrangements for staffing precincts, which Gosnell describes, seem to have been typical in the communities which had substantial foreign immigration:

In the areas where there is a concentration of Negro population, both the Republican and Democratic parties had Negro committeemen. In the areas where persons of Polish descent are found, the parties kept a Zintak, a Konkowski, a Rosenkowski, a Kucharski, a Golusinski, and a Peska as committeemen; and in areas where many persons of Italian extraction are located, the committeemen bore such names as Serritella, Pacelli, Vignola, and Porcare.[19]

Other avenues of mobility into the ranks of respectability might be barred for the young man with a strange-sounding name or an unpopular skin pigmentation, but on election day all votes counted alike.

Plunkitt felt that his efforts to identify with all of the groups in the heterogeneous Fifteenth District made him a true cosmopolitan:

> When I get into the silk-stockin' part of the district, I can talk grammar and all that with the best of them. . . . As for the common people of the district, I am at home with them at all times. When I go among them, I don't try to show off my grammar, or talk about the Constitution, or how many volts there is in electricity or make it appear in any way that I am better educated than they are.[20]

Moreover, he did not confine himself to *group* recognition:

> I know every man, woman, and child in the Fifteenth District, except them that's been born this summer—and I know some of them, too. I know what they like and what they don't like, what they are strong at and what they are weak in, and I reach them by approachin' at the right side.
>
> For instance, here's how I gather in the young men. I hear of a young feller that's proud of his voice, thinks that he can sing fine. I asked him to come around to Washington Hall and join our Glee Club. He comes and sings, and he's a follower of Plunkitt for life. Another young feller gains a reputation as a baseball player in a vacant lot. I bring him into our baseball club. That fixes him. You'll find him workin' for my ticket at the polls next election day. Then there's the feller that likes rowin' on the river, the young feller that makes a name as a waltzer on his block, the young feller that's handy with his dukes—I rope them all by givin' them opportunities to show themselves off. I don't trouble them with political arguments. I just study human nature and act accordin'.[21]

THE DECLINE OF URBAN MACHINES

Plunkitt's happy view of the benevolence of organizations such as his was by no means shared by the better-educated, more prosperous residents of the cities. Spurred by revelations of corruption and favoritism on a grandiose scale, reform movements aiming to obliterate "bossism" rose with increased frequency by the later years of the nineteenth century. But in Plunkitt's day it was axiomatic that "Reform Administrations Never Succeed Themselves." Reformers, Plunkitt felt, were "only mornin' glories" because to them politics was a periodic spurt of ill-organized emotional fervor, rather than a year-round business. At the root of the short-run failure of the turn-of-the-century reformers was the limited nature of their appeal to the urban electorate of the day—antiseptic pleas for clean government, efficiency, and leadership by the well-born and well-bred. One might have been slightly more successful selling mink coats in the tropics.

More recently, however, the decline of city machine has been widely heralded. Because of the absence of reliable trend data, this decline cannot be documented with precision—although it does seem to have taken place. The withering away of old-style political organizations seems to have been only partly a direct consequence of attempts to reform urban politics. Rather, events have conspired to sap the traditional resources of party machines and to make voters less interested in those resources which the parties still command.

Decline in the resources of urban machines.   Even though the short-run impact of reform movements on local party organizations was minimal, the ebb and flow of these movements led to gradual changes in governmental procedures—changes that were to deprive the machines of key resources. Everywhere, party organization probably was weakened by loss of federal patronage resulting from the growth of a merit-based national civil service. In some states and localities, public jobs have not been insulated from politics to a great degree, but in others civil-service reform is complete and city and state employees no longer man the wards and precincts. Under the latter circumstances, a party politician may be able to do no more than seek some minor form of preferment for an otherwise qualified job applicant. Furthermore, the technical requirements of so-called patronage positions are often sufficiently complex to make it inexpedient—in today's climate of opinion and publicity—to fill them with unqualified personnel.[22] For these and other reasons related to contemporary affluence and educational levels, when the growth of urban redevelopment and antipoverty programs in the 1950s through 1980 opened up new kinds of appointive positions in the cities, the holders of these new jobs did not automatically become the loyal underlings of party leaders.[23]

In addition to undermining the power of local political machines, the Community Action Programs (CAPs) of Lyndon Johnson's War on Poverty had yet other effects on local urban politics. In an ironical twist to conservative demands that decision-making on local issues be returned to the local level, the CAPs did just that—local areas were encouraged to submit locally unique proposals to Washington for funding. Thus, some decision-making was returned, as political conservatives wished, to the local level. The difference was that it was not returned to traditional and tradition-minded decision-making groups. A longer lasting effect of the CAPs on American politics resulted from their getting those who were poor and often apathetic involved in discussing and deciding what they thought would improve their lot. The CAPs have disappeared, but the experience of these organizational efforts and the lessons learned from them are still a part of the structure of American politics.

Good-government procedures for auditing municipal funds, purchasing supplies, and letting contracts reduce the possibilities not only of outright corruption but also of what Plunkitt called "honest graft."[24] Tendencies on the part of local politicians to wink at violations of such good-government procedures are inhibited by the increased possibility of federal prosecution of local malefactors.

The federal government has weakened local machines in still another, and probably more fundamental, respect. Since the New Deal years, administering social-welfare programs has become a major formal task of government. Unemployment insurance, workmen's compensation, Social Security, collective-bargaining rights—none of which requires voting for machine candidates—have ended the local party's monopoly on the role of public benefactor.

Some reform legislation—for example, the New Deal welfare programs—was not introduced with an explicit view toward weakening the parties. Other reforms, such as the establishment of civil service, were. Nomination of candidates in primary elections and the use of nonpartisan procedures which bar party labels from the ballot in local elections are other examples of laws which have been passed with a view to restricting traditional party powers. By themselves such procedures do not necessarily hamper organizational activity, as can be seen from Kent's description of party tactics in a primary election (pp. 64–65). Combined with other party-weakening forces, however, such anti-party legislation often seems to have had the desired effect.[25]

Decline in voter interest in machine resources.   As we shall see shortly, not all contemporary voters are uninterested in receiving traditional machine benefits. Nevertheless, to the extent that countless changes in the past few generations have increased the material security of urban Americans and widened their psychological vistas, opportunities for bosses to control blocs of voters have been reduced. Few if any of today's urban citizens are as economically deprived, or as enmeshed in time- and energy-sapping work routines, as were garment-industry employees in the 1890s. For many industrial workers, union contracts have brought wage scales and a degree of job security which exceed even middle-class expectations of 50 years ago. Patronage jobs with the Department of Sanitation, therefore, are no longer overly desirable. Even non-union workers are often protected by minimum-wage legislation and the other types of governmental welfare benefits referred to above. And, at least at the higher levels of appointive political office, the problem may be more that of persuading a job candidate to make the financial sacrifice entailed in public service than that of rewarding the faithful for services rendered.

Partly as a consequence of the new material security, public attitudes seem to have undergone substantial transformations. More citizens would now find it repugnant to trade their votes for a mess of patronage—or to ignore the mess in City Hall. Contributing to this development have been rising educational levels and the diffusion of values and standards congruent with the good-government philosophy that reformers once found so hard to sell. Ironically, the machines themselves, by helping to incorporate such underprivileged groups as the immigrants into American society, encouraged the development of the kinds of attitudes which make voters immune to the boss's blandishments.

Does all this taken together mean that parties are no longer relevant at the local level? Far from it! It could be that today's voters are too sophisticated to "trade their votes" for favors. But, there is no easy characterization of today's voters, for this encompasses a wide variety of beliefs, backgrounds, and life circumstances, as we showed in Chapter 3. For instance, earlier we suggested that the increasing black and Hispanic populations of our nation's largest cities increases the potential for the development of machines on the nineteenth-century model, *if* local leadership emerges which is acceptable to the community.

One could also argue that there is a great potential and a great need for local party development in the fabled American suburbs. Too often we have found that increased education does not necessarily mean increased civic education. For instance, many citizens are not aware of the services to which they are entitled, or how to gain access to them. As has been shown in at least one urban setting, party leaders can provide valuable and valued services to the public, pushing the buttons in local government to make sure that garbage is collected on time, that streets and sewers are kept in good repair, and the like.[26] What could result from local party development of this kind in the suburbs would not be trading votes for favors so much as trading inactivity and non-voting for favors.

As more conservatively governed cities have moved to single-member city-council districts, under pressure from the Supreme Court and the Justice Department, the levels of locally available governmental services to the poor have improved. The addition of just one or two members politically responsible to the poorer districts of a city often results in a significant increase in city services. It is not necessary that the poorer areas control a majority of the positions on a city council or that their representatives be militant and abrasive—their mere presence is sometimes enough to improve basic services. And if voters choose to reward the party that best serves them in an immediate and visible sense, one could ask it this is truly worse than either non-voting or voting in an uninformed manner!

THE RANGE OF CONTEMPORARY URBAN POLITICS

Traditional Party Organization

In earlier editions, we suggested that one evidence of the withering away of party organization was the relatively low proportion of people who reported having been contacted by party workers in the campaign (10 per-

TABLE 4-1   Who's at the Door? Who's on the Phone?

YEAR	N	DEMOCRATS	REPUBLICANS	BOTH
1952	1,691	4%	4%	3%
1956	1,641	6	6	6
1960	1,708	8	9	5
1964	1,575	14	18	8
1968	1,344	16	18	8
1972	1,013	13	8	8
1976	2,316	11	6	7
1980	1,384	8	9	5

Source: Center for Political Studies, University of Michigan. Cell entries represent the percentage of respondents indicating that they had had contact during the campaign with a representative of a party or a candidate.

cent in 1956, and nearly 20 percent in non-southern cities of 100,000 or more). An examination of Table 4-1 is revealing and very suggestive. Far from the relatively low contact once noted, there seems to have been at least a temporary increase in voter contacts in recent years. This increase *may* be attributable to a minor change in the wording of the question about contacts with party workers—the question now includes a reference to telephone calls as well as to face-to-face contact. However, it could also be argued that telephone contact is much more common these days; it has come to be a highly refined form of campaigning and "phone banks" often replace personal contact by party or campaign workers.

Furthermore, there is a good bit of local variation. Some cities have active local party organizations, and others do not. The nature of local candidate-based campaigns can also account for further variation in the accounts of personal contact. Regardless, it would seem that, by the standards of a Plunkitt, there is comparatively little party contact made with the voters, especially contact of a continuing variety. These reports of party contact are inherently concerned only with soliciting votes. Plunkitt, on the other hand, knew for a certainty that his contacts would result in votes, almost without asking.

In the 1950s, in Detroit, only 6 percent of the public remembered having been approached by political-party workers; in fact less than a fifth knew that there were party precinct officials in their district. Detroit is a city which elects its municipal officials on a nonpartisan basis, a practice which may account for the fact that its precinct organizations (which were still needed to work for state and national party candidates) had become ramshackle and ineffective. Only a fifth of the Detroit precinct leaders had at their disposal such an elementary tool as a card file of their party's supporters and of the precinct's independents; less than a third had conducted door-to-door canvassing or called meetings of their precinct workers during the 1956 campaign.[27]

In Seattle, another nonpartisan city, Professor Bone found that "although [precinct] committeemen are elected at the general election . . . , contests for the position are infrequent and the county chairmen commonly fill many posts by appointment after the election. It is generally recognized that the job of precinct captain is as easy to obtain as that of scoutmaster or Sunday-School teacher." Many of the party leaders were housewives, some evidently participating out of a vague sense of duty ("I certainly didn't seek this job and would like to give it to someone else. But I will do my best.") or for social reasons ("to get acquainted more with the residents of the precinct"). One such woman completely reversed the classical pattern in which the precinct leader is the individual most intimately familiar with the district. Her reason for seeking the post, she explained, was "to help me get acquainted with my new neighborhood."[28]

On the other hand, in the city of New Haven, Connecticut (a state which, as we shall see in the next chapter, has shied away from party-weakening legislation), 60 percent of a sample of voters reported that representatives of the parties had contacted them during election campaigns. The importance of parties in the politics of this municipality has been extensively documented by Robert A. Dahl and his associates.[29] New Haven's Mayor Richard C. Lee, in the early '60s, was able to obtain support for a massive urban redevelopment program, in spite of many obstacles to favorable action on such programs elsewhere, in large part because of the capacity of an old-style party organization to weld together the government of a city with a set of formal mayoral powers designed to impede effective action by the chief executive. During the crucial period of ratification of his program, Lee commanded a substantial majority in the city legislative body, a majority that he was able to wield with the confidence that British Prime Ministers can have in the votes of members of their parliamentary majorities.[30]

Further evidence of the continuing potential for old-style organization, at least in areas where there are many low-income citizens and not too much party-weakening legislation, has come from other studies. For example, one study of party leaders from eight New Jersey counties yielded numerous reports that the parties were continuing to perform traditional voter services. Seventy-two percent of these leaders reported that they often help "deserving people get public jobs"; 54 percent said they frequently explained government procedures (how to get Social Security benefits or unemployment compensation, for example); and 62 percent said they often helped citizens "who are in difficulty with the law."[31] A study of "Stackton," a midwestern industrial city, reports the performance of similar "social-service" party precinct work, especially in the lower-income black areas of the community. The authors of the study note the following differences between the experiences of precinct leaders in the white and black sections of town:

> Aside from having larger number of requests for aid, the kind of aid requested by Negroes differs from the requests by white constituents. Negro

requests are for (1) jobs, (2) relief money from the township trustee or welfare agency, or (3) aid in dealing with the law enforcement agencies. In a majority of white precincts, the requests are for (1) a summer job with the park district for a high-school age son, or (2) information about how to contact the city government agencies. The problems Negroes bring to their committeemen are usually pressing: Often the applicant is hungry, and several precinct workers . . . said that they had paid grocery, electric, and other bills out of their own pockets on occasion. No white committeeman reported he himself had given aid of the sort or had ever been asked for such aid.[32]

Two Kinds of New-Style Urban Political Patterns

Two of the newer American urban political patterns are the politics of *nonpartisanship* and the rise in many localities of *issue-oriented amateurs*. These are developments of very great intrinsic interest to students of local government. For our present purpose, however, we shall look at them mainly for the further perspective they provide on the strengths and weaknesses of old-style urban politics.

The politics of nonpartisanship.   We have already noted the presence of nonpartisan institutions in such weak-party cities as Detroit and Seattle. About two-thirds of American cities over 25,000 in population are nonpartisan in the sense that they are legally obliged to elect their public officials without reference on the ballot to the candidates' party affiliations. The nonpartisan movement was one of the many "direct-democracy," anti-machine procedures advocated during the waves of reform and progressivism early in the century. Since the 1920s, there has been little active agitation for nonpartisanship, but the proportion of localities using nonpartisan elections has consistently increased, largely because nonpartisanship is part of the package of governmental arrangements associated with the popular council-manager institutions; as communities adopted council-manager institutions, nonpartisan elections tended, as it were, to slip in the back door.

In some communities where nonpartisanship has been introduced, the old parties have continued to operate much as in the past; in others, new local parties have sprung up to contest the nonpartisan elections. Finally, in still others, nonpartisanship takes the form originally intended by the progressives who invented this device: no organized groups contest elections, and voters choose from a more-or-less self-selected array of candidates. Whether the nonpartisan selection process has effected the sort of government its original supporters wished is questionable. In many cities the elimination of partisan elections has resulted in city governments being taken over by nonpartisan business, particularly banking, insurance, real estate, and newspaper interests. How good this has been for American urban development is not as yet settled. We shall examine the research on the consequences of this last form of nonpartisanship in the next chapter, since these urban no-party systems provide an interesting framework for examining the levels and degrees of actual party competition in the various states. But to anticipate our conclusions, we may note that when nonpartisanship works it sometimes has quite unintended side-effects—notably voter confusion. Without the familiar device of party labels to aid in candidate selections, voters are thrown back on various, often quite haphazard, means of making their choices. Furthermore, the candidates themselves may be less able to bring their case to the electorate, since they no longer have the resources of political parties at their disposal. Paradoxically, a political form which is defended as a means of eliminating the partisan "barrier" between citizens and their officials often in fact serves to attenuate connections between them.

Issue-oriented amateurs. Old-style party politicians have sometimes been known to refer, perhaps cynically, to college graduates and "intellectuals"[33] as a "new ethnic group" on the American political scene. It would seem inevitable that there might be political consequences from the explosion of higher education in the post-World War II United States. Increasingly, college graduates—many of them much more receptive than most citizens to the appeal of abstract political issues—have become a major population group. And even as undergraduates many of them acquire strong, idealistic commitments to political participation.

Ideologically motivated grassroots party organizations first began to form within the Democratic party, especially during the 1952 election campaign, when that party nominated Adlai Stevenson, a candidate capable of arousing great enthusiasm among liberal-leaning college graduates. In spite of their candidate's defeat, the liberal Democratic Stevenson forces took root in some parts of many cities in the 1950s and 1960s, sometimes carrying out voter mobilization tasks that increasingly had been ignored by the decaying traditional party organizations, and sometimes even defeating the traditional organizations.[34] In 1968, these groups—along with college students—helped provide the core of workers behind the campaign to secure the Democratic presidential nomination for Senator Eugene McCarthy of Minnesota. The fervor of their commitment to the issues, and the distaste with which they viewed the practices associated with "the old politics" (such as bargaining and compromise), paralleled the attitudes of the newer activists in the Republican party—the issue-oriented amateurs who had been especially articulate in supporting Barry Goldwater's 1964 presidential campaign, and then in the Democratic Party with the 1972 nomination of Senator George McGovern. It is not entirely coincidental that these two candidates suffered the most resounding defeats in American political history. These sorts of ideologically motivated candidates have a strong appeal to the political activists who control most party structures and who dominate the voting in the party primaries and caucuses. The general electorate, however, is much less ideologically oriented. In short, to become president a candidate must convince the general public that he is fit to be president.

It is largely the Democratic rather than the Republican amateurs who have attempted to establish themselves at the level of local party organization. Differing from the reformers of the past both in that they are willing to use partisan institutions and that they are devoted to specific policies such as civil rights or urban renewal (rather than merely to "efficiency" or "clean government"), they nevertheless share one characteristic with their reform predecessors—an enmity to "bossism" and "machine tactics." And in at least one respect they also resemble the old-style organization men they seek to replace: in contrast to the situation that seems to result from nonpartisanship, both old-style and new-style urban party politicians rely on extensive face-to-face contact with voters. Where new reformers have been successful, it often has been by beating the boss at his own game of canvassing the election district, registering and keeping track of voters, and getting them to the polls.[35]

A classic example of this is the 1963 Chicano political takeover first of the small Texas town of Crystal City and eventually of the county government. The first electoral victory for the Mexican-American majority came about partially because the new and inexperienced (in the ways of maintaining political control in South Texas) city manager failed to note that the number of Mexican Americans who had paid their poll taxes (this was before the Twenty-fourth Amendment) was higher than the number of Anglos who could vote. The subsequent balloting was along ethnic lines. The Anglo minority came back with an ethnically balanced ticket in the next city council election and won. However, a new group of Chicano activists had become involved in Crystal City politics. By a skillful blend of the new (to Mexican Americans) politics of ethnic consciousness with traditional voter registration and get-out-the-vote drives, by 1970 they were able to regain and consolidate control first of the city council, then of the school board, and finally of the county government.[36]

But much of the day-to-day style of the traditional urban politician is clearly distasteful to the new reformers: they have generally eschewed the use of patronage and, with the exception of campaigns for housing-code enforcement, they have avoided the extensive service operations to voters and interest groups which were central to old-style party organizations. For example, when election-district captains and other officials of New York's Village Independent Democrats—the reform group which deposed New York Democrat County Leader Carmine DeSapio in his own election district—were asked the same set of questions about their activities used in the New Jersey study noted above, the responses were strikingly different, as can be seen from Table 4-2.

The successes of this class of new-style urban party politician have vindicated a portion of the classical strategy of urban party politics (the exten-

TABLE 4-2   Services Performed by New Jersey Old-Style Party Politicians and by New York City Issue-oriented Amateurs

Service	PERCENTAGE PERFORMING THE SERVICE "OFTEN"	
	New Jersey Professionals	New York Amateurs
1. Helping deserving people get public jobs	72	0
2. Showing people how to get their Social Security benefits, welfare, unemployment compensation, etc.	54	5
3. Helping citizens who are in difficulty with the law	62	6

Source: Richard T. Frost, "Stability and Change in Local Politics," *Public Opinion Quarterly*, 25 (Summer 1961), 221-35. The New York politicians were surveyed in the 60s by Goetchus; see note 35.

sive reliance upon canvassing and other personal relations) and also have shown that under some circumstances it is possible to organize such activities with virtually no reliance on patronage and other material rewards. The new reformers have tapped a pool of political activists used by parties elsewhere in the world—for example, in Great Britain—but not a normal part of the American scene.

New reformers are successful where material resources available to the parties are limited—for example, in California—and where voter interest in these resources is low. In practice, however, the latter condition has confined the effectiveness of the new-style reform Democrats largely to the more prosperous sections of cities; neither their style nor their programs seem to be successful in lower-income districts.[37] The areas of reform Democratic strength are generally *not* the areas which contribute greatly to Democratic pluralities in the cities. And, in many cities, the reformers' clientele is progressively diminishing as higher-income citizens move outward to the suburbs. Therefore, though fascinating and illuminating, the new reform movement must be considered, at least for the moment, as only a single manifestation in a panorama of urban political practices.

FUNCTIONS OF OLD-STYLE PARTY ORGANIZATIONS

Several conclusions can be distilled from the somewhat schematic analysis in this chapter of old-style party organizations and of certain of the latter-day alternatives to them. Returning to our basic question about the functions served by American political parties, what can we say about the past—and to some extent continuing—functions of urban party machines?

First, we may ask whether the urban machines contributed to the effectiveness of governmental policy-making. If we use narrow standards to evaluate this aspect of the parties' performance, our judgment certainly must be negative. The annals of machine politics are studded with examples of extravagant and corrupt use of public funds. Nevertheless, the cities were built, administered, and maintained. Although urban growth followed a largely hit-or-miss pattern, and cities today are suffering from the lack of planning during their years of expansion, party organizations succeeded in unifying and coordinating city governments. Given the formal governmental institutions of the nineteenth-century cities, it is not certain that these tasks would otherwise have been performed.

The effects of party machines on popular control have been rather complex. In Chapter 3 we saw that parties are a valuable instrument for simplifying the tasks of the voter. They provide him with a device for consolidating his perception of governmental officialdom and thus greatly reduce the costs in time and energy of making political choices.

Old-style party organizations, by nominating slates of candidates, consolidated and simplified political perception and choice. Still, it would be difficult to maintain that the greenhorn immigrant, exchanging his vote for a Thanksgiving Day turkey, was exercising effective control over party leaders. Even from the limited standpoint of the nineteenth-century city resident's desire for physical security, machines had their deficiencies. Party benevolences, after all, were not the citizen's as a matter of legal right. They might always be withdrawn. Furthermore, the party's favors to the voter's employer might negate its services to him—for example, by permitting the continuation of hazardous working conditions in a factory.

In time, however, the immigrant or his children were able to use the party as an effective vehicle for increasing their own leverge in the political system. Since in the final analysis the parties were dependent on winning elections, they found it necessary to accommodate to the changing desires of voters. After the early demands for minimal material security came strivings for group recognition. Therefore, each wave of new immigrants gradually worked its way—and was recruited—into the ranks of party leadership.

Professor Elmer E. Cornwell, Jr., in a study of the incorporation of ethnic groups into the parties in Providence, Rhode Island, found that within about three decades after representatives of a group first appeared in the community, the group began to obtain representation in political-party councils. Figure 4-1, which summarizes his findings, shows that by the end of the ninteenth century the city's Democratic party had come under thorough Irish control. The next major immigrant wave, which was from Italy, found an especially sympathetic reception in the Republican party, probably largely because the Yankee Republican leadership realized that its chances for electoral success were dependent on support from immigrant groups, and the Democrats had successfully won much of the Irish vote. By the post-World War II years, Italians were dominant in the Providence Republican party and in 1958 the state had its first Republican Italian governor.[38]

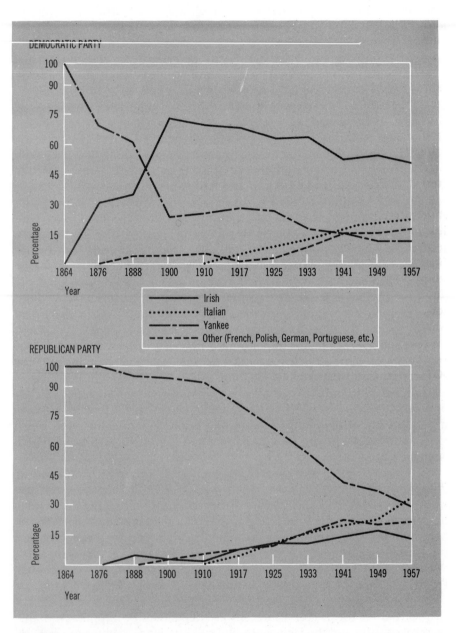

DEMOCRATIC PARTY

Irish
Italian
Yankee
Other (French, Polish, German, Portuguese, etc.)

REPUBLICAN PARTY

Source: Elmer E. Cornwell, Jr., "Party Absorption of Ethnic Groups: The Case of Providence, Rhode Island," *Social Forces*, 38 (March 1960), 207.

FIGURE 4-1 Incorporation of immigrant groups in party ward committees, 1864-1957.

Of the three criteria we have selected to assess the functions of parties, the urban machines stand highest in their contribution to political stability. The machines were corrupt. They squandered public funds. But machine practices ameliorated the harsh consequences of industrialization and urban growth—they eased the conditions of life for people who might otherwise have become deeply embittered, opening up avenues by which depressed groups could rise in American life. Even the inordinate brokerage fees accepted by machine politicians for their services were a vehicle for broadening the power base of American society. Over the years, the son of an immigrant laborer might become a freewheeling machine politician. His granddaughter might become a presidential advisor; his great-grandson might, as happened in the case of John F. Kennedy in 1960, become president.

It is striking that of all the major nations undergoing rapid industrialization in the past century, only the United States—which had the added task of incorporating an unprecedented influx of immigrants—failed to develop class-conscious political parties. It would be an oversimplification to attribute to the city machines alone the failure of a revolutionary spirit, other than that of 1776, to gain more than a modicum of strength in the United States. But it would be a conspicuous oversight to explain the nation's political stability without reference to the role played by George Washington Plunkitt and his ilk.

NOTES

[1] David Easton, *A Framework for Political Analysis* (Englewood Cliffs, N.J.: Prentice-Hall, 1965), p. 57.

[2] Mike Royko, *Boss: Richard J. Daley of Chicago* (New York: Signet, 1971); Milton L. Rakove, *Don't Make No Waves, Don't Back No Losers* (Bloomington: University of Indiana Press, 1975).

[3] Wallace S. Sayre and Herbert Kaufman, *Governing New York City: Politics in the Metropolis* (New York: Russell Sage Foundation, 1960), pp. 538–42.

[4] Lyle W. Dorsett, *The Pendergast Machine* (New York: Oxford, 1968).

[5] *Lewis* v. *Illinois State Employees Union.* 410 U.S. 943 (1973).

[6] *Elrod* v. *Burns,* 427 U.S. 347 (1976); *Branti* v. *Finkel* 445 U.S. 507 (1980).

[7] Daniel Elazar, *American Federalism: A View from the States* (New York: Crowell, 1966).

[8] For additional information see Floyd M. Clay, *Coozan Dudley LeBlanc: From Huey Long to Hadacol* (Gretna, La.: Pelican, 1973). For a study of a much less benign local boss see Glen Jeansonne, *Leander Perez: Boss of the Delta* (Baton Rouge, La.: Louisiana State University Press, 1977).

[9] Although the past is commonly assumed by political analysts to be "lost," recent historical scholarship has been attempting reconstructions of early urban patterns. See, for example, the contrary viewpoints developed from a wealth of data in Leo Hershkowitz, *Tweed's New York* (Garden City, N.Y.: Anchor Press/Doubleday, 1977); Alexander B. Callow, Jr., *The Tweed Ring* (New York: Oxford, 1966); Seymour J. Mandelbaum, *Boss Tweed's New York* (New York: Wiley, 1965).

[10]For an excellent brief discussion of the range of contemporary local political patterns—including machines—see James Q. Wilson, "Politics and Reform in American Cities," *American Government Annual, 1962–1963* (New York: Holt, Rinehart, 1962), pp. 37–52. For a fuller discussion see Edward C. Banfield and James Q. Wilson, *City Politics* (Cambridge, Mass.: Harvard University Press and MIT Press, 1963), and Herbert Kaufman, *Politics and Policies in State and Local Governments* (Englewood Cliffs, N.J.: Prentice-Hall, 1963). Also see Fred I. Greenstein, "The Changing Pattern of Urban Politics," *Annals of the American Academy of Political and Social Science*, 353 (May 1964), 1–13, portions of which have been incorporated into the present chapter by permission of the publishers.

[11]Charles F. Adams, ed., *The Work of John Adams* (Boston: Little, Brown, 1850), Vol. II, p. 144.

[12]See, for example, Edward A. Shils, *The Torment of Secrecy* (Glencoe, Ill.: The Free Press, 1956); Stanley M. Elkins, *Slavery* (Chicago: University of Chicago Press, 1959; 2nd ed., 1968).

[13]John DeWitt Warner, "The 'Sweating System' in New York City," *Harper's Weekly*, 29 (February 9, 1895), 135–36, reprinted in Oscar Handlin, ed., *Immigration as a Factor in American History* (Englewood Cliffs, N.J.: Prentice-Hall, 1959), pp. 64–66.

[14]The term "precinct" is used by most large cities to describe the several city blocks using a single polling place. In most cities the fundamental political units, and therefore the basis of party organization, are the constituencies of city-council members—the *wards*. Ward chairmen are ordinarily the chief lieutenants of a city boss. They, in turn, supervise and appoint precinct officials. There are minor variations, however. In New York City, for example, the basic party unit is the *district* from which state assemblypersons are elected.

[15]Frank R. Kent, *The Great Game of Politics* (Garden City, N.Y.: Doubleday, 1923), p. 21.

[16]William L. Riordon, *Plunkitt of Tammany Hall* (New York: Dutton, 1969, originally published in 1905), pp. 36–37. It is generally conceded that Plunkitt's remarks were somewhat embellished by Riordon in the reporting, but as the frequency of quotation from this little volume by political scientists attests, Riordon-Plunkitt remain among the standard commentators on old-style urban politics.

[17]*Ibid.*, pp. 123–24.

[18]For an interesting discussion of the growth of European identity in the United States, see Robert E. Park, *The Immigrant Press and Its Control* (New York: Harper, 1922).

[19]Harold F. Gosnell, *Machine Politics: Chicago Model* (Chicago: University of Chicago Press, 1937), pp. 44–45. In 1968, a welcome second edition of this classic work appeared with an epilogue by the author and a foreword by Theodore J. Lowi.

[20]Riordon, *Plunkitt*, pp. 62–63.

[21]*Ibid.*, p. 34

[22]Frank J. Sorauf, "State Patronage in a Rural County," *American Political Science Review*, 50 (December, 1956), 1046–1056.

[23]Among other things, under contemporary circumstances, the political leader may sometimes be as anxious to persuade the potential appointee to accept a choice position as the latter is to receive it. A 1968 investigation by *The New York Times* of the variety of resources then at the disposal of parties in New York City and State pointed to the decision of Republican Mayor John Lindsay to appoint the brother of a key leader of the Democratic-controlled State Legislature to a $14,000-a-year post in a city government bureau. But it was clear that Lindsay could not command the automatic obedience of this individual—much less his brother—in the manner of the traditional boss described by Frank Kent. A Lindsay associate indicated that the Mayor was simply somewhat wistfully hoping that the legislature would look on the city's case more favorably ("The fact that you do a favor. . . is like casting bread upon the waters"). Furthermore, the legislative leader's brother soon resigned the city position. The basic point of the *Times* story was that increasing federal government activity had led to a new burgeoning of patronage. But there was no evidence whatsoever that this latter-day development—another of the "trends" that is in need of further documentation—could be easily and invariably turned to strenghtening decaying party organizations. Martin Tolchin, "Political Patronage Rising at Fast Rate, Study Finds," *New York Times*, June 17, 1968.

[24]Plunkitt felt that there was no need for a politician to break the law in order to make his fortune, since there were numerous opportunities for him to use his inside knowledge to advantage. "My party's in power in the city and it's goin' to undertake a lot of public improvements. Well, I'm tipped off, say, that they're going to lay out a new public park at a certain place. I see my opportunity and I take it. I go to that place and I buy up all the land I can in the neighborhood. Then the board of this or that makes its plan public, and there is a rush to get my land, which nobody cared particular for before. Ain't it perfectly honest to charge a good price and make a profit on my investment and foresight? Of course it is. Well, that's honest graft." Riordon, *Plunkitt,* p. 4. Opportunities to use party connections for money-making purposes—without breaking the law—still do exist. For example, public building projects must be insured. Since the insurance rates are regulated, there is no need for competitive bidding, yet the agencies receiving such contracts receive very large commissions. For this and other examples of opportunities for "honest graft" see the *Times* article referred to in note 23.

[25]As we shall see, these reforms also may have had quite unexpected side-effects.

[26]H. Hertzberg, "Hi, Boss, Send the Judges to Meade Esposito," *New York Times Magazine,* December 10, 1972, pp. 33 ff.

[27]Daniel Katz and Samuel J. Eldersveld, "The Impact of Local Party Activity upon the Electorate," *Public Opinion Quarterly,* 25 (Spring 1961), 1–24.

[28]Hugh A. Bone, *Grass Roots Party Leadership* (Seattle: University of Washington Bureau of Governmental Research and Service, 1952), pp. 5, 27.

[29]Robert A. Dahl, *Who Governs?* (New Haven: Yale University Press, 1961), p. 278 and *passim*; Nelson W. Polsby, *Community Power and Political Theory* (New Haven: Yale University Press, 1963); Raymond E. Wolfinger, *The Politics of Progress* (New Haven: Yale University Press, 1970).

[30]Lee was far from being the creature of his party, however. Party leaders often find it desirable to choose visible, appealing public figures to head their tickets and to bring in votes for the less-distinguished party regulars running for lesser offices. Examples are the contribution of the Ed Flynn machine of the Bronx for the gubernatorial and presidential candidacies of Franklin D. Roosevelt, and the support of Chicago Democratic leader Jacob Arvey for the ascent of Adlai E. Stevenson from the Illinois governorship to the 1952 and 1956 Democratic presidential nominations. When Lee attempted to revise the city charter so as to make the mayor's dependency on the party less necessary, he was skillfully defeated by the party regulars. Raymond E. Wolfinger, "The Influence of Precinct Work on Voting Behavior," *Public Opinion Quarterly,* 27 (Fall 1963), 387–98. By the late 1960s Lee and the party organization had become estranged and, as in many other cities, there had been an insurgence of additional forces that were under the control neither of the mayor nor of the party organization—for example, a nationally based poverty program (see Russell Murphy, *Political Entrepreneurship and Urban Poverty* (Lexington, Mass.: Lexington Books, 1971). and militant black-power organizations, both of which illustrate contemporary trends that work to weaken old-style parties capable of exercising centralized urban leadership.

[31]Numerous other services were reported in response to an ingenious questionnaire which was carefully worded in order to avoid implying that respondents were to be censured for indulging in "machine tactics." Richard T. Frost, "Stability and Change in Local Politics," *Public Opinion Quarterly,* 25 (Summer, 1961,) 221–235.

[32]Peter Rossi and Phillips Cutwright, "The Impact of Party Organization in an Industrial Setting," in Morris Janowitz, ed., *Community Political Systems* (Glencoe, Ill.: The Free Press, 1961), p. 93.

[33]A term which we can loosely use in the American setting to refer to various kinds of professionals: university instructors; people associated with the communications industries and the arts; social workers; etc. We do not mean to imply that everyone connected with these endeavors is a serious user of the intellect, or that people from other social categories are not, but simply use the term roughly to distinguish a class of individuals long conspicuous in politics elsewhere and increasingly so in the United States.

[34]The best general account is James Q. Wilson, *The Amateur Democrats* (Chicago: University of Chicago Press, 1962). For a useful review of a number of studies of the motivations of old-style and new-style politicians, see Robert H. Salisbury, "The Urban Party Organization

Member," *Public Opinion Quarterly*, 29 (Winter 1965–66), 550–64. Also see M. Margaret Conway and Frank B. Feigert, "Motivation, Incentive Systems, and the Political Party Organization," *American Political Science Review*, 62 (December 1968), 1159–1173.

[35]There is another interesting point of resemblance between old- and new-style urban party politics. In both, an important aspect of the motivation for participation seems to be the rewards of sociability. Tammany picnics and New York Committee for Democratic Voters (CDV) coffee hours probably differ more in decor than in the functions they serve. An instructive indication of this is provided by the committee structure of the Greenwich Village club of the CDV; in addition to the committees dealing with the club newsletter, with housing, and with community action, there is a social committee and a flight committee, the latter being concerned with arranging charter flights to Europe for club members. See Vernon M. Goetcheus, *The Village Independent Democrats: A Study in the Politics of the New Reformers* (unpublished senior thesis, Honors College, Wesleyan University, 1963), pp. 65–66.

[36]For an excellent detailed account of this story see John Shockley, *Chicano Revolt in a Small Texas Town* (South Bend, In.: University of Notre Dame Press, 1974).

[37]DeSapio, for example, was generally able to hold on to his lower-socioeconomic status Italian voting support in Greenwich Village; his opponents succeeded largely by activating the many middle- and upper-class voters who had moved into new high-rent housing in the district. Similarly, in the various 1968 presidential primaries, the efforts of the late Senator Robert F. Kennedy were far more successful in areas populated by blue-collar workers, blacks, and other voters in the traditional core Democratic party constituencies than was the college student-staffed campaign of Senator Eugene McCarthy.

[38]John O. Pastore, who later served in the United States Senate, was elected governor as a Democrat in 1946, and was the first Italian to hold that office in the State.

chapter 5 ———————————

STATE POLITICS:
The Varieties of American
——————————— Party Systems

If the methods of the physical sciences could be neatly transferred to the social sciences, we might conceive of a quite elementary experiment which would help establish what functions are served by political parties. We would assemble a large sample of political units and divide it in two so that both halves were common in all characteristics. Into the political systems of the first half of our sample we would introduce political parties; the second subsample, our control group, would elect its officials and run its government by the same procedures as the first, but without recourse to parties. After a period of careful observation, we would note the shape that politics takes in each subsample, attributing the ways the first differed from the second to the effects of parties.

We might even imagine a more sophisticated experiment, dividing our sample into three comparable groups: one of them with a party system in which the parties were intensely competitive; one with a party system in which one party tended to dominate elections; and the third a control group with no parties. Further experimental possibilities could involve introducing variations in the number of parties in the party system, or in the contexts in which the parties operate—for example, the amount of basic social consensus or the distribution of interest groups.

TYPES OF PARTY SYSTEMS

Needless to say, complex political units cannot be manipulated experimentally like the white rats that are run through mazes by psychologists. Yet something crudely approximating our controlled experiment actually exists in the United States, because of the remarkable panorama of partisan practices in the fifty states and thousands of localities of the nation.

In a number of the states and in many of the localities, two-party competition of the sort we think of when we hear the phrase "the American two-party system" is full blown. Some states—for example, Connecticut, in the years between 1930 and 1956—have experienced closer election outcomes and more frequent alternations in party control of the government than even the federal government. With the exception of a few sparsely settled western states, high levels of party competition have been most common in the large industrial states, where urban blue-collar workers who tend to vote Democratic are balanced by the Republican pluralities rung up in suburbs, small cities, and rural areas.

The highly competitive states may be thought of as being at one end of a scale measuring party competition. Adjacent to them we find states which lean slightly in the direction of favoring Republican or Democratic candidates. Further along are states in which one party almost always elects the public officials, but the minority party has sufficient support to be within a hop, skip, and jump of taking office if the dominant party fails to keep its fences mended. Finally, at the far end of the scale are the one-party states—the states that have not elected officials or supported presidential candidates of the other party in living memory.

Historically, non-competitive states have been those which lacked the underlying social heterogeneity of the two-party states. We use the cautionary "historically" since there appear to be changes currently underway, but we are not at all certain that we should dismiss the idea of non-competition as a relic of earlier days. Depending on the time period studied, the offices which we consider, and our criteria for competition and non-competition, it would be possible to arrive at startlingly different conclusions for any given state.[1] If we were to take Texas as an example, and consider only the 1980 presidential election, Ronald Reagan's 56 percent showing might suggest to some that this once one-party Democratic state had shifted over to the Republicans. This impression might be fortified if we were to lengthen our period of observation and include other statewide offices, since a Republican won the governor's mansion in 1978, and a Republican was reelected to the U.S. Senate as well. Yet, in 1978, the Republicans won only four House seats, and could increase this to only five in the wake of Reagan's 1980 victory. Do we now classify Texas as one-party for some offices and two-party for others? If we were to include other offices, such as members of the two houses of the state legislature, it would be possible to confuse ourselves even further.

The tendency toward one-party domination in certain states—largely thought of as southern but not exclusively so—is often also encouraged by the traditions of sectional conflict which developed in the aftermath of the Civil War. Thus, in the eleven states of the Old Confederacy, Democratic ascendancy was a device for preserving a solid regional front in national politics, with the goal of preserving white dominance in the South.[2]

General elections ordinarily decide nothing in the one-party states. In the South, for example, Republicans have often failed even to contest the elections for many state and local offices. But this does not mean that one-party states are without political conflict. Election contests are "pushed back" to the nominating stage. Under such circumstances a candidate's party affiliation has little meaning—the party is neutral, serving as the arena within which individual politicians and factions vie for office. It was partly in response to the meaninglessness of general elections in the one-party states that in the late nineteenth and early twentieth centuries the uniquely American institution of primary elections developed.[3]

Since primaries are in effect no-party elections, and also the only real elections in the one-party states, it is rewarding to compare politics in the one-party states with politics in the states which have active parties. We also can add to our understanding of the functions of parties by glancing briefly at actual *nonpartisan elections*. In all of the American states, political parties play at least a nominal role in elections, even though in some states one party is of no practical significance. But, as we saw in the previous chapter, political parties are barred from being listed on the ballot in numerous American cities (indeed, the majority). And in many cities the goals of the proponents of nonpartisanship[4] have been achieved, in that parties have in fact withdrawn from local electoral politics and make no effort to use the nonpartisan ballot. In addition to local nonpartisanship, one American state—Nebraska—elects its legislators (though not its other state officials) without recourse to party labels. Basically, however, nonpartisanship is a local rather than a state phenomenon. The reason for considering it in a chapter on *state* politics is that it provides an analytically instructive limiting case for considering one of the key sources of variation in state political behavior—the presence or absence of organized political competition.

The reader should realize that the observations which follow are, strictly speaking, *not* comparable to a controlled experiment. We have already shown that the one-party states differ from the two-party states in respects other than degree of party competition. They differ, often profoundly, in characteristics such as the heterogeneity of their populations, per capita income, economic resources, and so forth. Therefore, the comparisons we make must be cautious; and we must occasionally resort to tentative inferences in an attempt to see whether differences relate to the presence or absence of competing political groups, or whether they relate to other factors, some of which are themselves responsible for the pattern of political competition in a state. The reader should also realize that party systems change over the years. What follows is not a *Mobilguide* to the most recent developments in the politics of the states to be discussed, but rather a series of illustrative accounts of party systems (and non-party systems) at particular points in time when they offered especially suggestive insights into the range of American partisanship. In considering this rich variation we shall move from what might be called "the state of nature"—the politics of non-partisanship and the one-party states—to contexts in which parties are important.

NONPARTISAN POLITICS

Political scientists had ignored the interesting possibility of comparing the politics of nonpartisan and partisan localities until the early 1950s, when Professor Charles R. Adrian pointed to the potential merits of such a strategy and reported evidence supporting a number of intriguing hypotheses concerning the unanticipated consequences of eliminating parties from politics. Although there are still gaps and inconsistencies in our information about the effects of nonpartisanship, a number of subsequent studies have been reported. Together, they mesh remarkably well with the findings of the voting research summarized in Chapter 3. As we saw, party labels serve in a number of ways to clarify the tasks of voters and politicians.[5] In the absence of partisanship—that is, in jurisdictions which are nonpartisan both legally and in practice—it of course becomes impossible for voters to rely on what we found to be the principal basis for voting in American national elections: namely, party identification. How then *does* the voter make his choices in nonpartisan elections?

(1) Personal qualities of the candidates—often wholly "trivial" qualities— become important. If the voter is unable to use his sense of identification with a political party as a basis for deciding how to vote, it follows from our analysis in Chapter 3 that he is thrown back on the two other general types of criteria that voters may employ—their issue orientations and their candidate preferences. But actually it seems especially to be response to the candidates—and sometimes response to what would seem, to most of us, to be extremely trivial characteristics of the candidates—that takes the place of party identification in the voter's deliberations.

In nonpartisan elections, not only are the candidates listed on the ballot unlabeled, but there also may be a great many of them. One function of parties, after all, is to narrow down the number of contenders for election. Since most voters do not follow politics closely and do not hold well-crystallized opinions on the issues of the day, the nonpartisan ballot presents a most puzzling stimulus—namely, a list of largely unfamiliar names of individuals running for office. *Anything* that makes a candidate's name stand out may be to his advantage under such circumstances, including:

(a) *Celebrity status.* Adrian refers, for example, to a successful candidate for Detroit's nonpartisan city council who "stood largely on the implicit platform that he had been an able shortstop for the Detroit Tigers baseball club."[6]

(b) *Political chameleon status.* Even having a name resembling the name of a celebrity may be sufficient for victory. In a 1954 Massachusetts primary election (a form close enough to nonpartisanship to be included in this discussion), a gentleman whose prior qualifications consisted of eighteen years of employment by a safety-razor company, culminating as head of the firm's stock room, won his party's nomination (and later the election) for state treasurer. His name was John F. (for Francis) Kennedy.[7] In yet another example, an attorney with a high likelihood of indictment and disbarment (he was subsequently indicted, convicted, and disbarred) won the Democratic nomination for Justice of the Texas Supreme Court. He had no Republican opponent but did win over a write-in candidate named Sam Houston. The winner's qualifications were simple—he had the same last name as both a former U.S. Senator and a candidate for governor of Texas.

(c) *Ballot order.* There is evidence that in some nonpartisan elections candidates get significantly more votes if their names happen to be located at the top of the ballot.[8]

(d) *Ethnicity.* Clear-cut patterns of ethnic bloc voting have been reported in nonpartisan elections—patterns that almost certainly were a pure and simple consequence of the nonpartisan ballot and the voter's need to search out some basis for selecting among the names on the ballot. Thus, in one Newark, New Jersey, nonpartisan city-council election, the major regularity emerging from an analysis of the election returns was that in those sections of the city where one Irish, Italian, Jewish, or black candidate did well, other members of the same ethnic group also did well; where one did poorly the others did poorly. Voters appeared to link together candidates of the same ethnic background without reference to the individual positions or parties of the candidates. But in Newark's partisan elections for the state legislature—elections that, apart from their partisanship, were quite similar to the nonpartisan elections in terms of such considerations as probable public awareness of the candidates' stands and records—Newark's citizens consistently ignored the possibility of voting along ethnic lines.[9]

(e) *Incumbency.* Finally, at least under some circumstances, nonpartisanship may encourage the re-election of incumbent public officials, especially if they hold positions that are both sufficiently inconspicuous so that the official's performance in office received little attention and sufficiently conspicuous so that his or her name tends to become familiar. Thus there appears to be a bias in favor of the re-election of officeholders in the Nebraska state legislature and in the city councils of at least the larger cities.[10]

(2) Under nonpartisan circumstances, influence shifts to non-party groups. This seeming bit of circular reasoning points to a second unanticipated consequence of nonpartisanship. The implication of the philosophy of nonpartisanship is that when the parties are eliminated *no one* will influence elections. But in fact, non-party groups pick up where parties leave off. Because of the importance of the familiar name in nonpartisan politics, the power of those who control the press and other channels for

conveying information to the public is increased. Candidates who are opposed by a nonpartisan city's newspapers may stand little chance of success; candidates who are *ignored* by the press may be even worse off. Without party resources for financing campaigns, and without the grassroots support of ward and precinct organizations, there is a greater likelihood that candidates will feel obligated to seek funds from other community groups. As a result, seeming independence may really signify hidden obligations to support the goals of various community interest groups.

(3) There is less campaigning.   Without party funds at their disposal, candidates are discouraged from bringing their case to the public. Massachusetts' "other John F. Kennedy" won his 1954 primary election on the basis of attendance at "three or four" rallies and a $10.50 outlay for automobile bumper stickers. In the campaigning which does take place, nonpartisan candidates may find it profitable to avoid discussing issues, especially controversial issues. The partisan candidate, on the other hand, cannot so easily ignore questions of public policy, since he or she is tied to a group that over the years has taken policy stands and acquired a public image. This may explain why mayors in the partisan cities have been more willing to take positions on the controversial issue of fluoridation of drinking water—and to guide that policy through to enactment.[11]

In the mid-1960s, when the city of Hartford, Connecticut, returned to partisan elections after 20 years of experience with nonpartisanship, a local political observer commented:

> Here was a system which, in theory, was beautiful. The theory was that every man should have a right to run for local office without having to go to a political party for nomination . . . In the first election under the new system in 1947, more than 60 candidates turned out for the Council, of whom nine were elected . . . Then . . . interest began to wane . . . Candidates began losing their interest in running when they found out how difficult it was to run on their own on a citywide basis, when they found out how much money it cost.[12]

(4) Voter turnout may decrease.   The observer who wrote of Hartford's experience with nonpartisanship comments that over the years voter interest in that city's elections became so slight

> that only about half the electorate was turning out for elections . . . Other cities in the state were showing 70 and 80 percent turnouts. There were no issues in local elections. There was no party responsibility. It was, simply, every man for himself.[13]

Low voter turnout appears to be a general tendency under nonpartisanship, judging from an analysis of 461 American nonpartisan and partisan cities, which shows an average voter turnout of 50 percent in the local elections of the partisan cities and of only 30 percent in the non-partisan cities.[14]

(5) Protest voting may be frustrated. To the degree that voter involvement is reduced and the automatic return of incumbents is fostered, government tends to be insulated from currents of public opinion. One period of ferment when American voters in many states replaced the "ins" with the "outs" was the early 1930s. But:

> No such changes took place in the nonpartisan Minnesota legislature during the same period, despite drastic changes in the partisan state offices. In 1931 when the Farmer-Labor radical Floyd B. Olson was swept into the governorship, the House Liberals were too weak even to have a candidate for the speakership. In 1933, fifty-eight percent of the House and fifty-five percent of the Senate were made up of incumbent hold-overs from the previous conservative era. Olson never held a working majority in either house, although he won three consecutive decisive victories for himself. The voters apparently did not know how to give him a legislative majority.[15]

TWO KINDS OF ONE-PARTY POLITICS

Surprisingly enough, the study of state political parties did not begin by focusing on the states in which competitive parties make an important contribution to politics. Rather, it began with the work during the mid-1940s of V. O. Key, Jr., and his associates, on the one-party southern states.[16] In these states, as we have seen, politics proceeds, in essence, without benefit of parties. One-party state politics bears many resemblances to nonpartisan city and state legislative politics.

The naive northern observer of one-party southern politics is likely to assume that the South is all of a piece—draped with Spanish moss and peopled with characters from the novels of William Faulkner, Erskine Caldwell, and Truman Capote. Key's work effectively punctures this image. Politically and socially, each of the southern states is distinct in numerous ways.

One political characteristic in which southern states vary is the pattern of their primary elections and governmental politics. Key found that politics in most southern states was fluid and "multi-factional." A typical gubernatorial or senatorial primary in such a state might see a half-dozen or more candidates in the field, each of them supported by his own temporary campaign organization and none of them very closely connected with any previous factional coalition. Under such circumstances, voting becomes so splintered that if (as is the case in most American elections) the candidate with a plurality of the vote were to take office, many government officials would represent no more than a quarter of the electorate. Therefore, most of the southern states have adopted a special election procedure, the run-off primary,[17] to preserve majority rule in the face of fragmented politics.

Some southern states—at the time of Key's writing these included North Carolina, Tennessee, and Louisiana—are not multi-factional. Factional politics in these states forms a rather rough approximation of a two-party system. Various factors contribute to what Key calls "bi-factionalism." In the neighboring states of North Carolina and Tennessee, for example, the effect of a strip of traditional southern "Mountain Republicans"[18] who dominate the politics of the hill areas between the two states has contributed to holding down Democratic party factional politics to a dual pattern. In each of these states one of the stronger Democratic factions (in North Carolina the "Shelby County Dynasty," in Tennessee Boss Crump's Memphis machine) allied itself, for patronage reasons, with office-hungry Democrats from the state's Republican-dominated areas. The combined strength of two such blocs was usually sufficient to stimulate other groups in the state to pool their strength in a second opposition faction, since only by unifying could they hope to win. In Louisiana, a traditionally powerful and unified New Orleans machine had a similar effect on factionalism; but even more important—after the early 1920s—was the tendency of prosperous citizens to band together in opposition to the flamboyant appeal made to redneck farmers and other economically and politically distressed folk by Huey Long and his kin.

Quite commonly, when southern politics does assume a bi-factional form (as is the case intermittently in a number of the normally multi-factional states), conflict has followed lines of cleavage similar to those in Louisiana: wealthy plantation owners and their urban industrial allies are represented by one faction; up-country, low-income farmers by the other. In Louisiana, correlations can be found between support for the Long faction and support for the Populists in the 1890s. Anti-Long voting has parallels which go as far back as the Whig opposition to Jacksonian Democrats in the distant pre-Civil War past, when true party competition existed in the southern states. Intuitively, the rough Long/anti-Long dichotomy still operates in Louisiana. If this is so, it could be argued that this state has the longest continuing tradition of political factionalism in the United States.

These two patterns of southern politics are of interest to the political scientist because they enable him to compare politics *sans* parties with a sort of quasi-party politics. It is, however, also necessary to compare the dual- and multi-factional varieties of southern politics with northern two-party politics, since (as we shall see) even stable, dual factions differ in at least one crucial respect from political parties.

Multi-factional Politics

One of the indicators of multi-factionalism is the number of contenders for office in the first primary. At Key's writing, Florida—partly because of its oddly dispersed population centers, but probably more basically because of its remarkable influx of new citizens—was the limiting case in multi-factional fluidity. It may be Florida that Key has in mind at one point in his overall assessment of factionalism, when he almost sputters an array of modifiers: "multifaceted, discontinuous, kaleidoscopic, fluid, transient . . ."[19]

None of the Florida candidates, Key found, had a statewide political organization; virtually anyone who could afford the filing fee might be found running for office. In the especially chaotic gubernatorial primary of 1936, fourteen men competed in Florida's first primary, the front-running candidate polling about 16 percent of the state's vote. Key and another student of Florida politics, Hugh D. Price, found evidence of a trend toward stability and dual factionalism in the state during the 1940s and 1950s,[20] but judging from the pattern of state voting in the mid-1960s, reports of the demise of fragmented politics in this and other states are premature. In the 1983 Arkansas Democratic gubernatorial primary, for example, there were five candidates. As Table 5-1 makes clear, the third-running candidate was eliminated from the run-off primary by about 6 percent of the vote. Elections of this sort, Key wryly comments, might better be considered lotteries. Another confounding factor can be what happens between the first and second or run-off primary. There is no assurance, as Table 5-2 demonstrates, that finishing first in the first primary, even by an apparently comfortable margin, will mean victory in the second contest.

Indeed, the late deLesseps Morrison led the first primary ticket in all of his races for the Louisiana governor's office. He was always beaten in the second primary. For that matter, one might expect that, with voter confusion diminished as the number of candidates drops to only two in the run-off primary, turnout would increase, but this is not always the case. In the 1978 Louisiana Democratic primary for governor, for instance, there were 136,000 more votes cast in the first primary, with seven candidates in the field, than in the second primary. Finally, since the Republicans left the Louisiana general election uncontested or with a candidate who was obviously not serious, it was not uncommon in many instances to see even fewer voters appearing at the polls for the actual election. Indeed, one could almost argue that the function of the first primary for some is to make moral

TABLE 5-1 Multi-Factional Fragmentation: Arkansas Democratic Gubernatorial Voting, First Primary, May 25, 1982

CANDIDATE	NUMBER OF VOTES	PERCENTAGE
Bill Clinton	228,245	41.9%
Joe Purcell	159,872	29.3
Jim Guy Tucker	124,855	22.9
Kim Hendren	20,876	3.8
Monroe A. Schwarzlose	11,295	2.1

Source: *Congressional Quarterly Weekly Report*, 40 (May 29, 1982), 1294.

**TABLE 5-2   Changing Places: The 1982 Georgia Democratic
            Gubernatorial Primary**

CANDIDATE	NUMBER OF VOTES	PERCENTAGE
	—First Primary—	
Bo Ginn	319,207	36.3%
Joe Frank Harris	213,125	24.2
Eight others	346,713	39.4
	879,045	99.9%*
	—Second Primary—	
Joe Frank Harris	498,973	53.8%
Bo Ginn	428,704	46.2
	927,677	100.0%

*Does not equal 100% because of rounding.

Sources: *Congressional Quarterly Weekly Report*, 40 (August 14, 1982), 1992 and 40
(September 4, 1982), 2217.

judgments; the second primary is to force the remaining voters to make
practical decisions.

When only two factions compete seriously in the politics of a southern
state, the candidates' election appeals and the geographic distribution of
votes often indicate that politics has made contact with underlying interest
and issue cleavages, such as the conflicts discussed above between owners
of large plantations and small up-country farmers. On occasion, voters will
be presented with a rather clear-cut liberal-conservative choice. Multi-
factionalism, on the other hand, is far less likely to tap such "gut" issues.
Distinctions in the ideologies, or group appeals, of some of the various candidates may be evident to politically sophisticated observers of the multiple-
candidate elections, but there is little evidence that these distinctions will
have reached the mass of the electorate.

"Friends-and-neighbors" politics—voting for the home-town candidate—is especially common in the multi-factional states. This pattern
(which is paralleled by wheeling and dealing, in which countless bargains
are struck between county leaders and factional candidates) is revealed
when each of several candidates wins 60, 70, or 80 percent of the vote in
counties near home, but receives no more than a fourth of the statewide
vote. Under these circumstances, special advantages may accrue to candidates who spent their youth in one locality and their adult years in another,
and who thus have two sets of friends and neighbors. In a politics of personalities, especially when much of the population is poorly educated, it
also often seems to be an advantage to be the politician with the loudest
hillbilly band and the saltiest jokes.

The tendency of friends-and-neighbors voting to blur issue considerations in a multi-factional state can be seen in Figure 5-1, which presents a

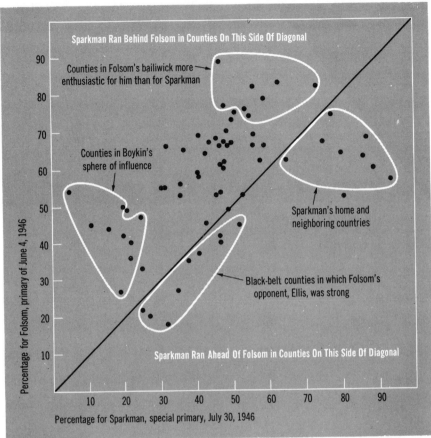

Source: V.O. Key, Jr., *Southern Politics* (New York: Knopf, 1949), p. 48. Each dot represents a county and is located at the point where the percentage of county support for Folsom and the percentage for Sparkman intersect. For further explanation, see text and *Southern Politics*, p. 47 n.

FIGURE 5-1 Voter inconsistency in one-party multi-factional politics.

scatter diagram plotting the relationship between the sources of strength of two liberal politicians from the small-farm northern portion of Alabama in gubernatorial and senatorial primaries held in succeeding months in 1946. As Key points out, if Alabama's factions "had any consistency," one would expect the counties which supported the liberal gubernatorial candidate, James ("Big Jim") Folsom, in the first election to back the state's liberal Senator John Sparkman in the second, especially since "many of Folsom's campaign workers moved over to labor in the Sparkman cause and in general the same crowd supported both." Voter consistency would be shown in Figure 5-1 if the dots in the diagram were arrayed in a straight line, indicating that where Folsom ran well Sparkman also ran well and vice versa. This is precisely what one finds in two-party states when the electoral strength of a party in one election is plotted against its strength in another. But in this pair of Alabama elections, Key points out, although

> a rough correspondence existed in the distribution of the Folsom and Sparkman strength, extraordinary exceptions also manifested themselves. Folsom carried the counties within his friends-and-neighbors sphere by huge majorities, but this strength could not be transferred intact to Sparkman. Similarly, in the counties in [Sparkman's opponent] Boykin's congressional district Folsom attracted much heavier support than Sparkman could.[21]

Key finds it especially indicative of the issue-free nature of multi-factional politics that Washington County (represented by the dot closest to the vertical axis in Figure 5-1) could cast "54.5 percent of its vote for Folsom, a progressive candidate, and sixty days later . . . only 5.4 percent of its ballots for Sparkman, a like-minded candidate, because of its preference for Boykin, known generally as a conservative."[22]

One consequence of friends-and-neighbors voting is that public officials of wondrously divergent types of ideological convictions may be elected simultaneously. Thus in one Florida primary the voters gave comfortable margins to a candidate who had acquired national repute for his liberalism and sympathy to the goals of organized labor and to another who was a vehement opponent of unions. Each candidate for statewide office and for the state legislature (as well as each candidate for local and federal office) runs independently of the others in multi-factional states. Each raises his own campaign funds (Key estimated in the 1940s, before television had added substantially to electioneering costs, that $100,000 was a conservative estimate of the necessary resources for a successful southern gubernatorial campaign) and acquires his own obligations to his supporters. As might be suspected, such an election arrangement is hardly conducive to close cooperative relations between elected officials. Therefore, one pattern noted by Key, closely resembling the experience of Minnesota in the 1930s referred to on p. 89, is the stymieing of "reform" governors by their state legislatures. A gubernatorial candidate may campaign and win office by attacking the existing state of affairs and proposing alternative policies. Once in office, however, he finds himself faced with legislators who have no special reason to feel committed to his version of the public interest. In fact, given the low visibility of legislators' activities and the unlikelihood of effective voter retaliation, the reform governor's legislature may be under the control of the very same "rascals" who were originally responsible for the castigated "existing state of affairs."

Bi-factionalism

The best available account of southern bi-factionalism is the extensive analysis by Allan Sindler of Louisiana politics.[23] Like the other southern states, Louisiana confined its intrastate politics to the Democratic primaries; but there are a number of clear-cut political differences between the Pelican State and its multi-factional neighbors. But, as we indicated in note 17, Louisiana no longer has a partisan primary system. Candidates from both parties run in a single primary, and there is no limit to the number appearing. Hence, it would seem that this aspect of Louisiana politics may have passed away. Yet to be determined, however, is whether voters are able to discern factional differences, and whether they wish to act upon them in casting their votes.

During the years covered in Sindler's research, each of the state's factions—Long and anti-Long—had distinct bases. As we have already noted, Long was unlike some of the South's other flamboyant political products in that he based both his appeal and his policies on specific social and economic goals, in addition to employing the ruthless manipulative skill and spell-binding stump performances for which he is better remembered. In a state which ranked at the bottom of the national heap in terms of the amenities of life available to its inhabitants, Long welded together a coalition of poor agriculturalists and, to a lesser degree, industrial workers and blacks. Well after an assassin's bullet had ended the Kingfish's life, the state's politics remained polarized in a bi-factional mold around issues of taxation, education, and welfare policy.

Louisiana had *some* of the appearance of the multi-factional southern states during its bi-factional period: several candidates contended in its first primaries, for example. But by the second primary the field was regularly narrowed down to representatives of the Long and anti-Long factions. Judging from the consistency with which the prosperous and poorer groups supported the "appropriate" factions and the lack of friends-and-neighbors voting in the state, the bi-factional alternatives must have been quite meaningful to Louisiana voters.

One indication of the strength of Louisiana factionalism is the use of a device seen nowhere else in the South—the ticket system. In most southern states, as we have seen, each candidate is on his own. The Louisiana tradition, originating with the old-time New Orleans machine and further developed during Long's years, is quite different. Candidates bound together on "tickets," much like the party slates offered to voters in northern states, run as common teams for the several statewide offices, for the legislature, and sometimes also for local offices. Technically, the ballot lists only names of individuals, but in fact many voters take to the polling place with them a list of the names on the "the Earl Long ticket" or "the Jimmie Davis ticket." This, however, is not as simple as it seems. Often candidates for lower level state positions will team with several candidates for the governor's office. Illiterate and other voters will often take a list of only candidates' numbers on the ballot to the polling place. Inasmuch as candidates for local office may have greater knowledge of which local voters can be "manipulated," statewide candidates may go to considerable effort to be on the same ticket with powerful and popular local office-seekers.

Tickets are a considerable asset to candidates, providing them with, in Sindler's words, "the benefit of a fully-organized campaign at cut-rate prices."[24] Since the candidates for such lower state offices as auditor, treasurer, and registrar of the state land office (and to a lesser degree legislators) campaign on the basis of their support for a gubernatorial candidate, the governor benefits by having a ready-made set of allies behind his program once he is elected. The voters also benefit, since—if they have a mind to do so—they can either elect a team or reject one.

The ticket system contributed to a politics of governmental activism, with factional alternation in office and attempts by each faction to woo the voter by providing him with services. Huey Long's ascendancy produced higher taxes, but also improvements in roads, education, hospitals, and other public services. When Longism went beyond this, producing egregious abuses of political power and corruption on a grand scale, the voters turned out the Long faction, replacing it with a conservative "reform faction." But the latter, in order to attain office, felt it necessary "to pledge liberal measures, which, in toto, made Huey's performance . . . appear conservative."[25]

This would seem to support one of Key's more interesting hypotheses concerning the effect of political parties or party-like organizations on the outcomes of politics. The results of a fluid, disorganized politics, Key believes, are that the "have-not" members of the population—the poor farmers, the sharecroppers, the textile-mill workers—suffer, and the groups likely to profit from the status quo gain. The former have few political skills and resources for advancing their interests. They are uneducated and without the kinds of experiences which would prepare them to follow government closely, keeping track of such recondite matters as the record of a state legislator in office. But they do have one vital asset, if they are able to use it effectively—their numbers.

Parties and stable factions like those in Louisiana simplify the problem of perceiving and evaluating government for such citizens, enabling them to reward their friends and punish their enemies. Probably more important, Key's argument runs, the competition between fairly coherently organized groups of factional politicians, each of them desirous of winning office, encourages competitive efforts to *anticipate* the needs of such blocs of voters. Each group tries to outdo the other in its promises and in its accomplishments in office. Organized politics also is potentially helpful to have-not groups because it increases the likelihood of organized government—that is, of cooperation between state officials and between governor and legislature. When government is stalemated, only those groups satisfied by the existing state of affairs are helped; when positive governmental action is possible, groups desiring new schools, larger welfare programs, and other active policies are at least in a position where it is possible in principle for them to achieve their goals.

Like many other intriguing theories, the argument that organized, competitive politics helps the disadvantaged is easier to enunciate than to document. No one has attempted to test Key's hypothesis for the bi-factional versus the multi-factional southern states. But there have been a variety of attempts, via statistical analysis, to determine whether states in which the political parties are closely competitive tend to spend more of their resources on programs—for example, aid to dependent children, high unemployment benefits, and progressive taxation—that especially help lower-income groups. The competitive two-party states are in fact more likely to adopt such policies than the states in which parties do not compete equally. But since, by and large, the competitive two-party states are also the wealthy industrial states, they therefore are the ones that can best afford such policies. Not fully conclusive results have proceeded from efforts to "control" for state wealth—to make state wealth a constant factor—and thus determine whether among states with equal capacities to pay the two-party states are more generous to their lower-income citizens. In general, such analyses suggest that party competition may in fact contribute to increasing state expenditure levels, above and beyond the state's capacity to pay for social services and similar programs. But it must be emphasized that further and more definitive investigations are needed.[26]

A bi-factional political system like Louisiana's differs from a two-party system in a number of important respects, Sindler argues. First, even a rather cohesive intraparty faction is likely to be muddier and less organized in its recruitment patterns that one might expect a party to be. In Louisiana, there were no clear-cut standards for deciding who in the Long group or who in the anti-Long group might be next to serve as the faction's standard-bearer. As a result, governors and lieutenant governors typically begin feuding toward the end of a governor's term in office.[27] Disagreements over who is to run for office are resolved in the first primary, but sometimes the period intervening before the second primary is not long enough for groups with common interests to forget campaign oratory and begin pulling together to win the election. Second, and related to this, the Louisiana factional politicians Sindler studied were less consistent in their allegiances than were the state's voters. There was a good bit of shifting of factional sides, accompanied by opportunistic bargaining and horse-trading. Instability seemed to be especially great in alliances between local politicians and the state factions. Since the connection between local and state levels is tenuous, political organization in bi-factional states is likely to resemble politics in states where most local elections are nonpartisan: in both cases the statewide political groupings are likely to command little solid grassroots support, and the channels of mobility from local political experience to higher office tend to be unclear.

Sindler also finds that although factional-ticket allegiances tied together the statewide officials—at least during the early portions of a governor's term—they were somewhat less binding on state legislators. The latter traditionally supported gubernatorial policy, but as much because of patronage arrangements as because of factional loyalty. Thus bi-factional politics, if more orderly than multi-factionalism, is still rather confused.

The confusion, Sindler's analysis suggests, may partly result from a seemingly minor, but probably vital, difference between factions and parties. *Parties have labels.* Shakespeare asked "What's in a name?" The political scientist can answer that the name of a party—if it becomes rooted in historical traditions, voter identifications, and politicians' professional experiences—may contribute remarkably to the coordination of disparate units in a political system.

Republican Factionalism?

Discussing southern factionalism up to this point, we have been guided by a simple fact—the historical dominance in that region by the Democrats. While it is still far too early to dismiss this dominance (note that all seven states listed as "Democratic dominant" in Table 5-3 are southern), there is no question but that the Republicans have emerged slowly to become somewhat competitive for certain offices. Where once it was to their advantage to keep their party small and non-competitive, gaining a few crumbs from the Democratic table (for example, partronage positions from the unchallenged Democrats as a reward for not contesting the general election), they have begun to find that they can indeed make a serious race for certain offices and occasionally win. In Georgia, for example, the Republicans never ran a candidate for governor in the 1880–1962 period. Yet when Howard Callaway ran in 1966, he beat Democrat Lester Maddox in the popular vote, although he was defeated in the Democrat-controlled state legislature since he had not had a popular vote majority.

Led by the conservative Republican presidencies of Richard Nixon and Ronald Reagan, and buoyed by what some saw as a rise in favor of the Republican brand of conservatism, more and more candidates began to emerge for the GOP. And, inevitably, this also meant that there would be contests in the Republican primaries, where once there had been no primaries at all in several of these states. In short, the unthinkable became more and more the normal means of operation for southern Republicans, as we can see in Table 5-4. What is not clear as yet is whether we are seeing emerging Republican bi-factionalism in some of these cases, or whether individual candidates, acting as political entrepreneurs, are creating a Republican version of multi-factionalism, all attributable to the sweet smell of potent electoral success. This upsurge in Republican activity is not necessarily bad for the Democrats. As Republicans perceive that they have a chance to gain major political offices, local Republican activists may file for local offices. The effect of this activity can be to force local incumbent Democrats to campaign in their areas of strength. This campaigning can result

TABLE 5-3 Measures of Party Competition for States, 1961–1982

| | YEARS OF CONTROL | | | | | | | |
| | Governorship | | Senate | | | House | | |
State	D	R	D	R	Tie	D	R	Tie
Democratic dominant:								
Ala.	22	0	22	0	—	22	0	—
Miss.	22	0	22	0	—	22	0	—
La.	20	2	22	0	—	22	0	—
Ga.	22	0	22	0	—	22	0	—
S.C.	18	4	22	0	—	22	0	—
Ark.	16	6	22	0	—	22	0	—
Tex.	18	4	22	0	—	22	0	—
Democratic majority:								
Md.	20	2	22	0	—	22	0	—
Hawaii	20	2	20	2	—	20	2	—
N.C.	18	4	22	0	—	22	0	—
Fla	18	4	22	0	—	22	0	—
Ky.	18	4	22	0	—	22	0	—
N.Mex.	16	6	22	0	—	22	0	—
Mo.	16	6	22	0	—	22	0	—
R.I.	16	6	22	0	—	22	0	—
Okla.	14	8	22	0	—	22	0	—
Tenn.	14	8	22	0	—	20	0	2
W.Va.	14	8	22	0	—	22	0	—
Competitive two-party:								
Calif.	14	8	20	0	2	20	2	—
Va.	10	12	22	0	—	22	0	—
Mass.	10	12	22	0	—	22	0	—
Conn.	18	4	20	2	—	14	8	—
Nev.	14	8	16	4	2	18	4	—
Alaska	10	12	14	6	2	18	2	2
Wash.	8	14	22	0	—	12	8	2
N.J.	18	4	10	12	—	16	6	—
Mont.	14	8	16	4	2	10	12	—
Oreg.	4	18	22	0	—	14	8	—
Del.	12	10	14	6	2	12	10	—
Pa.	10	12	10	10	2	12	10	—
Utah	18	4	8	14	—	8	14	—
Wis.	12	10	8	14	—	8	14	—
Mich.	2	20	10	8	4	16	4	2
Nebr.*	14	8	—	—	—	—	—	—
Minn.†	12	10	—	—	—	—	—	—
Ill.	12	10	8	12	2	8	14	—
Ariz.	10	12	10	12	—	8	14	—
Maine	12	6	2	20	—	10	12	—
N.Dak.	20	2	0	22	—	4	18	—
Ohio	6	16	6	14	2	10	12	—
N.Y.	8	14	2	20	—	12	10	—
Iowa	6	16	8	14	—	6	16	—
Ind.	8	14	8	14	—	4	18	—
Kans.	12	10	0	22	—	2	20	—
Idaho	12	10	0	22	—	0	22	—

TABLE 5-3   (Continued)

State	YEARS OF CONTROL							
	Governorship		Senate			House		
	D	R	D	R	Tie	D	R	Tie
Republican majority:								
Colo...................	10	12	2	20	—	6	16	—
Vt.....................	10	12	0	22	—	2	20	—
Wyo...................	10	12	0	20	2	2	20	—
S.Dak.	8	14	4	18	—	0	20	2
N.H.	10	12	0	16	6	0	22	—

*Nebraska's senate and house have been nonpartisan.
†Minnesota's senate and house have been mostly nonpartisan.

Source: Malcolm E. Jewell and David M. Olson. *American State Political Parties and Elections* (rev. ed.; Homewood, Ill.: Dorsey Press, 1982), p. 27. The classifications are based not only on years of control, but on additional factors such as size of majority in state legislature.

TABLE 5-4   Contested Republican Primaries in the South, 1960–1982

STATE	GOVERNOR	U.S. SENATOR
Alabama	1972[a]	1972[a], 1980
Arkansas	1974, 1976, 1980, 1981	
Florida	1960, 1970[b], 1978	1968, 1970, 1974, 1976, 1980[b]
Georgia	1974[b], 1978, 1982	1968, 1978, 1980[b]
Louisiana	1979[c]	1960, 1980[c]
Mississippi	1972, 1978	
North Carolina	1964, 1968, 1972[b], 1978, 1980	1962, 1968[b], 1974[a]
South Carolina	1974, 1976[b], 1978, 1980[b]	
Tennessee	1970[a], 1974[a], 1978[a]	1964, 1966, 1970, 1972, 1978[a], 1982
Texas	1960, 1968[a], 1970, 1972[b], 1974, 1978[a]	1964[b], 1970, 1976[b]
Virginia	—nominates by convention—	

[a]More than two candidates.
[b]Run-off primary needed.
[c]In the 1979 gubernatorial "non-partisan primary," David Treen was the only Republican in a nine-person race which also included one Independent. Two Republicans entered the senatorial primary in a five-person contest which was won by the incumbent Democrat, Russell Long.

Sources: *Guide to U.S. Elections* (Washington/Congressional Quarterly, Inc., 1975), pp. 897:918; *Guide to 1976 Elections* (Washington: Congressional Quarterly, Inc., 1977), p. 45; selected issues of *Congressional Quarterly Weekly Report*, 36 (1978), 38 (1980), and 40 (1982).

in higher voter turnout, with the formerly complacent non-voters casting straight Democratic tickets.

TWO KINDS OF TWO-PARTY POLITICS

The work of Key and Sindler suggests that, within the one-party states, dual-factional systems have certain advantages over multi-factional systems in terms of their contribution to popular control of government and effective policy-making. But even the dual-factional systems, it is argued, fall short of two-*party* politics.

For a decade after the appearance of Key's *Southern Politics,* the second of these hypotheses remained totally in the realm of speculation. There were no available studies of two-party states that considered the same questions raised by Key and Sindler about southern politics. The first systematic effort to fill this gap was in the work of Duane Lockard on New England politics. Three of the six New England states—Massachusetts, Connecticut, and Rhode Island—seem, at least during the period of Lockard's analysis, to have been competitive two-party states.[28] Of these we shall focus on Connecticut, a state in which the parties have had an especially substantial (and, Lockard believes, valuable) effect on politics. Then we shall glance briefly at another northern two-party state, Michigan, where the consequences of party competition have on occasion been less satisfactory.

Connecticut—Party Competition and Effective Policy-Making

Up through the 1920s, Connecticut was a safe Republican state. Following the shifts in political loyalties of the Depression and New Deal years, the Democratic party sprang to life in Connecticut, as it did in many other northern industrial states. During the years from the Depression through the mid-1950s, the Connecticut parties were remarkably competitive:

> In the 12 gubernatorial elections between 1930 and 1956 the Democrats have won seven times to the Republicans' five. The average Democrat percentage of the two-party vote in these elections has been a scant 49.9 percent. . . . In ten of the 12 elections the margin of victory was less than 25,000 votes and in three the margin was less than 3,000.[29]

At the same time, each of the parties was internally cohesive and disciplined to a degree which is unusual in the United States. By the 1970s, Connecticut no longer had strong and cohesive parties. However, we take the earlier strong competition as instructive in terms of how party competition can relate to policy-making.

The closeness of Connecticut's party competition was not a consequence of the desire of party politicians to hew to an ideal model of competitive politics. Two decades after Lockard's analysis, when the state had begun to shift toward what appeared to be a predominantly Democratic disposition, there was no sign that leaders of the party profiting from this change had any regrets. The even division of the state during the years of Lockard's research appeared to result from its even social division. Democratic support came from urban groups—industrial workers, labor unions, and ethnic minorities. (In Connecticut, it is almost better to speak of ethnic "majorities," since as recently as the 1980 census, 10 percent of the state's population spoke Italian as a first language. Add to this the Irish, Hispanics, and Eastern Europeans, and the point is clear.) The base of Republican power was small-town New England Yankees, suburbanites, and businesspeople.

Neither party was monolithic. Labor-oriented Democrats did not invariably agree on policy with Democrats of the city machines, or with such ethnic organizations as the Polish Pulaski Clubs. Suburban Republicans and rural Yankee Republicans sometimes found themselves at odds. Furthermore, each party had at least some supporters in the other party's areas of strength, so there were both urban, ethnic Republicans and rural, Yankee Democrats. Nevertheless, the population groups and interests aggregated by each of the Connecticut parties were considerably more consistent in outlook and background than those represented by Republican and Democratic politicians nationally.[30] This consistency helps to explain why the Connecticut parties could maintain rather clear-cut lines of authority and generally recognized leaders, making them in some way appear more like the well-disciplined political parties of Great Britain than the disorderly formations elsewhere in America.

A number of other factors are relevant to party unity in Connecticut. These included the keenness of state party competition (a considerable stimulus for politicians of each party to pull together in order to defeat the common foe); the failure of the state to adopt such party-weakening measures as nonpartisan local elections and statewide primaries,[31] and accidents of history which at various times brought to the fore in each party skillful leaders who held office for many years and helped inculcate traditions of disciplined politics into the thinking of the state's politically active citizens, even after competition became less intense and the leaders were gone or less active.

Another factor which seemingly bears on Connecticut's effective integration of party competition and policy-making is the absence of a strong pressure-group system. One of the truisms of American government is that where parties are strong in the organizational sense pressure groups will tend to be weak, and vice versa.[32] There is something of a "chicken and egg" controversy here, since strong parties may tend to pass restrictive legislation when they are in office. On the other hand, strong pressure groups may work to keep the party system relatively weak, by assuming some of the traditional functions of party. Nonetheless, it has been shown that the same pressure group in two states, Alabama and Connecticut, with the same resources of votes and money, was poles apart in strength.[33]

The behavior of Connecticut politicians once in office was profoundly affected both by the internal cohesion of the parties and by the competitiveness of the party system. Connecticut legislators hammered out party policies in caucus, often in consultation with the state party chairman and with the governor (if he was of the same party). Each party's legislators voted together and opposed the legislators of the other party with much greater frequency than is the case in Congress, or in most other states.

The unity of Connecticut's parties and the state's slender electoral balance, Lockard believes, created a situation in which the parties contributed in a major way to effective policy-making. Unified parties, as we have seen, can contribute to policy-making by enabling a single group to control both the legislative and executive branches. Party government in Connecticut at the time of Lockard's research did not operate this simply, however. Malapportionment of the state legislature had prevented the Democrats from control of the lower house in any twentieth-century election, and the upper chamber was to some extent gerrymandered to the detriment of the Republicans.[34] Furthermore, because of the closeness of elections during that period, even the tendency of Connecticut voters to follow party lines could not prevent a situation in which the governor was of one party and some of the lesser statewide officeholders (such as comptroller or treasurer) were of the other.

One would expect party cohesion and split party control of government to have produced political stalemate, rather than effective policy-making. Yet this was not the result. Lockard observed that much of the necessary legislation to keep the state operating was passed because Republican and Democratic leaders succeeded in compromising their differences and agreeing to support each other's bills. More important, Lockard felt, although the parties had the capacity to obstruct policy-making, they were in fact not obstructive. Because of the closeness of the electoral balance, party leaders found it vital to establish a record that would appeal to members of both their party's and the other party's coalition. And because they had considerable influence among their colleagues, state party leaders were able to persuade legislators to take a broader outlook than might be expected from their ideological and constituency orientations.[35]

Connecticut's small-town Republican legislators, to take an example, were in no danger of being voted out in their heavily Republican districts. Nevertheless, it was often possible to persuade them of the desirability of voting for policies that would appeal to the urban areas, since the votes of these areas were necessary for statewide party success. This, Lockard argues, is one reason why this state has "been among the vanguard in accepting new and relatively radical programs (as, for example, labor and anti-discrimination laws)." Lockard writes:

> But none of those laws ever got on the books without the affirmative vote of most of the rural small-town Republican legislators, whose general outlook is hardly daring. They are mostly true conservatives; they will wait awhile, thank you, and would rather not spend the money anyhow. But they voted yes on a good many innovations . . . [many of which] came when the Republicans had complete control over both Houses and the governorship. Many a law for which Democrats pleaded in vain when they shared power was rejected only to be passed the next session when the Democrats were out of power entirely. "Let's act now, when there can be no doubt of who gets the

credit," is the plea of the Republican leadership. Among others the following acts got passed in just this manner: the first fair employment practices law in the state, minimum-wage increases, and the repeal of prohibitory taxes on oleomargarine.[36]

Connecticut's politicians, Lockard concluded,

> do not behave responsibly solely out of the goodness of their hearts any more than General Motors tries to build better cars out of sheer altruism. One seeks a payoff in the market, the other at the polls. The important thing is to facilitate the means by which the votes can influence the politicians.[37]

Michigan—Party Competition and Political Deadlock

The Connecticut experience seems to offer a simple recipe for popular control of government and effective policy-making—electoral competition between cohesive political parties. Unfortunately, the case of Michigan suggests that matters are not quite so simple.

We are somewhat limited in our ability to compare Michigan with the other states we have discussed, for none of the several studies of Michigan politics[38] fully parallels the work of Key, Sindler, and Lockard. This much, however, is clear: the Michigan party system has many of the same ingredients as the Connecticut party system. Furthermore, during the years that will concern us here, the Michigan constitutional arrangements also were similar to Connecticut's, in that malapportionment made it virtually impossible for the Democratic party to control the legislature. But the response of the parties to this constitutional situation was radically different in the two states.

Although both of Michigan's parties have had their share of internal disagreements, party cohesion in the state legislature has been high. Describing the situation as of the early 1960s, Professor Norman C. Thomas commented that "The party caucus dominates roll call votes in the State Senate to a degree that is almost unparalleled in American politics. The situation in the House of Representatives is almost as rigid."[39] As in Connecticut, Michigan's politics became competitive in the 1930s with the rise of the Democratic party. Alternation in office was not quite as frequent in Michigan. By 1962, partly as a consequence of the vote-getting ability of G. Mennen Williams, the Democrats had controlled the governorship for fourteen years. There was no question, however, that the Republican potential was sufficiently great that sooner or later they would break this string of victories. The Republicans demonstrated this in November, 1962, when their candidate, George Romney, was elected governor.

Much of Governor Williams' career in office was marked by feuding with the Republican legislature. Conflict between the parties finally reached a head in a financial crisis that received nation-wide attention. This chain of events is best described by Professor Thomas:

> The recession of 1958 caused the state's sales tax revenues to fall far short of the estimated amount. Additional revenues were urgently needed if the state was to meet its obligations and if the current level of state services was to be maintained. The Democrats . . . proposed the adoption of a personal income tax. Republican leaders countered by advocating an increase in the sales tax from 3 to 4 percent. Neither side would yield. . . . [Each side persisted in blocking the other's proposals.] State employees suffered a "payless payday," the Administrative Board held biweekly sessions at which the General Fund was drained, and the fight raged on.
>
> After months of struggle, a temporary compromise was effected in December, 1959. Assorted "nuisance" taxes amounting to approximately $65 million, an amount far short of the state's financial needs, were adopted. A referendum proposal to increase the sales tax was placed on the November ballot. But the state had acquired a monumental deficit, essential services had been neglected, and Michigan's national reputation had suffered grievous damage that will take years to repair.[40]

The factors that cause a Michigan to differ so much in political style from a Connecticut are by no means obvious. Perhaps if, in the previous years, the state's electoral margins had been as thin as Connecticut's, Michigan politicians would have been willing to compromise their differences in order to maintain voter support. The Republicans may have felt that, because of the long string of Democratic victories, they no longer were in the running for the governorship. The Democrats may have felt confident of continued statewide victory, and embittered at their inability to surmount the state's malapportionment. Another confounding factor is that of pressure-group strength which, like that in Connecticut, can be considered weak.[41] Michigan indeed has a strong party system, but the deadlock in policy-making which has often been noted there cannot be attributed to pressure groups neutralizing either each other or the major parties. A more fundamental explanation of Michigan's difficulties, however, seems to involve the ideological and interest bases of the two parties.

Much the same kinds of population blocs are aggregated by Michigan parties as by Connecticut parties: Democrats base their support on urban, ethnic, and labor voters; Republicans draw on rural, old-stock citizens and on businesspeople. But the groups seem to be qualitatively different in their goals in Michigan, and they are combined in different proportions. Party competition to a considerable extent pits the heavily Democratic Wayne County (Detroit) against the "outstate" areas. Much of Detroit's working population is organized by unions which operate in the militant CIO tradition of aggressively liberal political action. Pragmatic, old-time politicians of the Boss Plunkitt variety (described in Chapter 4) have largely disappeared in Detroit. Precinct work is carried on by union political committees. On the Republican side, executives in the state's big businesses—especially the automobile industry—allied with outstate interests largely set the party's tone. Party competition, therefore, was to a considerable extent a simple projection into the political arena of the conflict between major economic interests.[42] Under these circumstances, unified, policy-oriented parties led to the kind of politics described by the French as *immobilisme*, rather than to popular control, political stability, and effective policy-making.[43]

THE FUNCTIONS OF STATE PARTY SYSTEMS

From the preceding it can be seen that no general assessment of the functions of the state party systems can be made: the variety of systems is far too great for this to be possible. What one *can* assess is *types* of party systems. For the purpose of making a few broad evaluative statements, we may distinguish between three patterns of state politics—no-party political systems, moderate dual systems, and divisive dual systems.

No-party systems. Politics without parties is the rule in the multifactional one-party states, whether southern or northern. The prototype at the local level is the politics of effectively nonpartisan cities. No-party systems are most striking, in terms of our criteria, for the barriers they place in the way of popular control of government. They fail to simplify the political choices which voters must make, and they impede the establishment of stable connections between politician and constituent. It is conceivable that in a world of perfectly informed and ideally involved voters the simplification functions of parties would be superfluous. In the real world, where citizens are parents, homeowners, jobholders, television viewers, and baseball fans, as well as voters, some procedure for facilitating political perception and evaluation seems essential. The no-party systems also have shortcomings, as we have seen, at the governmental level: they fail to encourage politicians to cooperate in making governmental policies.

Moderate dual systems. Our model of moderate two-party politics is the Connecticut political system of the period of Lockard's analysis, although by stretching a point the Louisiana of the Longs might be placed in this category. Connecticut politics was not simply the antithesis of, say, Florida politics, but the contrast between the states was considerable. Connecticut voters were provided with reasonably distinct alternatives by their state's party system. At the same time, the character of their politicians, and the setting in which politicians found themselves, engendered active attempts on the part of leaders to anticipate and meet public desires.

Politicians saw politics as an arena for applying workmanlike skills and sought to implement the policies which seemed necessary, even in the face of a politically obstructive constitutional system.

There seem to be two general prerequisites for a politics of moderation in a dual system such as Connecticut's. First, the politicians must be sufficiently flexible to "rise above principle" when this seems necessary to make the system work. Second, the groupings which each of the parties represents must contain enough "give" to permit this kind of flexibility. This situation can be realized in several ways. There may be moderate differences in the policies advocated by leaders of the core groups of each party's coalition, so that party leaders have to become accustomed to striking a balance between diverse viewpoints. Also a state may contain sizable groups—such as white-collar workers—which are not securely located in either coalition and which, because their views fall between those of the two parties, encourage leaders of each to move toward the center in the policies they support. Finally, each of the parties may find it necessary to appeal to at least some members of groups in the other party's coalition and, therefore, to moderate—or at least make ambiguous—its goals.

Divisive dual systems. The conception of Michigan politics circa 1959 presented above meets neither of the two prerequisites for moderation. Michigan's parties cannot be accused of failing to offer clear choices to the voters, but choices are illusory if there is no chance that they will find their way into the statute books.

It is doubtful that barricades would have been raised in the streets of Kalamazoo and Grand Rapids if the 1959 Michigan financial crisis had been further prolonged. Nevertheless, a divisive dual politics, which arouses public expectations and fails to meet them, probably possesses the greatest potential for instability of the three classes of systems we have crudely designated.[44] No-party politics would seem also to present problems of stability, but more over the long run, as a consequence of short-run stagnation due to governmental inactivity. In both the short and long run, a moderate dual variant seems most likely to preserve public order.

A further point—one relevant to our examination, in the next chapter, of the curious creatures known as the national parties—may be drawn from this tour of the American states. Evidently, a great many factors determine the kind of politics which develops in any locality, state, or nation. One such factor seems to be the statutes governing the conduct of politics. Party-weakening legislation, such as the laws requiring nonpartisan elections, sometimes succeeds in its stated purposes. (As we have seen, it may also have other, unexpected side-effects.) But non-legal factors have an even more fundamental effect on the shape of politics. These include the ethnic balance of a body politic, its historical traditions, and the kinds of economic interest groups it contains. Unlike laws, these factors are not readily manipulable.

Therefore, although one or another style of politics (for example, moderate dualism of the sort found in Connecticut, or English-style party government) may seem to us desirable, there is no guarantee that what we believe to be an ideal party system will fit into a particular real world political unit. One must work with the available raw materials.

NOTES

[1]A number of ways of classifying states in terms of the degree to which their parties are competitive have been proposed. For a general discussion of the classification proposals see David G. Pfeiffer, "The Measurement of Inter-Party Competition and Systemic Stability," *American Political Science Review,* 61 (June 1967), 457–67. On variations in state "styles" of politics and parties see Samuel C. Patterson, "The Political Cultures of the American States," *Journal of Politics,* 30 (February 1968), 187–209, and R. S. Childs, "Inside 100 State Parties," *National Civic Review,* 56 (November 1967), 568–71.

[2]See V. O. Key, Jr., *Southern Politics in State and Nation* (New York: Knopf, 1949), especially Chs. 16–17.

[3]We saw in Chapter 4 that the direct primary was one of the procedures proposed by turn-of-the-century reformers to weaken party machines. The argument, as one leading reformer put it, was that the primary "takes away the power of the party leader or boss and places the responsibility . . . upon the individual. It lessens party spirit. . . . Partisanship blinds not only the public official but the ordinary citizen and tends to lead him away from good government." George W. Norris, "Why I Believe in the Direct Primary," *Annals of the American Academy of Political and Social Science,* 106 (March 1923), 23.

Even non-reform groups seem to have favored primaries in the one-party areas, however, since without them there was no effective appeal to the voters. V. O. Key, Jr., *American State Politics* (New York: Knopf, 1956), pp. 87–97.

[4]A typical pro-nonpartisanship assertion: "To be effective and self-reliant cities must be emancipated from the tyranny of the national and state political parties. Good citizens who agree on vital local issues should not be divided by blind loyalties that serve only to confuse these issues." "Revolt of the Independents," editorial in *National Municipal Review,* 40 (December 1951), 564–65.

[5]Adrian's original statement, "Some General Characteristics of Nonpartisan Elections," *American Political Science Review,* 46 (September 1952), 766–76, was later revised and reprinted in Oliver P. Williams and Charles Press, *Democracy in Urban America* (Chicago: Rand McNally, 1961), pp. 251–63. Except where indicated, our assertions on nonpartisanship are drawn from Adrian's revised article. Other useful analyses of nonpartisanship include Charles R. Adrian, "A Typology for Nonpartisan Elections," *Western Political Quarterly,* 12 (June 1959), 449–58; Eugene C. Lee, *The Politics of Nonpartisanship* (Berkeley: University of California Press, 1960); Charles E. Gilbert and Christopher Clague, "Electoral Competition and Electoral Systems in Large Cities," *Journal of Politics,* 24 (May 1962), 323–49; Robert L. Crain and Donald B. Rosenthal, "Structure and Values in Local Political Systems: The Case of Fluoridation Decisions," *Journal of Politics,* 28 (February 1966), 169–95; Eugene C. Lee, "City Elections: A Statistical Profile," *Municipal Yearbook* (Chicago: International City Managers Association, Vol. 30, 1963), pp. 74–84; A. Clarke Hagensick, "Influences of Partisanship and Incumbency on a Nonpartisan Election System," *Western Political Quarterly,* 17 (March 1964), 117–24; Gerald Pomper, "Ethnic and Group Voting in Nonpartisan Municipal Elections," *Public Opinion Quarterly,* 30 (Spring 1966), 79–97.

[6]"Some General Characteristics of Nonpartisan Elections," p. 263 n.

[7]Jack Burby, "The Other John F. Kennedy," *The Reporter,* April 14, 1960, pp. 31–32. In 1962, another politically unknown Kennedy (Richard) won the nomination for Ohio's congressman-at-large seat by 2,582 votes out of 530,404 cast in a field of eleven. Civil-rights-minded party leaders were mortified to learn that this Kennedy—who had won the party's nomination in spite of an almost complete failure to campaign—was an ardent *segregationist.* William H. Hessler, "Taft *vs.* Kennedy in Ohio," *The Reporter,* October 25, 1962, pp. 40–42. (The Ohio Kennedy was defeated in the general election.) Massachusetts' "other Kennedy" is said to have turned in a creditable performance as treasurer. Other political chameleons who succeeded in being elected seem to have been far less satisfactory public servants. See Key, *op. cit.,* pp. 162–64.

[8]Henry M. Bain and Donald S. Hecock, *Ballot Position and Voter's Choice* (Detroit: Wayne State University Press, 1957). There is evidence that ballot position may affect partisan contests as well, particularly for lower offices. See Jack L. Walker, "Ballot Forms and Voter Fatigue: An Analysis of the Office Block and Party Column Ballots," *Midwest Journal of Political Science,* 10 (November 1966), 448–64, and Delbert A. Taebel, "The Effect of Ballot Position on Electoral Success," *American Journal of Political Science,* 19 (August 1975), 519–26.

[9]Gerald Pomper, *op. cit.,* pp. 79–97. Further supporting evidence for the interpretation of the Newark findings as a rather direct consequence of the nonpartisan ballot comes from an ingenious Canadian election survey reported by Leon J. Kamin, who included in a public-opinion poll the names of several *imaginary* candidates for an *imaginary* political office. Kamin varied the order in which the names were listed on the ballot and also used both English- and French-sounding names. He found that candidates who were listed low on the ballot received significantly fewer votes than higher candidates. He also found that English-speaking and French-speaking voters chose names of their own ethnic group. *But when parties were listed on a comparable set of ballots, neither ballot order nor ethnicity had any effect on voters' choices.* "Ethnic and Party Affiliations of Candidates as Determinants of Voting," *Canadian Journal of Psychology,* 12 (December 1958), 205–212. For a similar study reporting similar findings see Robert A. Lorinskas, Brett W. Hawkins, and Stephen D. Edwards, "The Persistance of Ethnic Voting in Urban and Rural Areas: Results from a Controlled Election Method," *Social Science Quarterly,* 49 (March 1969), 891–99.

Another clever use of quasi-experimental technique to show that certain aspects of the candidate and his image affect nonpartisan voting is reported by Dean Jaros and Gene L. Mason in "Party Choice and Support for Demagogues: An Experimental Examination," *American Political Science Review,* 63 (March 1969), 100–10. Jaros and Mason gave their respondents the choice of a series of hypothetical election contests, asking them which contest they would like to vote in and for which candidate or side. Included was a candidate whose "demagogic" status was established by attributing to him rather crude and extravagant statements in support of a position with which the respondent was known to sympathize. (That is, for civil rights opponents, a demagogic anti-civil rights assertion was presented, and so forth.) The half of the sample for which there was no possibility of making a partisan choice was more likely to choose the demogogic alternative. This may not be wholly unrelated to the Gallup Poll finding that support for the presidential candidacy of former Alabama Governor George C. Wallace in 1968 was more than twice as great among voters who considered themselves independents as among party identifiers. *Gallup Opinion Index,* December 1968, p. 5.

[10]Gilbert and Clague, *op. cit.,* 340–347. But Gilbert and Clague find no differences in the return rates of incumbent mayors in the partisan and nonpartisan cities, probably because mayors *do* get sufficient publicity to be assessed on the basis of judgments of their performance. A preliminary report of data from 574 cities of 25,000 or more in population fails to show the same differences in the tendency of incumbents to stay in office, but the partisan and nonpartisan cities reported on differ in a variety of respects other than partisanship and these need to be analyzed in order to assess the implications of the findings: Eugene C. Lee, "City Elections," p. 77. A further consideration is that if nonpartisanship is introduced in a one-party area it may have the general consequence—at least at first—of increasing the diversity of officeholders since dependents and members of the minority party have a chance of election. For an instance when the introduction of nonpartisanship had such an effect see Aaron Wildavsky, *Leadership in a Small Town* (Totowa, N.J.: Bedminster, 1964), pp. 47–51.

[11]Crain and Rosenthal, *op. cit.,* 169–195.

[12]Jack Zaiman, "The Theorists Lose," *Hartford Courant,* November 13, 1967.

[13]*Ibid.*

[14]Lee, "City Elections," p. 83. Data evidently were available from only 461 of the 574 cities referred to in note 10. For a further analysis of the same data showing that nonpartisan cities are lower than partisan cities in turnout even when a variety of further ways in which such cities differ from each other are controlled, see Robert A. Alford and Eugene C. Lee, "Voting Turnout in American Cities," *American Political Science Review,* 62 (September 1968) 796–813, especially 808.

[15]Adrian, "Some Characteristics of Nonpartisan Elections," pp. 259–60.

[16]V. O. Key, Jr., *Southern Politics* (New York: Knopf, 1949). Where not otherwise indicated, the observations which follow are based on Key.

[17]Only two of the eleven southern states have plurality nominations. In the others, there is a second primary two to five weeks after the first primary, in which the two leading first-primary candidates compete. As we shall see, the differences in support between candidates who win enough votes to make the second primary and those who do not may be very small. *Ibid.,* pp. 416–23. In 1975 Louisiana adopted a "non-partisan" primary that is really not non-partisan at all. Candidates of both parties, and Independents as well, enter a single primary. If one gets a majority of the votes cast, that person is elected. If there is no majority, then a run-off primary takes place between the top two candidates, who may both be Democrats! The winner of this second primary is elected.

[18]These pockets of hill-country Republicans are a curious throwback to the Civil War. Their ancestors were poor, non-slaveholding farmers who objected to secession. One such county even attempted to secede from the Confederacy! *Ibid.,* p. 282. After the war they sided with the party of Lincoln. The persistence of these southern Republicans is striking evidence of the stability of voters' party identifications.

[19]*Ibid.,* p. 302.

[20]Hugh D. Price, *The Negro and Southern Politics* (New York: New York University Press 1957), pp. 93–103.

[21]Key, *Southern Politics,* pp. 47–49.

[22]*Ibid.,* p. 48.

[23]Allan P. Sindler, "Bifactional Rivalry as an Alternative to Two-Party Competition in Louisiana," *American Political Science Review,* 49 (September 1955), 641–62; and *Huey Long's Louisiana* (Baltimore: Johns Hopkins Press, 1956).

[24]"Bifactional Rivalry," 654.

[25]*Ibid.,* 644.

[26]For work to date, see, for example, Thomas W. Casstevens and Charles Press, "The Context of Democratic Competition in American State Politics," *American Journal of Sociology,* 68 (March 1963), 536–43; Richard E. Dawson and James A. Robinson, "Inter-party Competition, Economic Variables, and Welfare Policies in the American States," *Journal of Politics,* 25 (May 1963), 265–89; John H. Fenton, *People and Parties in Politics* (Glenview, Ill.: Scott, Foresman, 1966), Chs. 2–5. Especially note the general points about these analyses made by Allan G. Pulsipher and James L. Weatherby, Jr., in their "Malapportionment, Party Competition, and the Functional Distribution of Governmental Expenditures," *American Political Science Review,* 62 (December 1968), 1207–1219. Also see John H. Fenton and Donald W. Chamberlayne, "The Literature Dealing with the Relationships between Political Processes, Socioeconomic Conditions and Public Policies in the American States: A Bibliographical Essay," *Polity,* 1 (Spring 1969), 388–404; and Duane Lockard, "State Party Systems and Policy Outputs," in Oliver Garceau, ed., *Political Research and Political Theory* (Cambridge, Mass.: Harvard University Press, 1968), pp. 190–220. For a sophisticated analysis concluding that party competition does have an effect on state policy output, but that the effect is complex and varies from policy area to policy area, see Charles F. Cnudde and Donald J. McCrone, "Party Competition and Welfare Policies in the American States," *American Political Science Review,* 63 (September 1969), 858–66. A major addition to this literature, certain to provoke further debate, is Sarah McCally Morehouse, *State Politics, Parties and Policy* (New York: Holt, Rinehart and Winston, 1980).

[27]At the time of Sindler's research, as in several other southern states at the time, factionalism was further exacerbated by an institutional factor—governors were prohibited by law from succeeding themselves and were therefore more likely to find their support disintegrating as election time approached. Currently, six states in the South have such a limit, three (including Louisiana) have a two-term limit, and two have none.

[28]Duane Lockard, *New England State Politics* (Princeton, N.J.: Princeton University Press, 1959). Lockard classifies New Hampshire and Vermont as bi-factional one-party states and Maine as a multi-factional one-party state. For Lockard's approach to the classification of state party systems see *ibid.*, pp. 324–26. Subsequent developments in the New England states are discussed in George Goodwin, Jr., and Victoria Schuck, *Party Politics in the New England States* (Durham, N.H.: The New England Center for Continuing Education), issued as a special supplement to the periodical *Polity*, 1 (Fall 1968).

[29]Lockard, *New England State Politics*, p. 231.

[30]For example, Connecticut has nothing comparable to the northern and southern wings of the Democratic party in Congress. In using the past tense above, We do not mean to imply that the bases of party support in Connecticut have changed markedly since Lockard wrote. Compare the articles by Murray S. Stedman, Jr., in Goodwin and Schuck, *op. cit.* Population changes and possibly also the failure of the Republicans to present strong nominees appear to be elements in the declining competiveness. In addition, the rise of issue-oriented amateurs—Goldwater Republicans in 1964, McCarthy Democrats in 1968, and McGovern Democrats in 1972—contributed to the lowered cohesion in each of the parties.

[31]The effects of primary elections on the distribution of power within a political party are too complex for detailed discussion here. See Key, *American State Politics*. In general, it may be said that nomination by primary election increases the possibility that the politicians in a state party will split up into a number of factions, each of which appeals directly to the small fraction of voters who turn out in primaries. Control by any single organization of a statewide primary is difficult. When state nominations have to be achieved by convention rather than primary election, politicians are more likely to reconcile their differences and maintain a degree of unity.

As of 1955, Connecticut was the only state without some form of statewide primary. In that year a "challenge" primary law was passed, permitting candidates who won at least 20 percent of the state convention votes to contest the nomination. For many years, although there had been many factional disagreements in both parties, neither party had fought a primary under this law, an indication of the strength of the state's traditions of party cohesion.

[32]Morehouse, *op. cit.*, p. 117.

[33]*Ibid.*, pp. 106–107.

[34]Rural—which in the north often means Republican—over-representation was one of the verities of state and congressional politics until the series of United States Supreme Court decisions requiring "one man, one vote," beginning with *Baker* v. *Carr*, 369 U.S. 186 (1962).

[35]Party leaders who have influence among their colleagues may also find that their stewardship of the party's record leads them to urge legislators to resist various kinds of interest group demands to which individual legislators might be disposed to succumb. But where parties are weak or nonexistent, legislators may hesitate to ignore the requests of such groups.

[36]Lockard, p. 334.

[37]*Ibid.*, p. 304.

[38]Useful studies of Michigan politics include Norman C. Thomas, "Politics in Michigan: The Curse of Party Responsibility," *Papers of the Michigan Academy of Science, Arts, and Letters*, 47 (1962), 311–24; Stephen B. Sarasohn and Vera H. Sarasohn, *Political Party Patterns in Michigan* (Detroit: Wayne State University Press, 1957); John P. White and John R. Owens, *Parties, Group Interests and Campaign Finance: Michigan '56* (Princeton: Citizens' Research Foundation, 1960); Robert L. Sawyer, Jr., *The Democratic State Central Committee in Michigan, 1949–1959* (Ann Arbor: University of Michigan Institute of Public Administration, 1960).

[39]Thomas, "Politics in Michigan," p. 316.

[40]*Ibid.*. p. 318.

[41]Morehouse, *op. cit.*, pp. 115–117.

[42]Evidently, even party factionalism on occasion follows rather monolithic economic lines in Michigan. It is reported that disagreeements between the moderate and "stand-pat" wings of the Republican party once boiled down to conflict between the executives of two major automobile manufacturing corporations. Duncan Norton-Taylor, "What's Wrong with Michigan?" *Fortune* (December 1955), pp. 142 ff.

[43]The reader should be reminded that not only the unified, uncompromising nature of the parties, but also the constitutional arrangements which prevented the Democrats from controlling the legislative as well as the executive branch, contributed to Michigan's *immobilisme*. Unified, policy-oriented parties, even when based on rather clear-cut cleavages in the population, are less likely to result in political stalemate when the institutional framework permits a single party to control government. This possibility does still arise, however, since the closer the party balance in any election, the greater the likelihood that minor variations in voting for different candidates will lead to party differences in control of the houses of the legislature and the various state offices. Furthermore, *immobilisme* may be replaced by a situation in which the parties make new policies without great difficulty only to have the policies changed radically when the other party takes office.

[44]See the analysis by Robert A. Dahl as to whether the American Civil War could have been averted if the national political system were better geared to avoiding stalemates and making decisions more expeditiously: *Democracy in the United States: Promise and Performance* (3d ed.; Chicago: Rand McNally, 1976), Ch. 27.

chapter 6 _____

NATIONAL POLITICS:
Presidential and
_____ Congressional Parties

The state and local party systems, and the social forces that shape them, provide the base of American national-level party politics. Congress is staffed by men and women who are locally nominated and elected and who, in many cases, have made their way into politics at the lower governmental levels. The president is nominated by national convention delegates from the states and localities; state and local politicians staff the wards and precincts in presidential elections.

The institutions that channel state and local partisanship up to the federal level have often struck one balance in the choice of the president and another in the selection and organization of the 535 members of Congress. Excepting of Carter, Democrats who have become president have usually been more likely to advocate active, "liberal" governmental policies than have the Democrats who guide the congressional party. With two notable exceptions, in 1964 and 1980, the Republicans also have tended to produce presidents and presidential candidates who were more activist and "liberal" than their party's congressional leaders. The 1980 exception (Reagan) was, however, temporarily accompanied by a wave of conservative sentiment in at least the Republican-controlled Senate which suggested that for the short run, at least, this may not hold. Congress need not be more conservative than the president. Hence, at the federal level, it has usually been useful to make not only the familiar distinctions between Democrats and Republicans, but also an additional distinction between the presidential and congressional wings of each party.

Neither the Democrats nor the Republicans are as unified at the federal level as their counterparts in Connecticut. Nor are they as divided as the factions within the Florida Democratic party (see Chapter 5). In general, each of the parties is sufficiently unified at the federal level to carry the policy-making process *part* of the way to conclusion. Intraparty cooperation is usually *necessary* for effective policy-making, but it rarely is *sufficient*. Partisanship must be supplemented by bargaining and compromising between parties and factions.

Let us consider these baldly stated propositions in further detail.

THE DEMOCRATS AND THE REPUBLICANS AT THE FEDERAL LEVEL

A common complaint about American politics is that the parties are not "really different" from each other. Consider the following assertion of a foreign journalist assigned to cover the 1968 presidential campaign:

> The first lesson that any European has to learn about American politics is that they are not "issue oriented"—and that is certainly only too clear this year. When former Governor George Wallace of Alabama announces that "There's not a dime's worth of difference between those two big parties of ours," he may not be speaking the literal truth, but it is hard to fault his use of politician's license. . . .
>
> There is scarcely an area of public policy in which Nixon and Humphrey do not make the same soothing noises. What division there is between them is not ideological or philosophical. It is purely personal—a Tweedle-dum-Tweedle-dee argument between the two of them as to which is better qualified to occupy the White House.[1]

As we pointed out in Chapter 2, this complaint is not limited to foreign observers: many Americans hold this point of view as well.

The most convenient place to start considering the assertion that the parties are virtually identical is with Congress. After all, both parties have members on Capitol Hill who span the entire gamut of political belief. At this writing, among those calling themselves Democrats are vigorous advocates of the programs that fall under the heading of "liberalism": for example, Senators Daniel Patrick Moynihan of New York and Teddy Kennedy of Massachusetts. But the Democrats also count among themselves such strong conservatives as Senators John Stennis of Mississippi and Howard Cannon of Nevada. Across the aisle, the Republicans exhibit the same diversity—from the liberalism of Senators Lowell Weicker of Connecticut and Charles Mathias of Maryland to the antithetical views of Senators Strom Thurmond of South Carolina and Jesse Helms of North Carolina.

Yet in spite of this variation within each of the parties, the claim that the congressional Republicans and Democrats are identical twins is far from the truth. The extremes of the two parties *do* touch; on some noncontroversial issues—for example, Mothers' Day resolutions—both parties tend to vote unanimously on the same side; and on issues like women's rights and veterans' benefits, which cut across the parties' constituencies, the divisions are within rather than between the parties. Nevertheless, when all of this is said, it is still true that there are frequent and continuing party differences in congressional voting.[2] The *centers of gravity* of the two parties are unmistakably different on the persisting controversial issues that can be roughly subsumed under the headings "liberalism" and "conservatism."

We would go far afield if we tried to assign precise meanings to terms as ambiguous and value-laden as "liberal" and "conservative." Fortunately, this is not necessary. Both terms have clear social meanings. A number of citizens' groups identify themselves as liberals or conservatives and are generally so recognized by other active political participants. One of their favorite pursuits is rating Congresspersons' voting records.

Table 6-1 shows the "liberalism" scores for senators and representatives in the first year of the Carter presidency (1977) and that of President Reagan (1981). The scores were calculated by the best known of the liberal

TABLE 6-1 **Liberalism Scores of Democratic and Republican Members of Congress, 1977 and 1981**

PERCENTAGE OF LIBERAL VOTES	SENATE			HOUSE		
	Repub-licans	Non-Southern Democrats	Southern Democrats	Repub-licans	Non-Southern Democrats	Southern Democrats
	NUMBER OF SENATORS			NUMBER OF REPRESENTATIVES		
1977						
0-9%	16	0	3	55	5	23
10-19%	6	0	4	40	4	19
20-29%	4	1	2	20	6	10
30-39%	0	1	4	7	17	11
40-49%	4	3	2	7	20	7
50-59%	1	5	0	10	34	1
60-69%	3	7	1	4	22	2
70-79%	1	8	1	2	33	4
80-100%	3	20	0	1	67	3
1981						
0-9%	6	—	—	68	1	14
10-19%	3	—	3	56	1	11
20-29%	3	1	2	28	5	13
30-39%	—	2	2	16	8	13
40-49%	—	2	2	9	13	6
50-59%	—	2	1	7	22	5
60-69%	—	4	—	3	13	1
70-79%	—	6	1	4	28	2
80-100%	—	18	1	—	67	5

Sources: Compiled from ratings of the Americans for Democratic Action, *Congressional Quarterly Weekly Report*, 36 (April 15, 1978), 914-916 and 40 (July 3, 1982), 1614-1617.

groups, the Americans for Democratic Action (ADA). Voting records approaching 100 percent signal "liberalism," by the standards of that organization. In 1977, for instance, ADA-defined liberals in the House supported such policies as prohibiting the development of the neutron bomb, "indexing" of the minimum wage, not requiring work to be done in order to obtain food stamps, and not refusing legal assistance to the poor by the Legal Services Corporation in cases involving homosexuality or gay rights. For the Senate in 1977, liberalism was construed as meaning support for the use of federal funds for abortions, halting the import of chrome from Rhodesia, strict requirements on the restoration of land after it had been strip mined, and opposing a requirement that food stamp recipients pay for a portion of their stamps.

We have chosen 1981 as a year for contrasting these scores. It was, like 1977, a new president's first year in office, but one would expect some sharp differences. President Reagan's fellow Republicans controlled the Senate for the first time since January, 1955. In both chambers, substantial numbers of "boll weevils" (southern Democrats who supported the Reagan tax and budget programs) crossed party lines in their voting. In 1981, the ADA took liberalism to mean, among other things, votes in favor of tax cuts for low- and middle-income taxpayers, and limiting military aid to El Salvador. The ADA also opposed certain domestic spending cuts, limits on busing and abortion, and defense programs such as chemical weapons research and the building of the B-1 bomber and the MX missile. The result of some of these votes is instructive.

	HOUSE		SENATE	
	Democrat	Republican	Democrat	Republican
Against B-1 bomber	121-106	21-157	23-23	5-43
Against MX missile	112-113	27-151	35- 9	44-6
Limits on abortions	—	—	19-24	33-19
Budget cut	63-176	190-0	37- 9	51- 1

The distribution of scores in Table 6-1 could be as easily presented in reverse order (although the items used were not always the same) by using the ratings of Senators and Representatives by various conservative groups, such as Americans for Constitutional Action (ACA).

In the 1977 Senate, twenty Democrats (none of them southern) and only three Republicans received scores of 80 percent or better by the ADA's rather stringent standards. For 1981, when legislators were apparently responding to a "conservative tide" in the country in the wake of President Reagan's victory, the figures were sharply lower—nineteen Democrats and no Republicans (two Republicans scored 55, the "high" for that party). In the House, scores of 80 percent or better were obtained by seventy Democrats (three of them southern) and only one Republican in 1977. For 1981, sixty-seven Democrats and no Republicans met this standard. The average liberalism scores for the four congressional parties for each year were:

	1977	1981
House Democrats	53%	59%
House Republicans	18%	16%
Senate Democrats	58%	65%
Senate Republicans	25%	17%

If a few further distinctions are made to account for some of the most obvious idiosyncracies of the American party system, the party differences stand out with even greater clarity. For example, in Table 6-1 a distinction is made between the non-southern Democrats and those from the eleven southern states, where both liberal and conservative views are still to a considerable extent expressed within the Democratic party. Northerners provide the bulk of the "illiberal" Democratic scores. Only rarely do southern Democrats receive "liberalism" scores in excess of 50, and the great bulk of the Democrats in the ADA's lowest categories were southerners. We might add that the South is no longer quite the bastion of the Democratic party that it once was, as southern Republicans cater to conservative voter tastes even more than do their Democratic brethren across the aisle (see Table 6-2). Of the Republicans who deviated from their party in the direction of liberalism, many were from the kinds of constituencies in which appeals to urban voters are necessary—big-city House districts and the industrial states. Massachusetts Republicans, for instance, are considerably more liberal in their congressional voting than are southern Republicans.

The views of presidential candidates cannot be compared in the tidy fashion of a tabulation of legislative voting records. To begin with, presidential candidates are not forced to vote on current legislation, unless they happen to have been nominated while serving in Congress; and even then they may modify their positions on assuming the new role of aspiring chief executive. Furthermore, the candidates often fail to join issues with each other—each candidate emphasizes his own strong points and ignores or "reinterprets" his opponent's more telling arguments. If, however, a version of Table 6-1 were devised, based on a careful analysis of the candidates' more specific issue positions and commitments, the great majority of the candidates of *both* parties in the modern, post-1930s era would be placed on the liberal side of the scale.

Such an analysis would certainly reveal differences between the Democratic and Republican presidential candidates in each election campaign—differences of the same sort that divide the members of the two parties in Congress. But the presidential candidates, even though they are far from

TABLE 6-2   Southern Representation in Congress, 1977 and 1981

	SENATE				HOUSE			
	Democrats		Republicans		Democrats		Republicans	
STATE	1977	1981	1977	1981	1977	1981	1977	1981
Alabama	2	1	0	1	4	4	3	3
Arkansas	2	2	0	0	3	2	1	2
Florida	2	1	0	1	10	11	5	4
Georgia	2	1	0	1	10	9	0	1
Louisiana	2	2	0	0	5	7	3	1
Mississippi	2	1	0	1	3	3	2	2
North Carolina	1	0	1	2	9	7	2	4
South Carolina	1	1	1	1	5	2	1	4
Tennessee	1	1	1	1	5	5	3	3
Texas	1	1	1	1	22	19	2	5
Virginia	1*	1*	1	1	4	1	6	9
Totals	17	12	5	10	80	70	28	38
Average Liberalism Scores	26%	40%	8%	7%	24%	29%	5%	6%

*Harry Byrd, elected as an Independent, but voting with the Democrats on organizational matters.

Source: Compiled from *Congressional Quarterly Weekly Report*, 36 (April 15, 1978), 914–16 and 40 (July 3, 1982), 1614–1617.

replicas of each other, would, in their very broad agreement on such matters as federal responsibility to maintain a prosperous economy, be closer to one another than the average congressional Democrat is to the average congressional Republican. At least this is the strong impression that most observers have had of the typical pairs of contenders that have emerged from the presidential nominating process: for example, Roosevelt and Willkie in 1940, Eisenhower and Stevenson in 1952 and 1956, and Nixon and Humphrey in 1968. Some readers might have difficulty with the idea of Nixon being seen as a "liberal" in even the broadest sense of the word, but it must be recalled that he was contested for the nomination in 1968 by Reagan, in part because Nixon was perceived by Reagan's supporters as being too centrist. The minor challenges he received in 1972, when he sought to build an "ideological majority" rather than a party majority, came from both right and left wings of his party, and were, of course, unsuccessful.

There have been five interesting exceptions in recent decades to the rule of picking both candidates from the liberal side of the political spectrum. Three occurred within the Republican party. The first of these was the 1964 nomination of Senator Barry Goldwater of Arizona, one of the party's more articulate spokespersons; the others were the 1980 and 1984 nomination and election of former California Governor Ronald Reagan.

The other exceptions were Carter's 1976 victory and his renomination in 1980. The latter nomination can be largely explained by pointing to the advantages of incumbency. Even though his presidency was marked by considerable conflict with the Democratic-controlled Congress, the inherent advantages of incumbency were difficult to overcome. Each of these five examples, it should soon be clear, is a classic example of the exception that "proves" a rule, in the sense of emphatically documenting the rule's underlying logic. In order to understand this more clearly, we must examine in some detail the forces, strategies, and motivations that come into play in American presidential nominations. This also will provide support for the first half of the assertion made at the beginning of this chapter that American national parties have tended to strike a balance between selecting the president and in choosing and organizing the Congress.

Having just supported our assertion, we must offer a counterargument. While the liberal–conservative balance would seem to be fairly valid through 1968, some significant changes have taken place, notably in the ways in which delegates are selected to the national nominating conventions. The number of states using the primary more than doubled from 1968 to 1980, before shrinking back somewhat in 1984. This, in addition to the increasing use of precinct-level caucuses by the Democratic party, has created a much broader base for participation by the average citizen. And when more people are involved in the selection of candidates, there is a potential for wider choice in the presidential nomination process. For instance, Jimmy Carter ran an outsider's campaign for the 1976 Democratic nomination. When he won both the nomination and the election, the potential existed for a new kind of "balance" between the legislative and executive branches, that between the amateur and the professional politicians. The same could very well be said about the 1980 election. In each case, the broadened base of the major parties nominated a candidate with a total of eight years of experience, and only at the state level.

PRESIDENTIAL-PARTY POLITICS

Every four years, party representatives from each of the states assemble in two conventions in order to perform the extraordinary feat of selecting the two major parties' presidential candidates. In the process, a few thousand convention delegates in effect foreclose far more than 99 percent of the choice of who will head the nation for the next four years. Of roughly 160 million voting-age Americans, only two become realistic contenders for leadership. In so radically reducing the options, the convention delegates perform the paradoxical service of enhancing choice, by winnowing the candidates down to a manageable set of alternatives.

The Politics of Presidential Nominations

To the casual TV viewer and newspaper reader, the national nominating conventions must resemble a curious tribal rite. At its best the rite seems to be a cheerful, if innocuous ceremony—with its flamboyant demonstrations for favorite sons and endless outpourings of florid oratory, more of a piece with an old-fashioned Fourth of July than with the slick ness of the contemporary mass media. And at its worst—as in the hooting of Governor Rockefeller in the 1964 Republican convention or in the bloody street clashes, at the time of the 1968 Democratic convention, between o pponents of Administration Vietnam policy and the Chicago police—the rit e may seem grimly primitive. But, there is much more to the conventions than their carnival trappings and their occasional headline-attracting departures from the level of rhetoric and debate.

The conventions, in spite of their raucousness, can be usefully thought of as ambassadorial conclaves.[3] The delegates are the accredited representatives of their state parties: they have normally included a goodly proportion of the most influential activists in American state and local politics. Some of them are members of Congress—the more so since the Democrats reserved a number of places for them starting with their 1984 convention. Some are governors and holders of other state and local public offices. Others are county chairpersons, long-time party workers, or financial backers—the Republicans being strong on business people and the Democrats on union leaders. And some delegates are dignitaries whose political influence is not great, but who have been chosen to add in some way to the aura of the state's delegation. Delegations from states with tightly organized parties like Connecticut are more often than not able to arrive unified in support of a candidate. Other delegations express as many preferences as there are factions in the state's Democratic or Republican party. Divided delegations are especially common in any year when a party's nominations have been hard fought throughout the period of the presidential primaries.

During the pre-convention months, press attention focuses almost exclusively on those states in which candidates for the nomination have entered into primary elections. Fairly recently, the primary states could have been described as only a handful, as Table 6-3 shows. However, as both parties have "democratized" their selection processes, and as states have become more eager to get their shares of the limelight, these numbers have increased significantly. This is also true for the states which use the precinct caucus-county convention-state convention method of delegate selection. In 1976, for instance, the Democrats held precinct or county caucuses in nineteen states; in 1980 the figure was up to twenty states; and in 1984 the Democrats scheduled caucuses in twenty-seven states and the Republicans in twenty-two. It should be understood that these caucuses are quite different from those which party leaders once dominated. The average citizen

TABLE 6-3   Convention Delegate Selection by Presidential Primaries, 1948-1984

YEAR	NUMBER OF PRIMARIES		VOTERS (IN MILLIONS)		PROPORTION OF DELEGATES SELECTED	
	Dem.	GOP	Dem.	GOP	Dem.	GOP
1948	13	12	2.1	2.6	36.3%	36.0%
1952	15	13	4.9	7.8	38.7	39.0
1956	19	19	5.8	5.8	42.7	44.8
1960	16	15	5.7	5.5	38.3	38.6
1964	16	16	6.2	5.9	45.7	45.6
1968	15	15	7.5	4.5	37.5	34.3
1972	21	20	16.0	6.2	60.5	52.7
1976*	15	27	16.0	10.4	72.6	67.9
1980*	34	34	19.5	12.8	74.7	74.3
1984	30	24	17.9	6.5	67.1	—

*Excludes Vermont (1976, 1980, 1984) and Texas (1980, 1984) which held non-binding primaries in which delegates were not selected.

Compiled from the following sources: for 1948-1972, *Guide to U.S. Elections* (Washington: Congressional Quarterly, Inc., 1976), pp. 342-349, and Austin Ranney, *Participation in American Presidential Nominations, 1976* (Washington: American Enterprise Institute, 1977), Table 1, p. 16; for 1976, Ranney, *ibid.*, and *Guide to 1976 Elections* (Washington: Congressional Quarterly, Inc., 1977), pp. 26-30; for 1980, *Congressional Quarterly Weekly Report* 38 (July 25, 1980), 1870-1871; for 1984, *Congressional Quarterly Weekly Report*, 42 (February 11, 1984), 252, and ibid. (July 7, 1984), 1620.

can participate in these affairs, which leads to quite a change in their style. Regardless of which method is used state-by-state, we are constantly treated to press assessments as to which candidate likely has the most delegates "wrapped up."

Although it is not proven, there might very well be an effect of the media in terms of the sequence of voting, on a state-by-state basis. One candidate can move into the lead, and be virtually "conceded" the nomination by the media to the point where supporters of other candidates may feel inclined to not vote in the primaries or caucuses. On the other hand, such treatment by the media can result in rather rapid oscillations in voting. A good example of this might be the 1984 race for the Democratic presidential nomination. Before he even declared his candidacy, Walter Mondale was conceded to be the likely winner. Not until Gary Hart carried several states did Mondale's organization and supporters get sufficiently active to be able to hold on to the lead in the delegate count, but only after the lead had shifted back and forth.

Other candidates will, of course, issue their own delegate counts and dispute the media until such time as they may surge into the lead themselves. Why is such emphasis placed on this? Simply put, as more and more delegates are selected through the "open" processes of primaries and caucuses, it is easier to figure out who might be ahead, and where that candidate's strength is located. A spectacular primary victory against strong odds—like John F. Kennedy's 1960 success in West Virginia, a state in which there was believed to be great resistance to the thought of a Catholic president—can be the beginning of a pre-convention bandwagon. Another example would be Jimmy Carter, a virtual unknown in 1976, winning the Iowa precinct caucuses and the New Hampshire primary, starting a bandwagon which one by one eliminated any serious contenders. More often than not, the delegate selection process serves to weed out first the long-shot candidates, whose failure to impress substantial numbers of party professionals has led them to turn to the primaries and caucuses in an attempt to demonstrate their potential as the party's ticket leader in November. The 1964 Republican convention choice of Barry Goldwater is the only instance in which a party has nominated a man who chose to contest primaries and then performed quite poorly in them. And in 1968, the Democrats nominated Hubert Humphrey, who had not entered a single primary!

These two cases occurred at a time when presidential primaries were not the principal means of selecting delegates to the national nominating conventions. Most were then chosen by means through which the party professionals could exercise a great deal of control. Depending on the party and the state in question, there is an almost Byzantine array of procedures for selecting delegates: primary elections, precinct and county caucuses, congressional-district conventions, and state conventions, in varying combinations. Needless to say, the campaign managers of the serious aspirants for the nomination follow delegate selection seriously, soliciting commitments, and encouraging sympathetic party personnel to offer themselves as delegates in either the caucus or primary process. In particular, campaign managers and candidates concentrate on politicians who have a large personal following and may be able to command the support of blocs of delegates: governors, chairpersons of unified state parties, and city and county bosses. In addition to specific bargains and attempts at persuasion, there occurs during this pre-convention period an imperfectly understood process of growing consensus during which the standings of the contenders with the delegates begin to become fixed—probably in ways that are not unlike the imperfectly coordinated market processes through which the prices of securities become set. Among the factors influencing delegates' judgments at this point are the performance of the aspirants, not only in the primaries but also in other public activities during the pre-nominating period, and the nature of their public reception, as shown, for example, in press reports and national public-opinion polls.[4]

When a first-term president is running for renomination, the convention outcome has come to be virtually preordained: no twentieth-century president has ever been denied nomination for a second term by his party. Even in 1968, when President Lyndon Johnson, facing strong opposition from within his party, chose not to seek renomination, most observers felt that he could have had the candidacy if he had chosen to run. There were two relatively close calls in recent history, however. Gerald Ford, who had not run for either president or vice-president in 1972, received 53 percent of the convention vote in 1976 against the challenge of Ronald Reagan. And, Jimmy Carter got 64 percent of the delegates in 1980 in his contest with Teddy Kennedy.

Sometimes non-incumbents succeed in building up enough pre-convention support to win the nomination without a contest, as in the cases of Richard Nixon in 1960 and of Herbert Hoover in 1928. Carter's relatively uncontested 1976 nomination could also be said to be of this variety. But ordinarily the nominating conventions are contested. Even when it is acknowledged that one of the candidates for nomination is well ahead, other names are also put in nomination, and there are active efforts to win over uncommitted delegates—often delegates who have held their votes in reserve by temporarily supporting a "favorite son"—and efforts to encourage committed delegates to defect. It is increasingly the case that a good bit of the business of the convention is settled before the convention actually meets—through the various processes of consensus formation, all of which tend to be fostered by modern means of rapid communication. Thus, in earlier political epochs, it sometimes took dozens of ballots to produce a convention winner.[5] But in the sixteen conventions held by the two major parties between 1956 and 1984 there was not a single instance in which the presidential voting went beyond the first ballot. This, however, is not to say that the convention has become some kind of rubber-stamping process, but rather that the delegates in effect have come to accomplish many of their purposes before formally convening.

The psychology of how delegates make their choices has yet to be definitively analyzed. But important clues are available from two major studies of the attitudes of delegates to the 1956 and the 1980 conventions and of party identifiers in the general public.[6] As can be seen from the selective summary of these findings in Table 6-4, there are consistent and quite distinct differences in the issue positions of the delegates to the two parties for each of the years studied. The differences parallel those between Democratic and Republican members of Congress, with the Democrats showing a much greater proclivity than the Republicans to support expansion of the scope of governmental activity, or to oppose budget cuts in certain programs. Since it is sometimes argued that the two parties ought to be more sharply distinguishable from each other ideologically, so as to represent differences in the electorate, it is also interesting to note what Table 6-4 reveals of voter attitudes. As we can see, the two groups of voters are much less sharply divided, especially in 1956, than are the party delegates, although in a very mild way the Republican and Democratic party identifiers show the same kinds of differences in issue preferences as do the politicians.

A further observation that emerges from Table 6-4 helps explain both the once-normal tendency of the two parties to nominate what we

TABLE 6-4   Views of Democratic and Republican National-Convention Delegates and Voters on Issues of the Day, 1956 and 1980

Type of Governmental Activity Favored	PERCENTAGE SUPPORTING INCREASE OF GOVERNMENTAL ACTIVITY			
	Convention Delegates		Voters	
	Democrats	*Republicans*	*Democrats*	*Republicans*
1. Social Security benefits	60%	22%	69%	57%
2. Federal aid to education	66	22	75	65
3. Slum clearance and public housing	78	40	80	72
4. Minimum wages	50	16	59	54
5. Public ownership of natural resources	58	13	35	31
6. Corporate income tax	32	4	32	23

Favor Budget Cuts for:	1980 PERCENTAGE SUPPORTING BUDGET CUTS			
	Convention Delegates		Identifiers	
	Democrats	*Republicans*	*Democrats*	*Republicans*
1. Defense	58%	6%	35%	18%
2. Social Security	8	17	4	10
3. Health/Medicare	14	57	8	17
4. Education	15	61	6	12
5. Welfare	38	89	48	66

Sources for 1956, Herbert McClosky et al., "Issue Conflict and Consensus among Party Leaders and Followers," *American Political Science Review,* 54 (June 1960), 406–27. For 1980, John S. Jackson, III, Barbara Leavitt Brown, and David Bositis, "Herbert McClosky and Friends Revisited: 1980 Democratic and Republican Party Elites Compared to the Mass Public," *American Politics Quarterly,* 10 (April 1982).

have been loosely referring to as "liberals," and the 1964 and 1980 Republican departures from this rule. As to the latter, it is clear that, while Republican delegates were as consistently conservative as they had been earlier, Republican voters had shifted dramatically. Hence, the delegates were nominating someone who, ideologically, fit what was no longer the "fringe" element of their party. For 1964, however, assuming the findings from 1956 apply, the Republican convention delegates were probably far more conservative than either their normal base of voters, or the voters to whom they had to appeal in order to win—Democrats and Independents. In 1956 (and most likely in 1964, considering their nomination of "Mr. Conservative") their stands were dramatically more conservative than those of their own voters on exactly the kinds of issues that are likely to be salient in an election campaign—namely, "meat and potatoes" matters such as Social Security, housing, and wages. Since, as we saw in Chapter 3, the Republicans have fewer supporters than do the Democrats, it is vital for the GOP to mount a presidential campaign that holds virtually every Republican party identifier and at the same time produces substantial Democratic defections, as happened in 1980.[7] Yet given their conservative ideological principles, the Republican delegates are under a standing temptation to nominate what Senator Goldwater proved to be: the minority candidate of the minority party.[8]

The Republican delegates are, however, under still another standing temptation. To the degree that they may be practical politicians, they may try to nominate someone who can be elected. Typically, there has been a strong presumption that this goal can only be achieved by choosing someone who is more favorable than is the typical Republican convention delegate to the kinds of social programs which Table 6-4 showed to have widespread public popularity—such programs as Social Security, aid to education, and the minimum wage.[9] Finally, in 1980, perhaps because of perceptions that these programs might no longer be as widely supported by the general public as they had been earlier, or perhaps because they saw that President Carter was vulnerable on a group of other issues, Republican conservatives had their chance again, and took it. With these exceptions, Republican delegates usually face a painful cost accounting, unlike Democratic delegates for whom political philosophy and political practicality frequently coincide (with the notable exception of McGovern, in 1972). They need to weigh the merits of backing a candidate whose beliefs they favor against those of backing one who actually stands a chance of taking office.

Calculations of this sort by the delegates are complicated by an additional practical concern—that of estimating not only whether a prospective candidate will do well nationally, but also how well he will do in the delegate's own bailiwick. Since the party's national candidate heads a slate of ordinarily much less well-known state, local, and congressional candidates, the candidate may lead the local ticket to victory or may sink it completely. This is a consideration that no local party organization can fail to ignore.

There are some Republican politicians represented at any nominating convention for whom the requirements of national victory and those of state and local victory tend to be the same. These are the Republicans from the big industrial states. By definition, successful politicians from such states want to win in their own jurisdiction, and the candidate who is best for their state ticket tends to be precisely the candidate who is most likely to lead the party to national success. Even a cursory examination of the census statistics shows why the populous industrial states exercise such a fascination for presidential strategists. The four largest alone—California, New York, Texas, and Pennsylvania—contain within their borders about a third of the nation's population. These four states account for roughly a quarter of the electoral vote. Furthermore, as long as state electoral votes continue to be counted on a winner-take-all basis, even a slight plurality in these four states—which, as competitive two-party states, are easily tipped to either side—brings *all* of their votes, about half the total needed to win the presidency. Ordinarily a successful Republican politician or presidential candidate in these states must add to the traditional Republican "outstate" vote from the smaller communities and suburbia a further increment of votes from great metropolises, which are heavily populated by such categories of Democratic core voters as union members, other manual workers, and members of the various ethnic groups. The candidate need not actually carry the cities, but needs to be sufficiently liberal to have a substantial urban appeal.[10]

Delegates oriented toward winning in the industrial states have prevailed in most Republican conventions, partly because these delegates have a large number of convention votes and partly as a result of their pragmatic appeals for a potential winner. At the very least, this Republican bloc has ordinarily been able to insure that the nominee will be, as Nixon was in 1960, 1968, and 1972, equivocal rather than militantly conservative on the standard issues that serve as the basis for the liberal–conservative rating scales. The classical example of Republican reluctance to extend the nomination to the party's spokesman for conservatism was the repeated convention rejection of Ohio Senator Robert Taft. In 1940, in 1948, and again in 1952, this personification of stand-pat virtues was rejected in favor of less conservative men—Willkie, Dewey, and Eisenhower—even though the majority of delegates probably found Taft much more congenial than his opponents within the party. Similarly, two successive Republican conventions rejected Reagan. In the 1968 convention, Reagan received only 182 first-ballot votes, or about 14 percent. By 1976 he had increased this to 1,070, or 47 percent. And, in 1980, he reversed the "rule" against the nomination of a conservative by winning all but 55 votes out of the 1,994 on the first ballot.[11]

The Reagan nomination of 1980 and Senator Goldwater's in 1964 show that there is no automatic process of Republican rejection of the party's militant conservatives. But the circumstances and consequences of 1964 are illuminating. The nomination of Goldwater occurred when there happened to be unusually great division among the industrial state Republicans over which candidate to support, and when that bloc's most promising prospect (New York's Governor Rockefeller) happened fortuitously to be a man suffering under the political disability of a recent divorce and remarriage. Goldwater's defeat in the general election was overwhelming. The only non-southern state to support him was his native Arizona. The GOP lost 38 House seats, 2 Senate seats, and 493 state legislative seats. The Eighty-ninth Congress, which as a result of the landslide included close to an absolute majority of non-southern Democrats, passed an array of liberal measures that had been blocked for years by a coalition of Republicans and southern Democrats. To many Republican politicians, this last consequence constituted the strongest argument for the party to return to its standard strategy of drawing from its liberal wing and appealing to the industrial states in making presidential nominations.[12] But sixteen years later a different story was told. In 1980, the South went Republican with a single exception—that of Georgia's native son Jimmy Carter. Running as a conservative, but less so than he had in 1976 when he sought the Republican nomination, Ronald Reagan evidently helped his party's candidates for lesser office. The Democrats lost 7 seats and control of the Senate, 33 house seats, and 197 seats in state legislatures. The Ninety-seventh Congress, 1981–1982, evidently read this as a move to the right, and supported a good deal of President Reagan's legislation. Was this indeed a conservative tide? Perhaps, but the voters in 1982 turned out some of President Reagan's strongest and most conservative supporters from Congress.

Presidential-Party Politicians

Both parties once normally drew their presidential candidates with an eye to their drawing power in the big states. From 1900 through 1968, involving eighteen elections and thirty-six major party nominating conventions, thirteen of the nominees were from New York, five from Ohio, three from California, and two from Illinois. This seems to be less the case in recent years, especially for the Democrats, who have nominated candidates from South Dakota (McGovern, 1972), Georgia (Carter, 1976 and 1980), and Minnesota (Mondale, 1984). More so for the Democrats than the Republicans, most nominees have had an initial commitment to liberal and activist policies.

Those who support such presidential goals may, for purposes of rough classification, be called "presidential-party politicians," as distinguished from "congressional-party politicians." The nucleus of the presidential party consists of politicians from the kinds of constituencies which nominate and elect the president—governors and party chairs of the industrial states and the big-city mayors, for example. Included in this category are also some members of each house of Congress,[13] but rarely enough members (the Eighty-ninth Congress being an exception) to guarantee the president an automatic majority for his legislative program. The Democratic party's presidential wing tends to enlist the loyalties of liberal intellectuals and labor leaders. Presidential Republicans are often executives of the nation's largest industries, publishers, professionals, and other citizens who are drawn to what President Eisenhower called "modern Republicanism."[14]

CONGRESSIONAL-PARTY POLITICS AND POLITICIANS

The procedures that lead to the staffing and organization of Congress have quite different consequences from those that determine who will be president and what political views will emanate from the White House. Those sections of the country and those political preferences that are especially strongly represented through the presidency—the industrial states and particularly their cities; the proponents of liberal legislation—tend if anything to be *under*-represented in Congress. And the reciprocal areas, interests, and views are especially well received by the legislators. This is a result partly of the way in which Congress is selected and partly of the nature of its two varieties of leaders.[15]

Political Consequences of the Basis of Congressional Selection

The populous states once so heavily represented as the home states of the presidential candidates have no more voting power in the Senate than such sparsely settled states as Nevada and Alaska, which combined contain about a third as many inhabitants as the Bronx. California, New York, Texas, and Pennsylvania may control a fourth of the electoral vote; but they make up a mere twenty-fifth of the Senate. The House of Representatives, of course, is apportioned by population. Until the Supreme Court's one-man-one-vote decisions of the 1960s, the urban areas were systematically and intentionally underrepresented in the House, as a result of the control over districting exercised by rural-dominated state legislatures. But even with the fairest of districting, the House is bound to contain numerous articulate conservatives, simply because in so many House districts there is no need for the representative to be responsive to urban interests, views, and groups. New York State, for example, typically casts its Republican as well as its Democratic convention votes for liberal presidential nominees; New York Senators, whether Republican or Democratic, usually receive "liberal" scores on the ADA and ACA yardsticks. But among the members of any New York State delegation to the House of Representatives are many upstate Republicans who yield to no one in the rigor of their conservatism. We saw in Table 6–1 that those who were rated in the highest categories of the ADA liberalism scale were principally non-southern Democratic members of Congress. But a "normal" Democratic majority in the House of Representatives—for example, the 243–192 division elected in 1980—rarely includes more than 175 northern Democrats, well under half the 435 members of the House.

In contrast to the advantage gained by a presidential nominee who comes from an area in which the two parties compete evenly with each other—especially in a big-city industrial state—the member of Congress who comes from such an area is at a profound *dis*advantage. The chairmanships of congressional committees, which as we shall see are exceedingly important positions, go to the legislators with the greatest seniority. The turnover in office of members from competitive areas reduces the likelihood that they will acquire enough continuous service ever to assume these key posts. In the House of Representatives not only do committee chairmanships often go to southern Democrats and rural safe-district Republicans, but they also are gradually coming to be earned by liberal northern Democrats from that party's safe urban districts.[16] Senate chairships, on the other hand, could scarcely be less responsive to the big cities if they had been assigned with the express purpose of ignoring them. In 1967–1968, nine of the sixteen chairmanships were held by southerners, although from the Civil War through 1964 the southern Democrats never supplied a single presidential nominee.[17]

The 1980 election of the Ninety-seventh Congress (1981–1983) did little to change this picture, even though the Republicans took control of the Senate. Granted, many of the new committee chairs were considerably less senior than were their Democratic predecessors, they still tended to represent states which were not very populous. In the Senate, for instance, the smaller states, traditionally more Republican than are the larger, dominated the chairmanships, with only two of the top ten most populous states represented (Texas and Illinois). Little changed in the House, however, as the Democrats retained control.

Elected Congressional Party Leaders

Among the foremost congressional actors are the first of the two kinds of congressional leaders alluded to above: the *elected leaders* of the two parties on each side of the Capitol—the Speaker of the House and his counterpart, the House minority leader, and the majority and minority leaders of the Senate. The elected leaders are voted on by the entire membership of their party in their chamber of Congress. Legislation which is strongly opposed by the Speaker or the Senate majority leader usually stands little chance of success. Even the minority party leaders may have effective veto power over policies if they are able to hold together their own forces and coalesce with dissident members of the majority.

The *veto* power of congressional party leaders is emphasized advisedly, for their power to insure affirmative action is much less certain. Leaders of Congress can cajole their colleagues. They can reward cooperative party members and impose minor deprivations on uncooperative members. They can do little more than this, however, since each member of Congress is dependent for nomination and election on local sources of support, not on the congressional parties. Congressional leaders lack the basic hierarchical power of hiring and firing subordinates.

The party leadership positions provide almost infinitely subtle opportunities for negotiation and maneuver. The Speaker and the Senate majority leader are at the center of communications in their chambers. They know the needs and desires of members. Because of their central position, they are able to serve first one faction and then another, exacting concessions and promises of cooperation. Representative *A* may be anxious to have a public-works project initiated in her district. Representative *B* may want to insure that the tariff on beet sugar, a source of livelihood for his constituents, is not reduced. By arranging for *A's* support of *B* and *B's* support of *A*, and seeing to it that both representatives' bills find a place on the crowded legislative agenda, the skilled party leader can win support for an important administration bill.

Tactics of this sort have their limitations. Broker activities can provide the decisive votes on close roll-calls and can ease the passage of minor legislation. But they will not work in the face of powerful constituency pressures. No amount of vote-trading or patronage once induced southerners to vote for civil rights legislation, or midwesterners to abandon farm supports.

The elected leaders are at the center of their parties in a second sense. The members of each party choose leaders whose views are somewhere near the party midpoint. Representatives of the extreme wings of either congressional party would find it difficult to serve the mediating role which congressional leadership requires. Since the congressional parties underrepresent the kinds of urban industrial constituencies to which presidents are oriented, those at their centers will normally be a good bit more conservative than presidents of the same party.

The contrast between the views of presidential and congressional politicians, oddly, is ordinarily most clearly evident in the party which does not control the White House. In recent years there has been a growing tradition of cooperation between presidents and the elected congressional leaders of the president's party. Leaders may work privately to persuade the president to moderate his programs. In public they support him. If in disagreement, they may attempt to make it clear that they disagree "as the Senator from California," rather than as party leader.[18] There are good reasons for the president and his party leaders to play down their differences. Congressional party leaders need the resources of the executive branch to help assemble majorities for the party's legislation and they need a satisfactory presidential record as a basis for conducting the next election campaign.

The differences between presidential and congressional politicians are most evident, therefore, in the party which is not inhibited by presidential leadership. Under these circumstances, an American party has no national spokesperson whose legitimacy is recognized by all party factions. The party's "titular leader," the defeated presidential candidate, carries the stigma of failure. The national chair, traditionally an appointee of the presidential candidate, can scarcely command more respect. In addition, the views of both are likely to be too liberal for the tastes of the party's highest elected officials, the congressional leaders. As a result, out-party politics may become something of a tug-of-war between congressional- and presidential-party politicians.

The Seniority Leaders of Congress

Presidents can generally count on the cooperation of their party's elected leaders in Congress. The members of their party who constitute the second kind of congressional leader—the *seniority leaders* who are their party's dominant members at the committee level—are far less predictably willing to back the president. As we have seen, the system of choosing committee chairs on the basis of seniority exaggerates the already considerable bias of congressional apportionment. Any president will find some allies among the chairs of the standing committees. He or she is equally certain to find other chairs who are skeptical of his or her program and bent on defeating it.[19]

Seniority, in Congress, which is taken to mean length of continuous service, has normally been the means by which committee chairs are selected. However, there has been a slight modification to the system. Following the 1974 congressional elections, when seventy-five freshman Democrats were elected, a "change" was instituted by House Democrats. Rather than going on the basis of strict seniority, anyone desiring to become a committee chair must be approved by the House Democratic caucus. As a result of this (then declared) "revolution," three long-time committee chairs lost their positions in early 1975. However, they were replaced by the next-most senior individuals on their committees. Since that time, the seniority system has gone unchallenged. Hence, seniority is still important, but it no longer guarantees that conservatives will chair committees. Peter Rodino (D., N.J.), for instance, is chairman of the House Committee on the Judiciary at this writing. Taking advantage of the seniority system in the Senate, conservatives actively backed the 1984 challenge to Senator Charles Percy (R., Ill.). By helping a liberal Democrat, they hoped to unseat Percy. Why would they do something like this? Assuming that the Republicans could retain control of the Senate, the next chairman of the Senate Foreign Relations Committee would be Jesse Helms (R., N.C.), a prominent conservative!

To understand the importance of committe chairs we must first consider the role of the committees themselves. It is difficult to exaggerate their significance. Even when facing the relatively simple tasks of nineteenth-century government, Congress found it advisable to delegate the framing and consideration of legislation and the oversight of administration to standing committees. The enormous work load of twentieth-century Congresses and the intricacy of contemporary legislation makes it unthinkable for the legislature to operate without such specialization today, unless it were to assume the rubber-stamp role of the British House of Commons.

With rare exceptions, all legislation is gestated in the committees. Because each member is informed mainly in the area of his or her committee specialties, the houses accept, or modify only slightly, a large proportion of the committee bills which come up for a vote; thus much of the statutory output of Congress essentially consists of a ratification of committee decisions.

Perhaps more important, a good bit of what Congress does *not* do is determined by the committees. As many as 10,000 bills may be introduced in a single session of Congress, and of these, only a very small fraction are reported from committee. The fatalities there inevitably include bills of considerable potential significance, some of them items on the president's list of "must" legislation. Committees are not necessarily accurate microcosms of the House and Senate; their memberships develop stalagmite-fashion by the accrual of new members and the defeat, decease, and transfer to other committees of old members. Therefore, bills often are killed in committee which would be passed if they had been reported and had come to the floor for a vote.

Among the committee members the chair is *by far* the most important. With a committee majority behind him or her, the chair is almost impossible to beat on an issue within the jurisdiction of his or her committee, except through extraordinary and embarrassing procedures which force the party leaders to admit their weakness and depart from the regular order of congressional business. Even without the support of their committee members, chairs are able to employ numerous parliamentary devices to block or modify legislation, including refusal to call committee meetings and hearings, failure to bring up or report legislation, and "stacking" subcommittees with the chair's allies and then directing key bills to these subcommittees.[20]

Both the elected and the seniority leaders, we have suggested, are in excellent positions to block policies. In constitutional theory, the veto is an instrument of the president. In American political practice, veto power is available to many people and groups throughout the political system. The possibilities for delaying or halting policy-making are nowhere better developed than in Congress. Each chamber in effect can exercise a veto over the other. In the House, the Committee on Rules has often defied the party leadership and prevented important bills from coming up for a vote. Filibustering in the Senate has had the same effect. The checkmating possibilities are so substantial that one wonders how any policies—especially on controversial issues—ever emerge from the Washington labyrinth.

POLICY-MAKING AT THE NATIONAL LEVEL

Party can, as we saw at the state and local levels, serve as the bridge between a legally separated executive and legislature. If members of the same party control both branches of government (or all of the semi-autonomous boards and commissions in a municipality), a basis exists for cooperation in the making of policy. At the federal level in the United States, however, party serves more as bridgehead than bridge.

Party as Bridgehead

To begin with, Congress and the president are not invariably of the same party. In presidential election years, the party that controls the White House ordinarily also controls both houses of Congress. We say ordinarily because there have been some exceptions. During the period of Democratic electoral hegemony that began in 1932, Republican presidents were elected in 1956 (Eisenhower), and 1968 and 1972 (Nixon) without carrying either house of Congress. In 1980 Republican Reagan carried the Senate but not the House. By the same token, Democrat Woodrow Wilson won re-election without carrying Congress.

The congressional election that occurs midway through the president's term scarcely ever fails to weaken his party in Congress. The party holding the presidency ordinarily loses congressional seats in the mid-term elections largely because Congressmen who represent areas of the other party's strength and who were carried into office on the president's coattails now have to run on their own.[21] In 1964, for example, President Johnson swept Democratic representatives into office from districts that had not returned a Democrat since Roosevelt carried forty-six out of forty-eight states against Landon in 1936, and before that not since the 1912 split in the Republican party. It was scarcely surprising, therefore, that the president's party suffered a sizable loss in seats in the 1966 mid-term elections. In general, the results of mid-term elections make it harder for the president to get his way with Congress. More often than not, the presidential party retains nominal control of Congress, but even this cannot be guaranteed: congressional-party control shifted in twelve mid-term elections between the Civil War and 1980.

Although presidents are far from assured of automatic ratification of their programs even when their party *does* control Congress, party is nevertheless of critical importance for the fate of the presidential program. Figure 6-1 shows levels of support by members of the two parties for President Johnson's program, during the historic 1965–1966 Congress that passed Medicare and so much of the rest of the traditional New-Deal–Fair-Deal–New-Frontier legislation. A president's fellow partisans, especially northerners in the case of Democratic presidents, provide the bulk of regular supporters of his program. Thirty-nine Democrats, only two of them from the South, backed Johnson on 60 percent or more of his recommendations. Only five Republicans supported him this often. House voting followed a similar pattern. But even in that remarkable post-landslide Congress, there were occasions when the President was defeated or was forced to modify his aims.

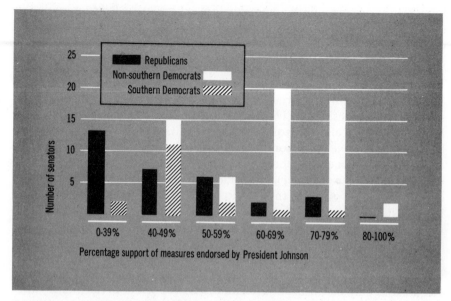

Source: *Congressional Quarterly Weekly Report*, January 5, 1968. Seven senators who for various reasons were unable to vote on the bulk of the relevant roll-calls are not included. Only two senators, a Republican and a southern Democrat, were lower than 30 percent in presidential support, since the president invariably recommends some non controversial legislation.

FIGURE 6-1 Administration support scores of Democratic and Republican senators, Eighty-ninth Congress (1965-66).

As a result of the 1966 mid-terms, the Democratic majority in the House was cut from its previous exceptional 295–140 advantage to a more typical 248–187 edge, and there was a somewhat less-pronounced decline of Democratic strength in the Senate. With the loss of the northern Democrats he had carried into office, Johnson had to manage with the normal level of support that a Democratic president can count on, drawing from his own wing of his party and from the minority of Republican liberals. The practical consequences of this shift in party strength between the Eighty-ninth and Ninetieth Congresses were estimated in the following way by *Congressional Quarterly's* professional Congress-watchers:

	FAVOR	OPPOSE	UNCOMMITTED
Rent supplements			
89th Congress	213	199	23
90th Congress	173	238	24
Poverty program			
89th Congress	240	191	4
90th Congress	191	225	19
Open housing			
89th Congress	234	199	2
90th Congress	205	216	14

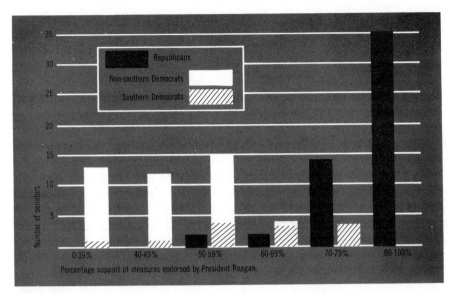

Source: *Congressional Quarterly Weekly Report,* 40 (January 2, 1982), p. 24.

FIGURE 6-2 Administration support scores of Democratic and Republican senators, Ninety-seventh Congress, first term (1981).

What better documentation that party normally is insufficient for national-level policy-making?

While party is not normally a sufficient guide for members of Congress in deciding how to vote, presidents at least often find that it is necessary. Examining another historic Congress, the Ninety-seventh, elected in 1980, we can see how President Reagan was able to develop his radical changes in tax and budget policy. Figure 6-2 shows the administrative support scores of the Senate, then under Republican control. Clearly, Republicans were more prone to favor many of the president's proposals than were the Democrats. Indeed, even though Democrats in the Senate showed less liberalism (according to ADA scores) than they had just four years earlier, and could often support the president, the Republican majority clearly provided the core of his support in the Senate. As before, however, southern Democrats again contributed to the conservative cause, supporting the president much more than did their northern colleagues.

Beyond Party: Bargaining

Where partisanship ceases, bargaining, compromise, and consensus-seeking procedures begin. An instructive example is the Trade Expansion Act of 1962, the most successful legislative achievement of President John F. Kennedy, whose extensive program of liberal legislation was by and large blocked in Congress in spite of the seemingly firm congressional majorities accompanying Kennedy's entry into office. (The Democrats controlled the House 263–174 and enjoyed a 64–36 majority in the Senate).

Tariff legislation is a classical example of the kind of public policy which places complex pressures on the political process. Since 1934, American foreign economic policy has been based on reciprocal trade legislation, which provides for tariff rates to be administratively set (within certain general legislative guidelines) and which places emphasis on encouraging low rates and the free flow of international trade. Before 1935, tariff rate-making was a congressional prerogative—and virtually a museum exhibit of log-rolling politics writ large. The difficulty with congressional rate-making, apart from sheer mechanical complexities, arises from the lack of congressional-party discipline and from the concommitant sensitivity of each individual member of Congress to any organized interest group in his or her constituency. Among the best-organized interests are those which are unable to operate efficiently in the world market and which survive only by virtue of the hidden subsidy of tariffs on foreign imports. Free-trade interests, on the other hand, are difficult to organize. Few industries are totally dependent on exports, and therefore industries which sell abroad are less aware of their stake in foreign trade than industries which seek to maintain their artificially protected domestic markets. The group which stands most to gain by free trade and lower price levels—the consumers—is not organized at all.

Congressional representatives may agree in principle that the nation's economic system will remain efficient only if the United States produces the goods it can manufacture economically and imports goods which can be produced more economically elsewhere. In practice, their impulse is to save their constituents—the beet-sugar farmers, the fluorspar-miners, or the candlestick-makers—from bankruptcy and unemployment.

Congressional rate-making contributed to generally rising tariffs during the period from the Civil War through the passage of reciprocal trade legislation in 1934. Once inefficient industries developed, they constituted permanent lobbies for perpetuation of the status quo. Other groups sought the same advantages and received them in exchange for their support of beet sugar, fluorspar, and candlesticks. With reciprocal trade, the power was granted the president to adjust tariffs downward in exchange for concessions from other nations. A three-quarter-century trend toward protection, culminating with the almost complete collapse of foreign trade during the Depression, was finally reversed.

Reciprocal trade legislation was extended periodically between 1934 and 1958. Congress always placed substantial limitations on the executive's power to revise tariffs, and many enclaves of protection continued to exist, but rates generally moved downward and foreign trade became increasingly important to the economy. In July 1962, the president's power to continue bargaining for lower tariffs was again due to expire. This time, in the administration's view, more than a mere extension of the 1934 legislation was necessary. A new and powerful element on the international trade scene, the European Common Market, seemed to call for a new response on the part of American foreign-trade negotiators.

The Common Market was a potentially valuable trading partner for the United States, but only it was argued, if the president were given increased tariff-bargaining power to negotiate mutual trade concessions. Otherwise, the six-nation customs union might successfully compete for America's foreign markets. More important, the political consequences of economic rivalry among the Western nations would be unfortunate, and, without additional American flexibility in tariff bargaining, Japan and the underdeveloped nations might lose their Western markets and be pushed toward dependence on the communist bloc.

The administration prepared its attack carefully, well aware of the congressional sensitivity to protectionist appeals. Traditionally, the tariff has been among the most partisan of issues. The pre-New Deal Democratic party, with its roots in the agricultural South, favored "free trade," whereas "protection" had been a pillar of old-time Republican policy. But by the 1950s tariff partisanship had begun to break down. Many influential Republicans—including President Eisenhower, representatives of the Republican party's presidential wing, and midwesterners from food-exporting farm districts—favored expanded foreign trade. The movement of textile manufacturers to the South, combined with the increased threat of Japanese and other inexpensive textile imports, created new protectionist advocates within the Democratic party. More generally, protectionists could be found in either party wherever congressional constituencies contained declining industries and pockets of unemployment which could be attributed to imports.[22]

The list of groups opposing trade expansion was lengthy, ranging from associations of almond-growers to the Window Glass Cutters League of America, AFL-CIO. Influential segments of the chemical and electrical industries demanded continued protection. But most important among the countless supplicants (the table of contents of the 1962 Ways and Means Committee hearings required 34 pages simply to list the group representatives who testified on trade expansion) was the textile industry. Textile manufacturing is located in over 100 congressional districts. The industry accounts for 2.2 million jobs, only about 3 percent of the national work force, but probably about half of the workers likely to be affected by trade liberalization.

A mammoth coalition of free-trade advocates was assembled under White House leadership, including such incongruent political bedfellows as the Chamber of Commerce and the AFL-CIO. Statements favoring trade expansion were obtained from former President Eisenhower and his former Secretary of State Christian Herter. By November 1961, the administration had begun to publicize its case in a concerted effort that included addresses by President Kennedy to the National Association of Manufacturers and the AFL-CIO conventions, and a battery of speeches and statements by other administration officials.

Much as if he were dealing with a foreign power, the president began negotiations with the moderately conservative chairman of the House Ways and Means Committee, where tariff legislation is initiated.[23] The negotiations were doubly sensitive, since the committee was also to handle two more of the administration's major measures: tax reform and medical care for the aged. Drafting the act required a delicate balancing of interests—certain provisions which were necessary for labor support were opposed by the farm and business groups, and vice versa. Unless both sides of the coalition were kept intact, the bill might easily have fallen prey to protectionist forces.

On February 15, 1962, a month before committee hearings were scheduled to begin, the administration unleashed its major weapon: the announcement of the successful negotiation of a nineteen-nation textile-import quota agreement which would keep foreign textile imports from rising much above prevailing levels. Further obeisance was paid to the textile industry in the form of liberalized tax-depreciation schedules. These spectacular concessions were a body blow to the protectionist coalition. The American Cotton Manufacturers Institute, representing 80 percent of the textile industry, swung to the support of the Trade Expansion Act, as did numerous protectionist-minded Congressmen. The expansionist camp had scored a remarkable coup. Yet at the same time, administration concessions made for something of a Pyrrhic victory. The quota restrictions canceled out a good bit of the effect which passage of the act could be expected to have. Textiles constitute one of the few industries which can be set up economically in underdeveloped nations. The quota, by denying American markets to these nations, would delay their development and also interfere with the goal of freeing them of dependence on American aid.

Even with the defection of the textile industry, congressional insiders doubted whether a majority of Congress could be persuaded to go along with expanded tariff-cutting powers desired by the president. Additional congressional support was won by discretionary presidential action raising tariffs on certain kinds of glass products and carpets. Both industries had congressional supporters whose backing might be crucial. The increases aroused a storm of protest in Belgium and Japan, where industries which were geared to sell glass products and carpets to the American market suddenly found themselves without customers; but they evidently won votes on Capitol Hill. Before the Ways and Means Committee had completed consideration of the bill, numerous modifications were made, softening the bill's tariff-cutting provisions. One of the key provisions of the act was retained by a 13–12 committee vote. The amendments were reluctantly accepted by the administration after committee spokesmen argued they were necessary to win House approval by a sufficiently large majority to impress the protectionist-minded Senate.

As the day for House voting approached, tension mounted. Shortly before, the House had dealt the administration a severe defeat by turning down Kennedy's farm bill. Lobbyists from both sides spread out through the corridors of the two House office buildings. In spite of a reported telephone call from Eisenhower, minority leader Halleck and other Republican party leaders decided to oppose the bill on the crucial roll-call—a motion to recommit to committee with instructions that the Reciprocal Trade Act be extended for a year. In effect, this would have denied the president any further tariff-cutting powers.[24]

The administration's months of careful planning, coalition-building, and concessions paid off. The motion to recommit was defeated 253–171. Halleck had lost the votes of a fourth of the Republicans, and Democratic defections had been held to 17 percent. The Republican leaders then supported final passage of the bill, as did almost half of their followers.

House passage occurred on June 28, 1962, but it was not until October 11 that a final version of the act reached President Kennedy's desk for his signature. During the interval, further compromising and bargaining were undertaken to insure the bill's safe transit through the Senate Finance Committee, Senate floor-voting, conference committee reconciliation of the differences in the Senate and House versions of the bill, and approval of the conference report by both houses.

A resurgence of the textile industry's fears concerning the effectiveness of the concessions granted by the administration led to informal agreements with Japan to halt export of certain textile goods and promises of administration support, in the next session of Congress, of legislation taxing textile imports. Similar gestures, though less far-reaching, were made to other protectionist groups—oil and coal producers and the timber industry, for example. On the Senate floor a bloc of 40 Democrats narrowly succeeded in beating down the efforts of 25 Republicans and 13 Democrats to reduce the flexibility of the president's tariff-reducing power, before the final Senate version of the bill was passed by a one-sided 78–8 majority.

Viewing the final legislative product, one journalist reported:

> Some free traders believe that the grand design of a "bold new instrument" has been impaired by the many administrative and legislative devices for dividing and conquering the opposition. The Administration's view, however, is that all the concessions and compromises fade into insignificance when viewed in the light of the legislation's potential effectiveness in expanding world trade. . . . The apparent consensus of impartial commentators is that the President has scored the biggest legislative victory of his career. The general feeling is that it is a substantive as well as a political triumph, despite all concessions and compromises.[25]

But, as in so many political matters, the issue, in its broadest sense, is far from resolved. Among the many problems besetting the Carter presidency was the great increase in imports of Japanese steel and automobiles, causing massive dislocations in employment and sales of two of our basic industries. These problems were essentially left to the Reagan administration, which, as this is written, was about to face another problem involving free trade, that of Japanese computer exports challenging American hegemony. To a very real extent, the success of President Reagan and his successors may hinge on their ability to translate economic and political needs of the country into popular support for what are likely to become greater efforts at protectionism. In doing so, it will be necessary for them to bargain, a procedure that is at the heart of the policymaking process. And, in doing this in turn, they run the risk of watering down their policy goals.

POLITICAL ACTION COMMITTEES—CHALLENGE OR HELP TO THE PARTIES?

Since our last edition, there have been some major changes in the ways political campaigns are financed and therefore run. In the first place, candidates for federal office must now file extensive reports on their receipts and expenditures, and these must be open for public scrutiny. Second, presidential campaigns are now partially financed through federal funds, "contributed" by those taxpayers who check off the appropriate box on their annual tax form (we might note that if you choose to do so, it neither increases your tax nor reduces your refund—it simply sets aside a dollar of your taxes to a special fund). And, the emergence of political action committees (PACs) comprises what some pundits believe to be the most significant change of all. What *are* these committees, and how have they come from seemingly nowhere? Why do many see them as a challenge to the parties?

There are essentially two kinds of PACs:

1. a separate segregated political fund connected to a corporation, trade association, or labor organization;
2. an independent political committee without any connected organization.[26]

PACs have been part of our political scene for some time, raising and spending money on behalf of candidates and parties. In one of those wonderful paradoxes of American politics, the scandals of the 1972 presidential campaign helped clarify their position and lead them to center stage. Briefly, direct contributions to campaigns by labor unions and corporations had been illegal, but it was found that almost $20 million in such contributions had been made to President Nixon's re-election campaign in 1972. When Congress in 1974 enacted public financing of presidential campaigns, it also provided for the establishment of more PACs (they had been present earlier) and defined their roles and limits. In effect, the embarrassments of illegality were swept away—what was illegal in 1972 was clarified, and therefore legal, two years later. Since then, their growth has been astonishing, in terms of sheer numbers and in the contributions they have made to campaigns, as Table 6-5 shows.

Clearly, the introduction of so many new sources of money, with a considerable amount to spend, can and does have an impact on political parties, as well as on the entire political process. However, evaluations of PACs and their influence range quite widely. Some see them as representing, if not bringing about, the absolute worst in politics, offering large sums of money masked as campaign donations in order to "buy" policy from candidates once they are elected. For instance, a senator can receive not just the $10,000 limit ($5,000 for the pre-nomination and $5,000 for the general election campaign) from a single PAC. Rather, that PAC, representing a certain industry, can put together a coalition of some two dozen other PACs representing that same industry. This can result in a combined contribution of $250,000, obviously a major contribution to the senator's re-election campaign. If that senator then votes for or against certain bills consistent with that industry's position, has he been "bought?" Things are seldom that clear-cut, no matter how much we might like them to be so. Rather, we might have a "chicken and egg" controversy here. It is quite possible that the senator got the money in the first place because he had often taken positions in the past, without ever receiving a campaign donation from that industry, which were favorable to the coalition of PACs. Thus, it would be possible to look on the $250,000 not so much as an attempt to buy a future vote, as an effort to help assure that an old friend would get re-elected.

Others are concerned not only about the industry- or labor-related PACs, but also about the independents. Their "independence" is maintained by having no formal relationship with either of the parties or their candidates. They are free to spend their money on any candidate, as long

TABLE 6-5 Political Action Committees: Growth and Contributions

TYPE	12/74	12/76	12/78	12/80	12/82
Corporate	89	433	784	1,204	1,570
Labor	201	224	217	297	380
Trade/Membership/Health	318	489	451	574	628
Independent	—	—	165	378	746
Other	—	—	36	98	47
Totals	608	1,146	1,653	2,551	3,371
Contributions to congressional campaigns (millions):					
House	17.1	22.4	24.8	28.9	
Senate	11.0	14.8	13.5	20.7	

Source: Federal Election Commission news releases.

as there is no communication between the PAC and the candidate's campaign. A good deal of this money has been associated with "negative" campaigns, waged against "liberal" candidates (typically Democrats, but not necessarily). However, it is doubtful whether these campaigns, usually waged on television, have as much impact as might be believed. Campaigns by the National Conservative Political Action Committee (NCPAC, or as it is sometimes known, NickPAC) were claimed to have been the major reason why seven liberal Democratic senators went down to defeat in 1980, thus giving control of the Senate to the Republicans for the first time since the results of the 1954 elections. However, in all seven cases, the incumbent Democratic senator pulled a higher share of the vote than did the nominal head of the ticket, President Carter. It would seem that one of the determining factors was a negative public attitude toward Carter, translated somewhat imperfectly into votes against other Democrats. Indeed, the negative campaign approach which NCPAC and some others try has become an issue in and of itself. In 1982, for example, Senator Paul Sarbanes of Maryland, whose re-election had been anything but a certainty, successfully made an issue of the fact that he was a victim of a hate campaign being conducted by "outsiders."

Why are PACs seen as a challenge to the parties? As far as party professionals are concerned, the most obvious answer is that PACs tap financial resources which might otherwise go directly to the parties themselves. This is very difficult to prove, however, since one would have to show that former donors to parties now give money to PACs instead. The greatest concern, however, stems from the sheer amount of money that PACs have injected into the campaign process. The laws that fueled the great increase in the number and types of PACs were created out of a concern with abuses of the public trust, as almost $20 million in corporate money helped to finance the "dirty tricks" aspect of the 1972 presidential campaign. Now, even more money is being spent on campaigns for members of Congress, most of whom are not highly visible public figures. Public regard for our government, its processes and outcomes, cannot be improved if large donations are made to candidates. Cynicism, and a proper concern for how our government operates, must inevitably lead us to ask why such large donations are necessary. What is being given in return for these donations? Why are donations necessary for candidates who are virtually unopposed?

There is another reason to be concerned—the potential role for PACs in nominations. In this day of the direct primary, running for office is no longer in the hands of party professionals as it was in the long-forgotten days of the legislative caucus. Candidates for public office often seek nomination without the help of the party organization. In some cases, they might even run for the nomination *against* the party, claiming that it is in the hands of "bosses" who are not interested in what the public wants. Nonetheless, the parties are always vitally interested in who gets the nomination. And, there seems to be a potential for PAC involvement in nominations such that neither the party nor the voters have any real say about who runs. Some anecdotal evidence has emerged which suggests that, when a coalition of PACs gets interested in a nomination, they may put up so much money for a certain candidate that other would-be challengers are scared off. This leaves the candidate in a position of having the nomination "bought" for him or her, by organizations which are not accountable to either the party or the voters. Nor can they be readily identified with the PAC.

> Political parties, by reason of their appearance on the ballot to identify candidates, are an integral part of the electoral choice. Voters have a direct opportunity to support or reject the party by supporting or rejecting its candidates. True, they can never be entirely clear whether it is the candidates or the parties they are judging, and indeed it is both: the "party in government." Voter control over political action committees by electoral choice is less direct. Without the PAC name or symbol on the ballot, problems of identification with the PAC are monumental.[27]

Hence, if only by default, parties are still important to the voter as a means of establishing control over government.

FUNCTIONS OF THE NATIONAL PARTIES

There is no shortage of pronouncements on the merits of the American national parties. The party system has its critics and its defenders, and neither side has been reluctant to express itself. Debate about the parties began as early as the 1890s, in the writings of Woodrow Wilson and A. Lawrence Lowell, among others. Books, articles, and pamphlets on the topic abound.

The critics of the parties usually conduct their assault on the basis of two of our three evaluative criteria—popular control of government and effective policy-making. Popular control, they maintain, is frustrated by the failure of the parties to provide clear-cut policy differences from which the voters might choose. Furthermore, the argument continues, even if the choices offered by the parties *were* clear, they would still be meaningless, for the parties are too disorganized to transform their promises into public policy. And those policies that they do make fail to meet the nation's overall requirements, because the parties find it necessary to placate so many veto groups.[28]

Occasionally—particularly during episodes of social violence, such as the labor–management conflicts of the 1930s and the ghetto upheavals three decades later—the critique of the parties has extended itself to our third criterion: political stability. The failure of the parties to cope with pressing needs and to reflect popular aspirations, it is argued, generates circumstances that compel aggrieved groups to seek to advance their purposes by resorting to physical means rather than the political power of persuasion.

Ordinarily, however, the criterion of political stability is cited by the defenders rather than the critics of the national parties. Most defenders of the party system do not confront the arguments that the parties fail to provide the voters with meaningful alternatives or to make sufficiently coordinated policies.[29] Instead, the defenders tend to concentrate their efforts on arguing that in a world in which democratic politics with freely contested elections is a minority phenomenon, no democracy has succeeded in holding together as large and diverse a population as that of the United States for any length of time approaching the American record. The absence since 1865 of further civil wars, according to the defenders' thesis, has resulted from the parties' success in maintaining a generally low-temperature political process. Decentralized, non-ideological parties are "the price of union."[30]

It has been said that the critics and defenders of the party system concur in their beliefs of how the system actually functions, but differ in their judgment of whether the way it functions is to be desired. This is not quite true. Both schools of thought agree with such broad assertions as "The American parties are decentralized." They differ, however, concerning important details and assign different weights to various observations. The same congressional roll-call may be treated by one observer as evidence that the congressional parties are "surprisingly" cohesive, by another as an indication of the failure of the parties to hold their forces together.

The critics and the defenders also disagree—sometimes radically—in their predictions of the consequences of decentralized parties and veto-group politics. "It is the party system," one pair of writers asserts, "more than any other institution, that consciously, actively, and directly nurtures consensus."

> [P]arties promise (and, on pain of not winning elections, deliver) to each group *some* but never all of what it wants, and so give each group a concrete reason for believing that what it regards as its legitimate needs and aspirations *are* getting a hearing, and that it has real chance of achieving all or most of its goals. No group, in other words, has reason to feel that the rest of society is a kind of giant conspiracy to keep it out of its legitimate place in the sun.[31]

Another writer points out with slightly different emphasis, the same attributes of the parties: "The bills and policies introduced by Senators and Congressmen from the areas of greatest popular concentration in America have almost without exception been substantially watered down according to the predilections and petitions of powerful minority interests in and out of Congress." But this writer concludes:

This is government by tollgate. [Its consequence is] the increasing danger of public cynicism and apathy toward the Congress, partly because its power is too diffuse or too subtle to comprehend; partly because when the power *is* clearly identifiable it seems to work more consistently for minorities than for the majority.[32]

Evidently, then, we do not have general empirical agreement concerning the nature of the parties. A major item on the agenda of students of parties is the search for criteria and evidence which will make it possible for us to clarify and resolve such points of contention. Do parties which permit veto-group politics breed "cynicism" or are they nurturers of "consensus"? Conceivably, the American parties have both effects, but this too remains to be demonstrated. The evidence which would enable us to answer questions of this sort with even a moderate degree of assurance has not been assembled. A *few* points are reasonably clear, however.

It is possible, for example, to deal with the assertion that the parties are merely two faces of the same coin and therefore frustrate popular choice and control. As we saw earlier in this chapter, in spite of the overlap between the parties, the midpoint of each is clearly set off from the midpoint of the other. We also noted that the party activists (the convention delegates) differ considerably in their views of the appropriate responsibilities of government. Since the activists differ much more sharply than do the party supporters in the electorate, it is difficult to believe that the parties are failing to express "natural" divisions in the electorate. (We noted in Chapter 5 that the "non-party" systems in some states and municipalities *are* open to this criticism.) Continental political scientists often argue that only multi-party systems, such as the French arrangement, offer the voters a full spectrum of alternatives, but recent research makes it clear that the cafeteria of French politics succeeds simply in puzzling and irritating the great mass of French voters.[33]

The argument of the party defenders that the flexibility of most American party politicians—their disposition to bend with circumstances—has contributed to stability is difficult to deny wholly, even though this is not a matter that can easily be assessed systematically. Since the Civil War the system *has,* after all, been stable, in the sense of persisting. This in itself is no small matter in the contemporary world. Changes in the basic structure of the system have occurred without revolution and coups. Yet the raw materials for additional wars between, among, or within the states clearly have existed in the dislocations brought on by industrialization, in America's extraordinary social diversity, and in traditions—beginning in frontier days—of physical violence.

Domestic violence, including violence directed toward political ends, did not disappear with the Indian Wars or even with the formation of national labor unions in the 1930s, needless to say. The year 1968 saw the assassination of two of the nation's leading political figures—Martin Luther King and Robert F. Kennedy. Earlier in the decade a president—the fourth in the nation's history—was shot to death. In the decade of the sixties there were also ghetto upheavals, campus violence, and the clashes at the 1968 Democratic Convention. One of President Johnson's last official actions was the appointment of a National Commission on the Causes and Prevention of Violence.[34]

On the other hand, the 1968 election, like all of its predecessors since the Civil War, and like those that followed, moved to a nonviolent conclusion, producing a new president whose legitimacy and power were promptly acknowledged by all of the actors on the political scene. And indeed, there was no sign that the nation's political figures viewed the violence of recent years with anything but remorse and a determination to return to more pacific means of social and political expression.

Leaders of this sort, who take it for granted that no domestic political difference is important enough to justify physical combat, emerged in this country in a setting of economic opportunity that appears to have fostered compromise rather than coercion, the meeting of voters' demands rather than the repression of the demanders. The fragmentation of the party and governmental systems has made it *necessary* for politicians and group leaders to bargain, if they are to hope to accomplish their ends. But fragmentation is far from being a *sufficient* condition for a politics of nonrepressive compromise. It appears to have been the pragmatic, ideologically mild orientations of the active participants that have made more or less easygoing bargaining politics possible. And it may be that the willingness of the party politicians to compromise and to be the engineers of compromise sets the tone for other groups in society. Thus there are labor leaders and business-association leaders in Washington who find it perfectly acceptable to work with each other in support of the Trade Expansion Act. And there are labor and business leaders who are willing to work together on the other side.

But what of the argument that a flexible, mediative politics fails sufficiently to meet the nation's long-run needs, and is in this sense detrimental to effective governmental policy-making—and in the longer run, therefore, to political stability? This may be the point at which the party critics have most acutely sensed the system's shortcomings. Bargaining politics has inevitable irrational components; and a political system which does not facilitate rapid policy-making may be too slow in responding to pressing needs. When policies emerge after having had to accommodate the demands of countless veto groups, they are likely to be internally inconsistent—as in the case of the textile concessions granted in connection with passage of the Trade Expansion Act.

In an ancient vaudeville routine a man who is asked "How is your wife?" replies "Compared with what?" Given the constraints imposed by the societal raw materials from which the parties are made, and given the performance of alternative systems,[35] it is not clear how much more can be done in the way of "rationalizing" American policy-making processes. During periods of war and depression, American politicians *have* been willing to reduce, temporarily, the amount of bargaining and vetoing in American politics. The future may see more circumstances under which this is necessary, for the political system appears to be not so well equipped to prevent crises as it is to respond to them after the fact. In the past, America has been able to afford whatever wastage results from the irrational consequences of bargaining politics. As Dahl and Lindblom point out, we cannot be confident the future will be so kind:

> So far, through two world wars, two periods of reconversion, a major depression, and a cold war, our resources have evidently been sufficient to offset losses resulting from breakdowns in coordination, and we have missed outright disaster. But if the survival of this country should ever come to depend upon squeezing the utmost from our resources, and hence on reducing conflicting policies to a minimum, the stark alternatives would be failure—or a drastic change in the policy process.[36]

American parties are in the process of significant change. They are not necessarily declining, as some would maintain, but there is evidence that they are more decentralized than ever, especially at the state and local levels. At the essential level of policymaking, parties are having a difficult time coping with the pressures of a changing environment in which to make policy. For example, despite his successes in getting Congress to accept his tax and budget policies, Reagan as president found that the formal and informal mechanisms of governance, including political parties, have been unable to cope with a rising deficit threatening not only our own economy but that of the rest of the world. Are parties alone to blame for this? Of course not. But they *have* been an essential element in governance, and they presently seem unable to cope with the demands placed on them. Thus it is not possible to rest in fat-bellied complacency, composing hymns to the best of all possible party systems.

NOTES

[1]Anthony Howard, "The Greatest Sham on Earth?" *The Observer* (London, England), October 6, 1968.

[2]For analyses of party voting in Congress, see David Brady and Philip Althoff, "Party Voting in the U.S. House of Representatives, 1890–1910: Elements of a Responsible Party System," *Journal of Politics*, 36 (August 1974), 753–75; Julius Turner and Edward Schneier, *Party and Constituency: Pressures on Congress* (Baltimore: Johns Hopkins Press, 1970); Duncan MacRae, Jr., *Dimensions of Congressional Voting* (Berkeley: University of California Press, 1958); David Mayhew, *Party Loyalty Among Congressmen: The Difference Between Democrats and Republicans* (Cambridge, Mass,: Harvard University Press, 1966); David Truman, *The Congressional Party* (New York: Wiley, 1959).

[3]This discussion draws heavily on the encyclopedic study of the national conventions by Paul T. David et al., *The Politics of National Party Conventions* (Washington: The Brookings Institution, 1960). For a considerably more readable account of these matters see Nelson W. Polsby and Aaron B. Wildavsky, *Presidential Elections* (5th ed.; New York: Scribners, 1980).

[4]The polls have become a major element in the pre-convention action. Like the primaries, they are especially important to the "outside" contender, in that they provide a potential lever for demonstrating that he is more likely to win election than is the frontrunner. New York Governor Nelson Rockefeller's 1968 nomination efforts put particular emphasis on poll ratings. Another modern development appears to be the publicized running tallies of delegate strength calculated by the news media during the period of delegate selection. These tallies provide politicians with advance information on relative candidate strength—information that in the past had to be established in the early convention balloting. In general the standard account of how presidents emerge neglects the importance of the press in contributing to the informal processes of consensus through which certain political figures become widely thought of as "available" presidential (and vice-presidential) candidates and certain others do not achieve this status. For a perceptive set of comments by a Washington correspondent see David S. Broder, "Political Reporters in Presidential Politics," *The Washington Monthly*, 1 (February 1969), p. 20–33. An especially useful compendium on the polls is the special issue of *Public Opinion Quarterly*, 44 (Winter, 1980) on "Polls and the News Media: A Symposium." Of particular interest in regard to the present discussion is, in that issue, C. Anthony Broh, "Horse-Race Journalism: Reporting the Polls in the 1976 Presidential Election," 514–29.

[5]In part this resulted from the Democratic party rule, abolished in 1936, which required a two-thirds majority for nomination. Nevertheless, the Republicans, who had no such rule, also had conventions that went into numerous ballots.

[6]Herbert McClosky et al., "Issue Conflict and Consensus among Party Leaders and Followers," *American Political Science Review*, 54 (June 1960), 406–427; John S. Jackson, III, Barbara Leavitt Brown, and David Bositis, "Herbert McClosky and Friends Revisited: 1980, Democratic and Republican Party Elites Compared to the Mass Public," *American Politics Quarterly*, 10 (April 1982), 158–80.

[7]The reader should review Fig. 3-2, which provides an elegant visual impression of the strategic requirements for Republican electoral success.

[8]Shortly before the Republican party gave its 1968 nomination to the man most preferred by national samples of Republican voters, Richard Nixon, the Gallup poll made the following statement regarding its findings since the period of the first national surveys: "The favorite candidate of the Republican rank-and-file in final preconvention polls has turned out to be the choice of the convention in all Presidential races since 1936, *with the exception of 1964.*" AIPO release, July 27, 1968, italics added. It is possible here to sketch only in a general way the events of the 1964 election, in which the Republican candidate polled only 38.7 per cent of the popular vote. See the following works and the further sources there indicated: Milton C. Cummings, Jr., ed., *The National Election of 1964* (Washington, D.C.: The Brookings Institution, 1966); John H. Kessel, *The Goldwater Coalition: Republican Strategies in 1964* (Indianapolis, Bobbs-Merrill, 1968); Bernard Cosman and Robert J. Huckshorn, *Republican Politics: The 1964 Campaign and Its Aftermath for the Party* (New York: Praeger, 1968).

[9]In 1964, many voters actually formed the impression that Senator Goldwater would abolish Social Security benefits. The Senator denied that this was his intention, but in general appears not to have been successful in repairing this and other negative aspects of his "image." See Angus Campbell, "Interpreting the Presidential Victory," in Cummings., *ibid.*, pp. 256–82.

[10]This assertion is much more applicable to New York, and Pennsylvania and Texas than to the less traditionally urbanized state of California. For an introduction to the complexities of voting in the Golden State see Raymond E. Wolfinger and Fred I. Greenstein, "Comparing Political Regions: The Case of California," *American Political Science Review*, 63 (March 1969), 74–85.

[11]*Guide to U.S. Elections* (Washington: Congressional Quarterly, Inc., 1975), p. 171; *Guide to 1976 Elections* (Washington: Congressional Quarterly, Inc., 1977), p. 15; *Congressional Quarterly Weekly Report*, 38 (July 19, 1980), 2067. See also Charles O. Jones, "Nominating "Carter's Favorite Opponent": The Republicans in 1980." in Austin Ranney (ed.), *The American Elections of 1980* (Washington: American Enterprise Institute, 1981), pp 61–98.

[12]In 1968, the Republican convention nominated Richard Nixon on the first ballot with 692 votes to 277 for Nelson Rockefeller and only 182 for the most explicitly conservative option, Governor Ronald Reagan of California. Nixon managed to achieve election without winning several of the big-city, industrial states—notably New York, Pennsylvania, and Michigan—but under the exceptional circumstances of a major Democratic factional division over foreign policy.

[13]The presidential and congressional parties must be thought of as overlapping, rather than mutually exclusive.

[14]The national chairs of the parties, since they are traditionally appointed by the presidential candidate, usually tend to be aligned with presidential-party politicians, even when they happen to be members of Congress. For useful accounts of the increasing role of national party officials see Hugh A. Bone, *Party Committees and National Politics* (Seattle: University of Washington Press, 1958), and Cornelius Cotter and Bernard Hennessy, *Politics without Power* (New York: Atherton Press, 1964).

[15]For a fuller discussion of the topics considered in this chapter, see Nelson W. Polsby, *Congress and the Presidency* (3rd ed.; Englewood Cliffs, N.J.: Prentice-Hall, 1976). See also Robert L. Peabody, *Leadership in Congress: Stability, Succession, and Change* (Boston: Little, Brown, 1976).

[16]Raymond E. Wolfinger and Joan Heifetz, "Safe Seats, Seniority, and Power in Congress," *American Political Science Review*, 59 (June 1965), 337–49; Barbara Hinckley, *The Seniority System in Congress* (Bloomington: Indiana University Press, 1971) and "Seniority in 1975: Old Theories Confront New Facts," *British Journal of Political Science*, 6 (October 1976), 383–99.

[17]And the 1964 nomination of a Texan—Lyndon B. Johnson—was of an incumbent, who had taken office via the vice-presidency. One of Johnson's first actions on replacing the assassinated Kennedy was to assert the priority of Kennedy legislation designed to guarantee black voting rights. No single act could have better symbolized his declaration of independence from the southern wing of his party. President Carter, who had served as a racially moderate governor of Georgia, 1971–1974, had significant black support in his 1976 bid for the nomination and then election. It may or may not be instructive to note that the only southern state he carried in 1980 was Georgia. Although he was clearly not of the older southern mold of Democrats, there were clearly many other issues in the campaign besides this.

[18]See Truman, *The Congressional Party*, p. 305.

[19]Committee chairmanships are held by the majority party member with greatest seniority on a committee. Ordinarily, a president will receive greater cooperation from chairs when the President's own party has a majority in Congress. Because of the vagaries of the seniority system, this is not invariably true. When the Republicans lost control of Congress in 1954, President Eisenhower's proposals were better received by certain of the southern Democratic chairs than they had been by chairs of his own party.

[20]The chair is also influential after his or her chamber has passed a bill. Traditionally the chair selects the members from his or her house for the conference committees which compromise the Senate and House versions of bills. At the conference stage there is leeway for revising legislation further or for killing it by refusing to agree. Conference reports may be accepted or rejected—but not amended—by the House or Senate.

[21]For documentation and a fuller discussion see Angus Campbell, "Surge and Decline: A Study of Electoral Change," *Public Opinion Quarterly*, 24 (Fall 1960), 397–418, reprinted in Angus Campbell et al., *Elections and the Political Order* (New York: Wiley, 1966), pp. 40–62.

[22]Richard A. Watson, "The Tariff Revolution: A Study of Shifting Party Attitudes," *Journal of Politics*, 18 (November, 1956), 678–701. The present account draws heavily on *New York Times* reports. The reader should also consult the important study of foreign-trade politics by Raymond Bauer, Ithiel de Sola Pool, and Lewis A. Dexter, *American Business and Public Policy* (New York: Atherton Press, 1963).

[23]This sentence was written for the first (1963) edition of the present work. Six years later the Washington correspondent of a knowledgeable British periodical wrote an account of a meeting between the same Ways and Means chairman (Wilbur Mills of Arkansas) and President-elect Nixon, and headed it with a similar allusion to international diplomacy: "Two-Power Meeting." (*The Economist*, January 4, 1969.) The *Economist's* correspondent observed:

"President Kennedy once visited Mr. Wilbur Mills' home state of Arkansas because Mr. Mills asked him to. A President from New England was humoring the most powerful of the southern barons in Congress. In contrast President Johnson said in November, 1967, that Mr. Mills, Chair of the Ways and Means Committee of the House of Representatives, would rue the day that he decided to obstruct the Administation's proposed surcharge on income taxes. But in the end it was Mr. Johnson who rued the day; he got the surcharge, but only by conceding a cut of $6 billion in the federal government's spending. The lesson has not been lost on the incoming President, Mr. Richard Nixon. He has already made a point of consulting Mr. Mills about his two chief taxation proposals. . . . " See also John F. Manley, "Wilbur D. Mills: A Study in Congressional Influence," *American Political Science Review,* 63 (June 1969), 442–64. Congressman Mills had a highly publicized incident with a striptease dancer in October 1974, but he won re-election comfortably four weeks later. Following another such incident, he resigned his chairmanship and served out his term, retiring from government service at the end of the 1975–1976 session.

[24]Many Republicans were opposed to the act in any form, but the Republican leaders evidently favored a watered-down version of the bill, which they hoped would emerge from a House-Senate conference. If the bill had been defeated in the House, however, chances of Senate passage would have been reduced.

[25]*New York Times,* September 23, 1962, Section 4.

[26]Larry Sabato, "Parties, PACs, and Independent Groups," in Thomas E. Mann and Norman J. Ornstein (eds.), *The American Elections of 1982* (Washington: American Enterprise Institute, 1983), pp. 86–87.

[27]Frank J. Sorauf, "Accountability in Political Action Committees: Who's in Charge?" paper prepared for delivery at the annual meeting of the American Political Science Association, Denver, September 2–5, 1982, p. 27.

[28]Among the better-known criticisms of the party system are E. E. Schattschneider, *Party Government* (New York: Rinehart, 1942); Committee on Political Parties of the American Political Science Association, *Toward a More Responsible Two-Party System* (New York: Rinehart, 1950); Stephen K. Bailey, *The Condition of Our National Political Parties* (New York: The Fund for the Republic, 1959); James MacGregor Burns, *The Deadlock of Democracy* (Englewood Cliffs, N.J.: Prentice-Hall, rev. Spectrum ed., 1963). See also David Broder, *The Party's Over* (New York: Harper, 1972) and William J. Crotty, *American Parties in Decline* (2nd ed.; Boston: Little, Brown, 1984).

[29]But not all defenders avoid these points. Since the critical view so often holds that the American parties should be more like those in Great Britain—that is, ideologically distinct from each other and capable of commanding the support of all of their elected officials— Professor J. Roland Pennock chose to compare British and American agricultural policies in some detail. Here, he reasoned, was a prototypical area in which the critics' theories held that the decentralized, undisciplined American parties failed to make coherent policies—and to reflect majority needs—because of congressional vulnerability to the special pleading of often quite small, economically unsound producer groups. His conclusion was that British agriculture was if anything *more* highly subsidized than American agriculture and that the main consequence of party discipline was to compel Members of Parliament of both parties to yield to their leaders' calculation that it would be too politically damaging not to subsidize the farmers. J. Roland Pennock, "'Responsible Government,' Separated Powers, and Special Interests; Agricultural Subsidies in Britain and America," *American Political Science Review* 56 (September 1962), 621–33. Also see Kenneth N. Waltz's attempt to compare the performance of the British and American political systems in a number of spheres—*Foreign Policy and Democratic Politics: The American and British Experience* (Boston: Little, Brown, 1967), especially pp. 19–35.

[30]Herbert Agar, *The Price of Union* (Boston: Houghton Mifflin, 1950). Defenses of the party system include Pendleton Herring, *The Politics of Democracy* (New York: Norton, 1940); Julius Turner, "Responsible Parties: A Dissent from the Floor," *American Political Science Review,* 45 (March 1951), 143–52; Austin Ranney, "Toward A More Responsible Two-Party System: A Commentary," *American Political Science Review,* 45 (June 1951), 488–99; Austin Ranney and Willmoore Kendall, *Democracy and the American Party System* (New York: Harcourt, Brace, 1956); Gerald Pomper, "Toward a More Responsible Two-Party System? What, Again?" *Journal of Politics,* 33 (November 1971), 916–40.

[31]Ranney and Kendall, *Democracy and the American Party System,* p. 508.

[32]Bailey, *The Condition of Our National Political Parties*, p. 5.

[33]Philip Converse and Georges Dupeux, "Politicization of the Electorate in France and the United States," *Public Opinion Quarterly*, 26 (Spring 1962), 1–23, reprinted in Angus Campbell et al., *Elections and the Political Order*, pp. 269–91. Also see the findings on lack of ideological cleavage among British voters (in spite of seemingly clear-cut policy differences between Britain's disciplined Labour and Conservative parties) in David Butler and Donald E. Stokes, *Political Change in Britain* (New York: St. Martin's Press, 1969).

[34]See Hugh Davis Graham and Ted Robert Gurr, eds., *Violence in America: Historical and Comparative Perspectives*, A Report to the National Commission on the Causes and Prevention of Violence, 2 vols. (Washington, D.C.: U.S. Government Printing Office, 1969), and James F. Kirkham, Sheldon G. Levy and William J. Crotty, *Assassination and Political Violence*, A Report to the National Commission on the Causes and Prevention of Violence (Washington, D.C.: U.S. Government Printing Office, 1969). On the alternation between moderate and severe conflict in American political history, see Robert A. Dahl, *Pluralistic Democracy in the United States* (3d ed.; Chicago, Rand McNally, 1976), especially Chs. 23–27.

[35]See note 27.

[36]Robert A. Dahl and Charles E. Lindblom, *Politics, Economics and Welfare* (New York: Harper, 1953), p. 348. See in general their discussion of bargaining, pp. 324–65.

chapter 7 _____

_____ A CONCLUDING NOTE

This analysis began with a sweeping question: "What does the American party system do for Americans?" Have the parties contributed usefully to life in the United States, or have they been neutral—or negative—in their effect? These questions having been raised, it was immediately necessary to descend to a more terrestrial perspective. In order to narrow the focus of our inquiry, the global query about the uses of the parties to Americans was divided into three more circumscribed but still reasonably sweeping questions asking how—if at all—the parties have contributed to democracy, political stability, and the "adequacy" of governmental policy-making.

In asking these questions, we were not operating in a vacuum, since parties must exist in an environment of public opinion as well as sustain challenges by other institutions to the performance of their traditional roles. In addition to the popular cynicism about parties which we have shown, there has also been a view which is increasingly held in both the popular press and in the scholarly community—that political parties may not ever have been very useful, but are certainly not of any use today.

In the face of such criticisms, we have sought to provide some provisional answers to our three questions. We stress that these are provisional, for the answers will change as the parties continue to change, along with public attitudes about the parties and government. The tentative answers at which we have arrived have been based upon certain aspects of partisanship in four political arenas:

(1)   At the level of *electoral partisanship,* we have noted the group constituencies of the parties and the effects of voters' party identifications on their voting behavior, placing the findings of contemporary voting research, which have shown changing answers to these questions, in the context of evidence about the citizen base of the political system.

(2)   At the *local* level, we have considered the activities of old-style party organizations, comparing them with two alternative patterns of urban politics—the politics of nonpartisanship and that of the issue-oriented amateur politicians who are increasingly evident at the local and higher levels.

(3)   At the *state* level, we spread before us an array of the party and non-party systems that have from time to time characterized various American states— the politics of multifactionalism in the one-party states and two types of two-party state politics.

(4)   At the *national* level, we have considered the perennial pushing and pulling between the presidential and congressional wings of the two major parties. This is taking place increasingly in a context which emphasizes non-party— some would say anti-party—politics.

As was stressed in Chapter 1, this introductory discussion cannot claim to provide a definitive assessment of the party system. In each of the four arenas, we have done no more than consider selective constellations of evidence especially relevant to illuminating how well (or badly) the parties perform in terms of our three evaluative criteria. Although the most recent available research evidence has been considered, it is in the nature of intellectual inquiry that "final" evidence is never available—one question always leads to another. Furthermore, the three evaluative criteria are not exhaustive, and would have to be submitted to far more extensive logical clarification than is possible here, if they were to be applied in a fully conclusive manner. To add a final caveat to this already formidable list, we must also note that some of the assertions we have been making are of a sort that does not in principle admit of certainty: the closer we approach to very broad, comprehensive evaluative judgments—that is, the more we move from judgments concerning, say, whether the Ford has a greater acceleration capacity than the Chevrolet, to judgments about whether the automobile has been a Good Thing for Civilization—the more our assertions must be treated as "mere" opinion.

A full statement of the qualifications applicable to every statement in each chapter would have proved a burdensome distraction from the thread of the argument. The kinds of qualifications most needed have been stated—namely, qualifications resulting from the gaps and inconsistencies in the presently available research findings. As of this writing, for example, there has not yet been a sufficiently clear and comprehensive analysis of the effects of party competition at the state level on the kinds of policies that are made by state governments. But there is less need to qualify the more general assertions—those that weave specific findings into larger interpretations of institutional functioning and, especially, those that reach overall judgments about the functions of the parties—simply because the reader should realize that *of necessity* these are bound to be speculative observations. The reader's task is to perfect his or her own standards for weighing, making, and defending such assertions.

Although the conclusions of this work must be treated as hypotheses rather than eternal verities, the importance in itself of explicitly stating one's hypotheses and other intellectual assumptions cannot be overestimated. The prime reason for stating hypotheses is to guide research. By stating our hunches as explicitly as possible we make possible further inquiry that can lead to their acceptance, rejection, or reformulation. Even if one is not directly involved in contributing to knowledge, explicitly stated hypotheses serve to sharpen one's newspaper reading and to help guide one's personal political participation. They provide a basis for making sense of the day-to-day flux of events, distinguishing the significant from the trivial.

THE PARTIES AND POLICY-MAKING

As we noted in the introductory chapter, the criterion "adequacy of policy-making," although vague, is a convenient piece of shorthand pointing to the variety of more specific questions that can be asked about the effects of the parties on the policy-making process and on the policies that emerge from it. The standard assumption is that parties make their contribution to policy-making by unifying governments—that is, by filling the major public offices with members of a team of like-minded partisans. In a system of separated powers, as in the American federal, state, and (frequently) municipal governments, there are legal provisions making the legislative and executive branches independent of each other, but preventing policy-making without their cooperation. Therefore, it would seem especially desirable for American parties to perform the task of unifying government.

Parties *do* sometimes serve as the unifiers of American governments. We saw how city machines were able to unite fragmented governments, thus meeting needs generated by urbanization and industrial expansion. And in states like Connecticut, parties sometimes have been able to transform party programs into public policy, by uniting the governor and the two houses of the legislature around a common program.

But frequently it is not possible for teams of partisans to unify the various components of American governments in order to make policy. In the competitive two-party states, the leadership "teams" often consist of members of opposing parties. In Washington, the same party ordinarily (i.e., about two-thirds of the time) controls both houses of Congress and the presidency. But the constituencies of the presidential and congressional wings of the parties are sufficiently different to preclude automatic cooperation between the branches.

Even when parties fail to unite the separated powers, they may nevertheless contribute to the making of policies. In Connecticut, during the period studied by Lockard, when there was divided control, the leaders of the two unified parties bargained with each other to accomplish certain of their policy ends. Lockard felt that the closely competitive nature of the state's electoral situation stimulated the leaders of both parties to seek an appealing record of accomplishments. Even at the federal level, where parties are much less united than in Connecticut, party is a vital element in the policy-making process. Our case study of Kennedy's successful campaign for trade-expansion legislation illustrated the typical state of affairs nationally: the president was able to begin with the support of a sizable bloc of members of his own party, and use this as a basis for the bargaining that enabled him to assemble a majority coalition.

The requirements of coalition-building in the United States have produced a class of gifted political mediators, experts at reconciling the irreconcilable. From Henry Clay—the Great Compromiser—through such twentieth-century figures as Sam Rayburn and Everett McKinley Dirksen, a political system studded with opportunities for minority veto of policies has called forth those who were expert at accommodating to the often inconsistent demands of countless minorities. The American politician, as A. Lawrence Lowell put it, "attempts . . . to conciliate all classes and delights in such language as 'a tariff for revenue only, so adjusted as to protect American industries.'"[1] Through such inspired ambiguities, politicians regularly strive to mix oil and water, to placate free-trader and protectionist, producer and consumer, management and labor.

The gauntlet set up by the veto groups in American politics delays policy-making. A program that impinges on many group interests—for example, road and highway redevelopment—will be held up for years, because the laborious work of assembling a successful coalition has not been completed. In the meanwhile, the nation fails to profit from desirable improvements. Or far worse, situations that might once have responded to modest remedial action became exacerbated and increasingly difficult to manage. Here, the obvious illustration is the cluster of urban malaises connected with unemployment, housing, transportation, and racial discrimination and conflict.

The patchwork policies that finally emerge from the American bargaining process—if they are not too little and too late—stand a good chance of remaining in force, by virtue of the bipartisan support they need in order to be adopted. Steel nationalization in Great Britain provides the standard example of the way in which unified, ideologically distinct parties can generate unstable policies. Nationalization of the steel industry was carried out in 1951 by a Labour government; the industry was denationalized when the Conservatives returned to power in 1953, only to be renationalized in the 1960s, when Labour was back in office. A similar example is the politics of secondary education in Britain at the time of this writing. The official Labour party view is that Britain's secondary schools should be more like American high schools, in that each school should strive to educate the full range of adolescents in the population. The Conservatives, on the other hand, favor continuing the present arrangements, under which the more promising students are selected at the age of eleven for special university-preparatory programs. Britain's local educational authorities face the dilemma of deciding whether to accede to the conservative government's pressure to continue the kinds of schools favored by the Conservatives, knowing, as they do, that there is a good chance that the next Labour government may reverse educational policies.[2]

THE PARTIES AND POLITICAL STABILITY

By now it should be clear that the distinctions between our three evaluative criteria are analytic: in the "real world," democracy, stability, and effective policy-making are closely interdependent. The experience of many new nations, and some older ones (such as France), points to the ways that internal instability can threaten democracy. The reverse of this causal sequence also can occur. In 1983, the assassination of a popular opposition leader in the Philippines unleashed a long period of political protest, both violent and nonviolent. Together with the assassination, the damming up of conventional channels of democratic expression appeared to be the major determinants of the unrest. To the degree that democratic practices are accepted as legitimate and that institutional channels for expressing and resolving conflicts are available, a nation is likely to produce leaders whose frames of reference simply do not recognize violence as an acceptable way of deciding who is to rule.[3]

Of the various permutations and combinations of ways that our three criteria can act upon one another, a particularly important though elusive connection is that between effectiveness of policy-making and stability. Consider the instability which would result if a nation were deadlocked for very long in the way that Michigan was deadlocked in 1959. Sooner or later the temptation to abandon constitutional procedures and turn to less gentle means of conflict resolution would be irresistible. Consequently, the familiar political flexibility of the typical national figures in American politics—their willingness to compromise their differences—contributes to political stability as well as to policy-making. V. O. Key quotes the politician who, after presenting his beliefs to his constituents, commented: "I have outlined my views without equivocation and those views will be my continued views unless the people at meetings and through cards and letters give evidence of the voters' opposition."[4] Assertions such as these provide an easy mark for ridicule. Inflexible politicians are less laughable, but also more difficult to live with.

But what if members of the electorate systematically fail to make their views known? One shortcoming of American party politicians, with their keen sensitivities to group pressures, is their tendency to neglect making needed policies if group pressures are not forthcoming. We have noted that the stimulus of party competition motivates politicians to anticipate—not merely respond to—group demands. But the parties are not competitive in all American political jurisdictions, and even where they are—as at the national level—politicians sometimes find sufficient employment in balancing and representing the groups that actually press their demands, without being solicitous of other groups. As Robert A. Dahl puts it, the political

> system makes it easy for political leaders to ignore groups of people whose problems lie outside the attention, loyalties, values and identifications of the great mass of voters, particularly if these groups lack bargaining power because of poor organization, low status, isolation, ignorance, lack of political incentives, and so on.[5]

And if unorganized groups—such as migrant workers, southern sharecoppers, and, at least until recently, a large proportion of the nation's black citizens—are unable to take the actions likely to elicit rewards from politicians, the members of these groups are likely to experience worsened conditions, at least relative to those of the rest of the population. When these unorganized citizens finally *do* express themselves—stirred by their deprived circumstances, unmellowed by previous experience with the normal political processes—their actions are not likely to contribute to political stability, at least not in the short run. The long-run consequences are more obscure, since violent upheavals sometimes may serve as a stimulus for reforms that have a stabilizing effect. At any rate, the presence of unorganized and deprived groups without an effective way of registering their views is a potential source of severe discontent with the political system.

THE PARTIES AND DEMOCRACY

The most satisfactory evidence presently available bearing on any of our three criteria relates to the effects of the parties on popular control of leaders. The parties do not, as we have just noted, enhance the political power of some of the more unorganized and deprived groups in American society. Nevertheless, in the research literature on voting and on state and local political systems there is considerable evidence pointing to the ways in which party systems offer the voter certain advantages over the various non-party alternatives.

In examining these research findings and their implications we began by considering what was described in Chapter 2 as a "photograph" of the citizen base of the political system. By way of illustration, a static presentation was made of data on levels of public political awareness and commitment to various democratic ground-rules. By implication, that chapter developed a direct-democracy model of popular control, stressing the importance of a politically competent, democratically competent citizenry, to the exclusion of other factors. We then used public-opinion data to show how far voters are from meeting the requirements of the model.

Fortunately, real-world democracy does not require that citizens control their leaders by carefully informing themselves on the issues of the day, inventing their own solutions to problems of public policy, and seeing to it that their solutions are adopted by government. Rather, there are institutions, the most important of which are political parties, which mediate between citizens and leaders. These institutions make it possible for the public, in spite of its seemingly limited resources for control of leaders, to have a profound effect on government.

Parties, as we saw in Chapter 3, aggregate voters into groups with roughly common interests. These interests of the voter groupings are loosely, but discernibly, linked with the policies advanced by groupings of politicians under the same party label. We saw, for example, that the socioeconomic groups at the heart of the Democratic constituency contain many citizens who profit from such policies as programs designed to alleviate urban distress. Among politicians, it is mainly the Democrats who strive to expand these programs.

A convergence of factors makes it possible for politician–constituency relations of this sort to operate, even in the absence of detailed scrutiny of the activities of politicians by the bulk of the electorate. Citizens vastly simplify their choice problems by holding a single, broad, "brand-label" preference—an identification with a party. Often little more than a fragmentary slogan is attached to the party preference—my party is "the party of economy and limited government"; mine is "the party of the common people." Nevertheless, since voters' party preferences are extremely stable and most voters are generally consistent in the party they vote for from election to election, politicians develop clear images of the groups supporting them. Therefore, they can be at pains to consolidate the support of their core constituents by meeting their expressed needs and by anticipating other possible needs. Nationally and in many state and local jurisdictions, neither party can count on sufficient votes from its regular supporters to win elections automatically, so there is a constant effort by the parties to meet the desires of other groups, whether the less committed supporters of the other party or individuals on the fence between the parties.

Paradoxically, by exercising much of the choice of who will be named to public office, parties *increase* the capacity of voters to control government. Party nominating procedures narrow down the number of candidates to two in most American general elections. Two candidates can be evaluated with relative ease by voters who are not professional students of politics, especially since each candidate is categorized in familiar terms by his party label. When the balance between supporters of the two parties is extremely close, we may expect the politicians to go to great efforts to select popular candidates.

Public control through the mediation of parties is complex and fallible. It falls short of civics-book standards of how public control should operate. Sometimes, even in the most competitive of party systems, questionable candidates are nominated and party politicians offer voters little more than a glorified shell game. Thus, on occasion, events seem to justify the argument that parties are more of a barrier than a link between public and government. Yet it has been instructive to consider the settings in which parties are not an important component of American politics—those communities where legal measures have been taken to eliminate the "barrier" and the multi-factional one-party states.

In both varieties of party-free politics voters seem to suffer. Electoral behavior more closely resembles the picture of voter irrationality and impotence presented in Chapter 2 than the conception of moderate voter rationality which emerged from our discussion in Chapter 3. Voters in the non-party systems are often exposed to a bewildering array of candidates about whom they know little. As a result, they rely on superficial criteria for choosing their leaders—the attractiveness of a candidate's name, or even his position on the ballot. In non partisan and multi-factional politics, the possibilities of successful protest against unsatisfactory governmental policies are limited by the difficulty of pinning responsibility on a team of "rascals" who might be thrown out of office. The absence of a governmental team also reduces the possibilities for cooperation between public officials in policy-making and therefore may frustrate the aspirations of groups seeking positive governmental policies that might alter the status quo.

IN CONCLUSION

On all three of our criteria, then, the American parties appear to make a substantial but far from "perfect" contribution. At a minimum, it is unlikely that effectiveness of policy-making, stability, and democracy would be better advanced if there were *no* American party system. Furthermore the *presently constituted* American party system makes contributions that do not readily meet the eye—a we saw, for example, when we compared nonpartisan with partisan politics.

Yet the balance sheet shows debits as well as credits. Rather than purring comfortably at the merits of the party system, the citizen would be advised to pitch in, participate, and attempt (in the light of his or her own values and preferences) to remedy the faults of the system. And for at least some small subgroup of the citizenry there is a further contribution to be made: more needs to be known about how the party system actually operates and what its consequences actually are. At a number of points in the preceding chapters, we have noted various continuing gaps in the available information about politics. Since appropriate political prescriptions are not likely to follow from inadequately informed descriptions, there is need for further recruits to the ranks of political science. They also serve who pause and analyze.

NOTES

[1]A. Lawrence Lowell, *Essays on Government* (Boston: Houghton Mifflin, 1897), p. 107.

[2]See the discussion of this dilemma in the *London Times Educational Supplement,* April 4, 1969. Also see *London Times,* February 5, 1970, p. 1.

[3]Note the universal expression of shock by the entire range of American politicians (as well as citizens) at the assassination of President Kennedy. Bradley S. Greenberg and Edward Parkers (eds.), *The Kennedy Assassination and the American Public: Social Communication in Crisis* (Stanford: Stanford University Press, 1965).

[4]V. O. Key, Jr., *Politics, Parties and Pressure Groups,* (4th ed.; New York: Crowell, 1958), p. 497n.

[5]Robert A. Dahl, "The American Oppositions: Affirmation and Denial," in Robert A. Dahl (ed.), *Political Oppositions in Western Democracies* (New Haven: Yale University Press, 1966), pp. 34–69 (quotation at p. 64). Dahl also remarks on two further shortcomings of the political (and by extension, party) system, both of them resulting from the considerable agreement among active politicians of both parties as to the nature and virtues of a variety of fundamental national institutions—agreement transcending the specify policy differences noted in Chapter 6. Such high levels of consensus, Dahl argues, contribute to a situation in which there is little fundamental critical examination of the functioning of the system; or at least little criticism that receives serious attention. Second, the minority of citizens who fall outside of the consensus—whether to the left or the right—are compelled "to choose between futility and the two-party politics of compromise, thereby increasing their sense of frustration and political alienation."

chapter 8 _____

_____ TO EXPLORE FURTHER

Our consideration of the American party system has dealt with selected aspects of electoral, local, state, and federal party politics. The topics discussed under these headings were chosen because they seemed especially well suited for illuminating how the party system contributes or fails to contribute to democracy, effective policy-making, and political stability. There has been no attempt to be "fully comprehensive" (whatever that might entail). Nevertheless, with the present discussion as a base, the student should find it possible to go on to a more general consideration of the nature of American party politics and the role of political parties in modern democracies. Some of the following suggested readings have been cited in the text of the book; others have not. The student who is seeking to launch a reading campaign should note both the relevant portions of this bibliographical essay and the footnotes to whatever chapters deal with the issues he or she proposes to explore further.

The contemporary literature on electoral behavior in the United States (and elsewhere) is largely an outgrowth of a technological innovation of the 1930s—the development of systematic public-opinion polling techniques. The recent development of the experiment as a means of measuring factors in voting and attitudes furthers the use of the questionnaire, borrowing somewhat from our colleagues in the related disciplines of psychology and social psychology. While this approach is beginning to bear intellectual fruit, there continue to be analyses of the behavior of the electorate based on census data and on the aggregate voting statistics for various political units, ranging from the precinct to the nation itself. However, the most reliable and intellectually productive insights into voting have come from very careful polling of the voters themselves. Three rather brief overall discussions of writings on electoral behavior and related issues are Donald E. Stoke's "Voting" in *International Encyclopedia of the Social Sciences,* vol. 16 (New York: Macmillan, 1968); David O. Sears' "Political Behavior" in Gardner Lindzey and Elliot Aronson, eds., *The Handbook of Social Psychology,* vol. 5 (2nd ed.; Reading, Mass.: Addison-Wesley, 1968); and Philip E. Converse's "Public Opinion and Voting Behavior" in Fred I. Greenstein and Nelson W. Polsby, eds., *Handbook of Political Science,* vol. 4 (Reading, Mass.: Addison-Wesley, 1975). All three contain extensive bibliographical references. In addition, see the very careful and clear short summary work by William H. Flanigan and Nancy H. Zingale, *Political Behavior of the American Electorate* (5th ed.; Boston: Allyn and Bacon, 1983), which makes extensive use of the priceless body of survey data on the American electorate that has been collected, beginning in 1948, by the University of Michigan Survey Research Center (and made available by the Center for Political Studies to the scholarly community for further analyses). Two of the many Survey Research Center (SRC) publications deserve special mention and should be studied by any serious student of electoral behavior— the magisterial general analysis in *The American Voter* by Angus Campbell et al. (New York: Wiley, 1960), and the collection of more specialized SRC studies, many of which attempt to link electoral behavior to the functioning of political institutions, in Campbell et al., *Elections and the Political Order* (New York: Wiley, 1966). For a critique of the SRC studies, see Norman Nie, "The Election Studies of the Survey Research Center," *British Journal of Political Science,* 1 (October 1971), 479–502. A major re-examination of these and other data, with some differing conclusions, can be found in Norman H. Nie et al., *The Changing American Voter* (enlgd. ed.; Cambridge: Harvard University Press, 1979). For an earlier but still profitable approach one might consult the pioneering research of Paul F. Lazarsfeld and Bernard Berelson and their associates, who conducted intensive studies of electoral behavior in single communities in the 1940 and 1948 elections. See especially Berelson et al., *Voting* (Chicago: University of Chicago Press, 1954).

Works on local politics and partisanship have become somewhat dated of late, perhaps reflecting a turn of scholars toward more visible subjects. For introductions, see James Q. Wilson, "Politics and Reform in American Cities," *American Government Annual, 1962–1963* (New York: Holt, Rinehart, 1962), pp. 37–52; Edward C. Banfield and James Q. Wilson, *City Politics* (Cambridge: Harvard University Press and M.I.T. Press, 1963); Herbert Kaufman, *Politics and Policies in State and Local Governments* (Englewood Cliffs, N.J.: Prentice-Hall, 1963); and Philip M. Hauser and Leo F. Schnore, eds., *The Study of Urbanization* (New York:

Wiley, 1965), especially Wallace S. Sayre and Nelson W. Polsby's "American Political Science and the Study of Urbanization," pp. 115–56. An instructive essay, notable for its extensive bibliography, is Robert C. Fried's "Comparative Urban Policy and Performance," in Fred I. Greenstein and Nelson W. Polsby, eds., *Handbook of Political Science*, vol. 6 (Reading, Mass.: Addison-Wesley, 1975). Among the studies of individual cities that transcend their locale of investigation are Wallace S. Sayre and Herbert Kaufman's *Governing New York City* (New York: Russell Sage Foundation, 1960), and Robert Dahl's *Who Governs?* (New Haven: Yale University Press, 1961). Another important study which focuses on aspects of community power such as those raised by Dahl is Robert E. Agger et al., *The Rulers and the Ruled* (New York: Wiley, 1964). For interesting analyses of a number of local political systems and their handling of controversial issues, see James S. Coleman, *Community Conflict* (Glencoe, Ill.: Free Press, 1957) and Robert L. Crain et al., *The Politics of Community Conflict* (Indianapolis: Bobbs-Merrill, 1969). For a report on boss politics as it once flourished, see William L. Riordon, *Plunkitt of Tammany Hall* (Garden City, N.Y.: Doubleday, 1963). More recent reports on the former Daley machine of Chicago are Mike Royko's *Boss: Richard Daley of Chicago* (New York: Dutton, 1971); Milton Rakove's *Don't Make No Waves . . . Don't Back No Losers* (Bloomington: Indiana University Press, 1975); and Thomas M. Guterbock, *Machine Politics in Transition: Party and Community in Chicago* (Chicago: University of Chicago Press, 1980). Of use for the wide number of topics considered, see Lee S. Greene, ed., "City Bosses and Political Machines," *The Annals of the American Academy of Political and Social Sciences*, 353 (May 1964). Also see William J. Crotty (ed.), *Approaches to the Study of Party Organization* (Boston: Allyn and Bacon, 1968), William E. Wright, *A Comparative Study of Party Organization* (Columbus, Ohio: Merrill, 1971), and the insightful article by Raymond E. Wolfinger, "Why Political Machines Have Not Withered Away and Other Revisionist Thoughts," *Journal of Politics*, 34 (May 1972), 365–98. An instructive work on patronage is Martin and Susan Tolchin's *To the Victor: Political Patronage from the Clubhouse to the White House* (New York: Random House Vintage Books, 1971).

As suggested in Chapter 5, the most influential of the studies of state party systems has been V. O. Key, Jr.'s *Southern Politics* (New York: Knopf, 1949). Although not the first study of state parties, it probably was the first to raise questions of theoretical interest which were then pursued by other scholars—for example, William C. Havard (ed.), *The Changing Politics of the South* (Baton Rouge: Louisiana State University Press, 1972). Much of the very extensive subsequent literature on individual states builds, as does Havard's volume, on *Southern Politics* and, to a lesser extent, on Key's *American State Politics* (New York: Knopf, 1956). Useful views on state parties in general can be found in Malcolm E. Jewell and David M. Olson's *American State Parties and Elections* (rev. ed.; Homewood, Ill.: Dorsey, 1982), and Robert J. Huckshorn's *Party Leadership in the States* (Amherst: University of Massachusetts Press, 1976). Some interesting collections on state politics and parties are James W. Fesler, (ed.), *The 50 States and Their Local Governments* (New York: Knopf, 1967); Virginia Gray, Herbert Jacob, and Kenneth Vines, (eds.), *Politics in the Ameican States: A Comparative Analysis* (4th ed.; Boston: Little, Brown, 1983); and Frank J. Munger, (ed.), *American State Politics: Readings for Comparative Analysis* (New York: Crowell, 1966). Of special interest for scope as well as commonality of approach is the series of volumes by Neal R. Pearce, all published by Norton (New York). Individual volumes include *The Deep South States of America* (1974); *The Mountain States of America* (1972); *The Border South States of America* (1975); *The New England States* (1976); (with Michael Barone) *The Mid-Atlantic States of America* (1976); (with John Keefe) *The Great Lakes States of America*; and *Megastates of America* (1972). Also see such studies of individual states and groups of states as Numan V. Bartley and H. D. Graham, *Southern Politics and the Second Reconstruction* (Baltimore: Johns Hopkins University Press, 1975) and Bartley's *From Thurmond to Wallace: Political Tendencies in Georgia, 1948–1968* (Baltimore, Md.: Johns Hopkins University Press, 1970); Jack Bass and Walter DeVries, *The Transformation of Southern Politics* (New York: Basic Books, 1976); Louis M. Seagull, *Southern Republicanism* (New York: Wiley, 1975); Duane Lockard, *New England State Politics* (Princeton, N.J.: Princeton University Press, 1959); Leon Epstein, *Politics in Wisconsin* (Madison: University of Wisconsin Press, 1958); Allan P. Sindler, *Huey Long's Lousiana* (Baltimore: Johns Hopkins Press, 1956); Jack D. Fleer, *North Carolina Politics: An Introduction* (Chapel Hill: University of North Carolina Press, 1968); John H. Fenton, *Midwest Politics* (New York: Holt, Rinehart, 1966); Edgar Litt, *The Political Cultures of Massachusetts* (Cambridge, Mass.: M.I.T. Press, 1965); Jack E. Holmes, *Politics in New Mexico* (Albuquerque, N.M.: University of New Mexico Press, 1967); and Malcolm E. Jewell and Everett W. Cunningham, *Kentucky Politics* (Lexington: University of Kentucky Press, 1968). For two very interesting studies, see the analysis of the Wisconsin political system in terms of that state's party finance practices by David Adamany in his *Financing Politics* (Madison: University of Wisconsin Press, 1969), and the broad investigation of the career patterns of state politicians by Joseph Schlesinger in his *Ambition and Politics: Political Careers in the United States* (Chicago: Rand McNally, 1966). One work which makes a case for the point of view that parties make a difference is Sarah McCally Morehouse, *State Politics, Parties and Policy* (New York: Holt, Rinehart and Winston, 1980).

Not all aspects of national-level party politics are equally represented in published works. For example, of the many books on the presidency, none considers in systematic detail the president's partisan role both in national policy-making and in the nation. Some overall sense of this emerges in Peter H. Odegard's "Presidential Leadership and Party Responsibility,"

The Annals of the American Academy of Political and Social Science, 207 (September 1956), 66–81. In this light, Gerald Pomper responded to the point of view advanced by President Nixon that the presidency should be "above politics." See his "Nixon and the End of Presidential Politics," *Transaction* 10 (March/April 1973), 14–16. A useful essay on the beginnings of this problem and its present state is Thomas E. Cronin, "The Presidency and the Parties," in Gerald M. Pomper, ed., *Party Renewal in America* (New York: Praeger, 1980), pp. 176–93. The partisan procedures that lead to the selection of presidents have received increasing attention. A useful start on this literature is the painstaking and extensive account of nominating politics past and present in Paul David et al., *The Politics of National Party Conventions* (Washington: The Brookings Institution, 1960); the supporting volume by Richard C. Bain, *Convention Decisions and Voting Records* (Washington: The Brookings Institution, 1960); and the updated volume of the same name, authored by Judith N. Parris and Richard C. Bain (Washington: The Brookings Institution, 1973). For more accessible accounts see Nelson W. Polsby and Aaron B. Wildavsky, *Presidential Elections: Strategies of American Electoral Politics* (5th ed.; New York: Scribner's, 1980) and Donald R. Matthews, ed., *Perspectives on Presidential Selection* (Washington: The Brookings Institution, 1973); James W. Ceaser, *Presidential Selection: Theory and Practice* (Princeton, N.J.: Princeton University Press, 1979); Caesar's *Reforming the Reforms: A Critical Analysis of the Presidential Selection Process* (Cambridge, Mass.: Ballinger, 1982); and Stephen J. Wayne, *The Road to the White House: The Politics of Presidential Elections* (2nd ed.; New York: St. Martin's, 1984). Also see such specialized works as James W. Davis, *Presidential Primaries* (New York: Crowell, 1967); William Keech and Donald R. Matthews, *The Party's Choice* (Washington, D.C.: The Brookings Institution, 1976); Austin Ranney, *The Federalization of Presidential Primaries* (Washington, D.C.: American Enterprise Institute, 1978); Judith N. Parris, *The Convention Problem: Issues in Reform of Presidential Nominating Procedures* (Washington, D.C.: The Brookings Institution, 1972); Denis G. Sullivan et al., *The Politics of Representation: The Democratic Convention 1972* (New York: St. Martin's, 1974); Denis G. Sullivan et al., *Exploration in Convention Decision Making: The Democratic Party in the 1970s* (San Francisco: Freeman, 1976); and James David Barber, (ed.), *Race for the Presidency: The Media and the Nominating Process* (Englewood Cliffs, N.J.: Prentice-Hall, 1978).

Although it has often been argued that cross-party alliances are of greater significance than partisanship in Congress, the various studies of congressional roll-call voting leave a quite different impression. See, for example, Julius Turner and Edward V. Schneier, *Party and Constituency: Pressures on Congress* (rev. ed.; Baltimore, Md.: Johns Hopkins University Press, 1970); Duncan MacRae, Jr., *Dimensions of Congressional Voting* (Berkeley: University of California Press, 1958); David Truman, *The Congressional*

Party (New York: Wiley, 1959); David R. Mayhew, *Party Loyalty Among Congressmen* (Cambridge, Mass.: Harvard University Press, 1966); Aage R. Clausen, *How Congressmen Decide: A Policy Focus* (New York: St. Martin's, 1973); and Cleo H. Cherryholmes and Michael J. Shapiro, *Representatives and Roll-Calls* (Indianapolis: Bobbs-Merrill, 1969). For a valuable general guide to earlier literature on all aspects of congressional partisanship see Charles O. Jones and Randall B. Ripley, *The Role of Political Parties in Congress: A Bibliography and Research Guide* (Tucson: Institute of Government Research and the University of Arizona Press, 1966). Ripley has also contributed two studies of special interest in this regard. See his *Party Leaders in the House of Representatives* (Washington, D.C.: The Brookings Institution, 1967) and *Power in the Senate* (New York: St. Martin's, 1969). Also see Robert L. Peabody, *Leadership in Congress: Stability, Succession, and Change* (Boston: Little, Brown, 1976); Lewis A. Froman, Jr., *The Congressional Process: Strategies, Rules, and Procedures* (Boston: Little, Brown, 1967). A Study which explores an important relationship is Aage R. Clausen, "State Party Influence on Congressional Party Decision," *Midwest Journal of Political Science*, 16 (February 1972), 77–101.

The financing of our national parties has been a subject of increasing concern, which has not abated with the advent of public financing of presidential elections. The most encyclopedic accounts of the financing problem are by Herbert E. Alexander, and of these the most recent are his *Financing the 1980 Election* (Lexington, Mass.: Lexington Books, 1983); *Financing the 1976 Election* (Washington, D.C.: Congressional Quarterly, Inc., 1979); *Financing the 1972 Election* (Lexington, Mass.: Lexington Books, D.C. Heath, 1979); and *Financing the 1968 Election* (Lexington, Mass.: Lexington Books, D.C. Heath, 1971). A recent short overview is provided in his *Financing Elections: Money, Elections, and Political Reform* (3rd ed.; Washington: Congressional Quarterly, Inc., 1984). Two works edited by Michael Malbin provide current views on selected aspects of the topic. These are his *Money and Politics: Financing Elections in the 1980s* (Chatham, N.J.: American Enterprise Institute and Chatham House, 1984) and *Parties, Interest Groups, and Campaign Finance Laws* (Washington, D.C.: American Enterprise Institute, 1980). Although dated, the nature of the problem is also well expressed in Alexander Heard's *The Costs of Democracy* (Chapel Hill: University of North Carolina Press, 1960). Two proposals for change are Lawrence Gitelson, *Money and Secrecy: A Citizen's Guide to Reforming State and Federal Practices* (New York: Praeger, 1972), and David W. Adamany and George E. Agree, *Political Money: A Strategy for Campaign Financing in America* (Baltimore: Johns Hopkins University Press, 1975). Additional aspects of national parties are considered in Hugh Bone, *Party Committees and National Politics* (Seattle: University of Washington Press, 1958); Cornelius P. Cotter and Bernard C. Hennessy, *Politics Without Power: The National Party Committees* (New York: Atherton 1964); Charles O. Jones, *The Repub-*

lican Party in American Politics (New York: Macmillan, 1965); and Ralph M. Goldman, *The Democratic Party in American Politics* (New York: Macmillan, 1965). For an unusual refutation of the thesis that the major American parties are identical peas in the same pod, see Herbert McClosky et al., "Issue Conflict and Consensus Among Party Leaders and Followers," *American Political Science Review*, 54 (June 1960), 406–27. This work has been essentially replicated as well as expanded upon by John S. Jackson in a series of reports in *American Politics Quarterly*. See his (with Robert A. Hitlin) "A Comparison of Party Elites: The Sanford Commission and the Delegates to the Democratic Mid-Term Conference," 4 (October 1976), 441–82; (with other writers), "Recruitment, Representation, and Political Values: The 1976 Democratic National Convention Delegates," 6 (April 1978), 187–221; (with Barbara Leavitt Brown and David Bositis) "Herbert McClosky and Friends Revisited: 1980 Democratic and Republican Elites Compared to the Mass Public," 10 (April 1982), 158–80. See also the able discussion "Democrats and Republicans: Who Are They?" in Clinton Rossiter's *Parties and Politics in America* (Ithaca, N.Y.: Cornell University Press, 1960).

Overall accounts of the party system tend to be classifiable under the headings "pro" or "con." The writers who express satisfaction with the parties (and they have been dwindling in number in recent years) tend also to see the parties as rather deeply rooted fixtures in the American political environment and therefore not readily susceptible to change. Critics of the party system, most of whom have judged the parties against the standard of British party politics, tend to assume that it would not be difficult to accomplish reforms which would increase the internal cohesion of each party and the degree to which the two major parties are clearly distinguishable from one another in their positions on public issues. Without doubt the most influential of the modern critiques of the party system is E. E. Schattschneider's *Party Government* (New York: Rinehart, 1942). See also the reform proposals by Professor Schattschneider's Committee on Political Parties of the American Political Science Association, *Toward a More Responsible Two-Party System* (New York: Rinehart, 1950). Reacting to the critiques in the committee's report, Austin Ranney's *The Doctrine of Responsible Party Government* (Urbana: University of Illinois Press, 1954) provides a useful review of pro- and anti-party theorists. Further criticisms can be found in Stephen K. Bailey, *The Condition of Our National Political Parties* (New York: Fund for the Republic, 1959) and David Broder, *The Party's Over* (New York: Harper and Row, 1972). Pendleton Herring's *The Politics of Democracy* (New York: Norton, 1940; reprinted with a new preface in 1965) is probably the most widely respected of the works of party defenders. Much attention has been paid in recent years to the questions raised by the reforms (those accomplished and those contemplated) of our major parties. Among such works are John G. Stewart, *One Last Chance: The Demo-*

cratic Party, 1974–1976 (New York: Praeger, 1974); Austin Ranney, *Curing the Mischiefs of Faction* (Berkeley: University of California Press, 1975); Gerald M. Pomper, ed., *Party Renewal in America: Theory and Practice* (New York: Praeger, 1980); and William Crotty, *Party Reform* (New York: Longman, 1983).

There is also a wide assortment of pro- and anti-party texts available to the reader. An able presentation of the defender's viewpoint and, as well, one of the best textbook descriptions of the party system is Austin Ranney and Willmoore Kendall, *Democracy and the American Party System* (New York: Harcourt, Brace, 1956). Also dated, but the most comprehensive of the party texts, is a work which remains relatively aloof from the defender-critic debate, V. O. Key's *Politics, Parties, and Pressure Groups* (5th ed.; New York: Crowell, 1964). This work contains a number of original analyses of aspects of party politics, such as congressional nominations, which set it apart from other texts. Other useful texts include Alan Gitelson, M. Margaret Conway, and Frank B. Feigert, *American Political Parties: Stability and Change* (Boston: Houghton Mifflin, 1984); Frank Sorauf's *Party Politics in America* (5th ed.; Boston: Little, Brown, 1984); Samuel Eldersveld, *Political Parties in American Society* (New York: Basic Books, 1982); Robert J. Huckshorn, *Political Parties in America* (2nd ed.; Monterey, Calif.: Brooks/Cole, 1984); and Ruth K. Scott and Ronald J. Hrebenar, *Parties in Crisis: Party Politics in America* (2nd ed.; New York: Wiley, 1984). There is a variety of shorter works of roughly the length of the present book, each of which refracts the American party system through the author's own particular interests and concerns. Allan P. Sindler's *Political Parties in the United States* (New York: St. Martin's, 1966) has an especially detailed account of state politics. John H. Fenton's *People and Parties in Politics* (Glenview, Ill.: Scott, Foresman, 1966) also focuses on state politics, with a special interest in the question of whether highly competitive political parties and issue-oriented politicians generate governmental policies that are favorable to low income groups. William J. Keefe's *Parties, Politics, and Public Policy in America* (3rd ed.; Hinsdale, Ill.: Dryden, 1979) takes a look at parties largely in terms of the policies which ensue when they govern. William J. Crotty, *American Parties in Decline* (2nd ed.; Boston: Little, Brown, 1984) traces some reasons for the difficulties American parties have been experiencing, as does David H. Everson, *American Political Parties* (New York: New Viewpoints, 1980). Another of the brief paperback volumes, Frank Sorauf's *Political Parties* (Boston: Little, Brown, 1964) pays particular attention to party organization. An edited work of contributions by Walter Dean Burnham, *The Current Crisis in American Politics* (New York: Oxford University Press, 1982) sets forth the various arguments by this able scholar that American parties are in decline.

Anthologies and "readers" have burgeoned in all areas of political science. While there has been something of a slowdown in the pace of production of anthologies on parties, a number are available which contain original contributions by scholars of selected aspects of American parties. Among these, examining the development of American party politics, is William Nisbet Chambers and Walter Dean Burnham, (eds.), *The American Party Systems: Stages of Political Development* (2nd ed.; New York: Oxford, 1975). An especially notable contribution to that work is Donald E. Stokes' "Parties and the Nationalization of Electoral Forces," pp. 182–202. Other readers focusing on more contemporary aspects of our party system include Joel L. Fleishman (ed.), *The Future of American Political Parties* (Englewood Cliffs, N.J.: Prentice-Hall, 1982); Robert A. Goldwin (ed.), *Political Parties in the Eighties* (Washington: American Enterprise Institute, 1980); and Seymour Martin Lipset (ed.), *Party Coalitions in the 1980s* (San Francisco: Institute for Contemporary Studies, 1981). A special variety of this genre provides relatively "quick" analyses of the most recent national election year. Notable among these have been Gerald Pomper (ed.), *The 1980 Election* (Chatham, N.J.: Chatham, 1981) and his *The 1976 Election* (New York: McKay, 1977). See also Ellis Sandoz and Cecil V. Crabb (eds.), *A Tide of Discontent: The 1980 Elections and Their Meaning* (Washington, D.C.: Congressional Quarterly, Inc., 1981), and Paul R. Abramson, John H. Aldrich, and David W. Rohde, *Change and Continuity in the 1980 Elections* (rev. ed.; Washington: Congressional Quarterly, Inc., 1983). Several readers reprint the better known and more influential articles from the scholarly journals, without always abbreviating them or deleting footnotes or tables. These include William Crotty (ed.), *The Party Symbol* (San Francisco: Freeman, 1980); Jeff Fishel (ed.), *Parties and Elections in an Anti-Party Age* (Bloomington: Indiana University Press, 1978); and David W. Abbott and Edward Rogowsky, eds., *Political Parties: Leadership and Linkage* (2nd ed.; Chicago, Rand McNally, 1978).

Compendia that deal with the United States plus the party systems of various other nations, thus providing a cross-national perspective, include Joseph LaPalombara and Myron Weiner, eds., *Political Parties and Political Development* (Princeton, N.J.: Princeton University Press, 1966); Seymour Martin Lipset and Stein Rokkan, eds., *Party Systems and Voter Alignments: Cross-National Perspectives* (New York: Free Press, 1967). Richard Rose, *Electoral Behavior: A Comparative Handbook* (New York: Free Press, 1974) includes an essay by Walter Dean Burnham, "The United States: The Politics of Heterogeneity," pp. 653–725, which warns of major shifts in the nature of our party system. A major research effort by Kenneth Janda provides comparative data on party systems in many nations. These data are directly available through the Inter-University Consortium for Political and Social Research at the University of Michigan. Some of the fruits of this research are in Janda'a *Political Parties: A Cross-National Survey* (New York: Free Press, 1980), and Robert Harmel and Kenneth Janda, *Parties and Their Environments: Limits to Reform?* (New York: Longman, 1982). A clear and thoughtful general comparative discussion of democratic party systems is contained in Leon D. Epstein's *Political Parties in Western Democracies* (New York: Praeger, 1967). Also see Epstein's essay "The Comparison of Western Political Parties," in Oliver Garceau (ed.), *Political Research and Political Theory* (Cambridge, Mass.: Harvard University Press, 1968) and Austin Ranney's "The Concept of 'Party'" in the same work.

Finally, no discussion of possibilities for further study would be complete if it did not urge on the reader careful day-to-day attention to party politics in his or her own locality and state, as well as in the nation. One should sample the newspapers in the area in order to compare both their coverage as well as their treatment of party politics, if possible checking them against the accounts of local party activists. A useful source of weekly reports in party politics is the second part of the first section of the Sunday *New York Times*. One can also consult, with profit, the national weekly edition of *The Washington Post*. Newspaper accounts of national party politics may be compared with articles in the various periodicals of news and opinions—for example *Newsweek, Time, U.S. News and World Report, The National Review, The New Republic, The Nation, The Washington Monthly,* and so on. An eclectic but illuminating source of miscellaneous national, state, and local political news, as well as news of Congress, is the *Congressional Record,* including its appendix. The *Record* appears while Congress is in session and often may be obtained free from one's representative or senator. *The National Journal* is also a valuable weekly source on national political trends in general as well as on party politics in particular. *Congressional Quarterly Weekly Report,* available at most well-stocked libraries, is indexed currently and then reorganized and transferred at the end of the year to a single volume called the *Congressional Quarterly Almanac,* a series dating from 1945. These, in turn, have been condensed in a series of massive summary volumes, *Congress and the Nation.* vol. 1 (1945–1964), and then quadrennially, through vol. 5 (1977–1980).

INDEX